The
Tracking Wars

The
Tracking Wars

*State Reform
Meets School Policy*

Tom Loveless

BROOKINGS INSTITUTION PRESS

Washington, D.C.

ABOUT BROOKINGS

The Brookings Institution is a private nonprofit organization devoted to research, education, and publication on important issues of domestic and foreign policy. Its principal purpose is to bring knowledge to bear on current and emerging policy problems. The Institution maintains a position of neutrality on issues of public policy. Interpretations or conclusions in Brookings publications should be understood to be solely those of the authors.

Copyright © 1999 by
THE BROOKINGS INSTITUTION
1775 Massachusetts Avenue, N.W., Washington, D.C. 20036
www.brookings.edu

Library of Congress Cataloging-in-Publication data

Loveless, Tom
  The Tracking Wars : state reform meets school policy / by
Tom Loveless.
    p.   cm.
Includes bibliographical references.
ISBN 0-8157-3636-3 (cloth : permanent paper)
ISBN 0-8157-3635-5 (pbk. : permanent paper)
1. Education, Urban—United States—Administration—Case studies.
2. Education, Urban—Political Aspects—United States—Case studies.
3. Educational change—United States—Case studies.   I. Title.

LC5131.H44 1998   98-25373
370'.9173'–ddc21   CIP

9 8 7 6 5 4 3 2 1

The paper used in this publication meets the minimum requirements of the American National Standard for Information Sciences—Permanence of Paper for Printed Library Materials: ANSI Z39.48-1984.

Typeset in Times Roman

Composition by G & S Typesetters
Austin, Texas

Printed by R. R. Donnelley and Sons
Harrisonburg, Virginia

Acknowledgments

I WANT TO THANK a number of people who provided support and assistance on this project. My work on tracking began in 1990 as doctoral research at the University of Chicago. There I enjoyed the benefits of a dissertation committee composed of patient teachers and distinguished scholars. Charles Bidwell, Larry Hedges, Kenneth K. Wong, and Dan Lortie were always helpful, and Robert Dreeben, my advisor and dissertation chair, was consistently generous with his time and right on target with his counsel.

After leaving Chicago, I continued the research as a faculty member at the John F. Kennedy School of Government at Harvard University. The Kennedy School offered the perfect environment for writing a book about the politics of tracking reform. Both the A. Alfred Taubman Center for State and Local Government and the Program on Policy and Governance were extremely supportive. The National Academy of Education and the Spencer Foundation have my gratitude for selecting me as a National Academy of Education Spencer Post-Doctoral Fellow in 1995; the fellowship allowed me precious release time to write.

Several people helped to prepare and mail surveys, code data, and prepare data for analysis. In 1990 I was assisted by a number of close friends, among them Kerry Chenoweth, Sandy Cognini, and Brigid Donaghy. While I traveled around California to visit schools in the study, home bases were graciously provided by Tom Kearney and Alice Frausto, Dennis and Marilyn Odin, and John and Louise Taft. At Harvard, Gregory Shilonsky, Miriam Udel, Maya Beasley, Wayne Williams, and Tina Choi served as student research assistants, and Kathleen Kaminski furnished clerical help. Irene Yarmak helped prepare data for analysis, and my faculty assistant during most of the book's writing, Greg Dorchak, helped me in a thousand different ways.

Several colleagues offered valuable comments on drafts of the manuscript. Robert Dreeben, Adam Gamoran, Michael Goldstein, Richard Murnane, Paul Peterson, Diane Ravitch, and Maris Vinovskis read all or most of the book and made suggestions that improved it immensely, and I profited tremendously from conversations with Alan Altshuler, Richard Elmore, Ron Ferguson, Thomas Kane, Richard Light, Gary Orfield, Donald Stewart, and Carol Weiss. Comments from seminar participants at the Kennedy school, the University of Chicago, the National Academy of Education, and the Hoover Institution at Stanford University forced me to sharpen my thinking. At Brookings, Nancy Davidson provided valuable advice; Paul Spragens copyedited the manuscript and Linda Webster prepared the index. The editorial crew's careful and thorough work is much appreciated.

I want to give special thanks to the principals and teachers who allowed me to visit their schools. Granting interviews on the tracking issue was a matter of trust. Tracking, like many topics in education, stirs deep feelings that can create bitter resentments. These educators trusted me not only to present their words accurately, but also to present their reasoning and circumstances truthfully and with sensitivity. I have tried to honor that trust. Where I have not done so, or where I've committed other errors of fact or interpretation, I assume sole responsibility for the transgression.

Contents

Figures

The
Tracking Wars

1

Implementing Tracking Reform

THIS BOOK IS ABOUT SCHOOL REFORM, one in particular: the effort to persuade schools to abandon or reduce tracking. The book's title refers to the bitter debate that has swirled around tracking throughout the twentieth century. It also refers to the conflict inherent in any state reform trying to influence school policy, especially policy as deeply entrenched and as locally rooted as tracking.

Tracking is the practice of grouping students into classes by ability and organizing curriculum by its level of difficulty. Tracking may occur within a particular grade, as when eighth graders who are still struggling to learn how to read and those able to devour Shakespeare's plays are grouped into separate English classes. Or it may stretch across grade levels, as when schools assign students to math courses progressing from the fundamentals of arithmetic to the abstractions of calculus.

Past condemnations of tracking are easy to understand. For most of this century, schools used IQ tests to sort students as young as thirteen years old into classes of vastly different curricula that predetermined their fates. But today's tracking systems function differently. Grouping takes place within each subject, not across an entire regimen of academic courses. Track assignments are guided by successful completion of prerequisite courses, prior achievement, and teacher recommendations, not IQ tests. Students move from track to track based on their grades and performance. Permanent track assignment is a thing of the past, and almost all schools allow parents to overrule and change students' placements.

Public opinion research conducted by the Public Agenda Foundation shows broad support for tracking among teachers, parents, and students. And yet, despite this popularity, and despite having shed much of its past rigidity and determinism, tracking generates fierce, protracted political

1

conflict in communities across the nation, bitterly dividing parents, educators, and the general public.[1]

In 1993 hundreds of parents in Alexandria, Virginia, protested the elimination of a ninth grade honors course in world civilizations, a dispute that, according to the *Washington Post,* revealed deep racial divisions on the tracking issue. In 1994 a group of angry parents in Vernon, Connecticut, protested their district's decision to abolish tracking in favor of mixed-ability classes. In 1996 a middle school advisory panel in Howard County, Maryland, conducted a local survey after implementing reductions in tracking. An avalanche of 5,000 responses moved the panel to conclude that heterogeneously grouped classes, which had been formed to boost the self-esteem of minority youngsters, were a dismal failure. In 1998 a California district settled a lawsuit in federal court by agreeing to withdraw letters of reprimand that had been placed in the files of three teachers who, two years earlier, had spoken out publicly against the proposed detracking of mathematics at their school.[2]

In the late 1980s and early 1990s the state departments of education in California and Massachusetts issued policy documents discouraging the use of tracking in middle schools. By taking this stand, the states weighed in on the side of tracking's critics, those who claim that the practice helps no one and hurts many, that it sorts students into immutable destinations correlated with race and social class and is therefore inherently undemocratic. Defenders of tracking, on the other hand, argue that classes formed by heterogeneously grouping students are practically impossible to teach, holding back academically talented students or leaving students with learning problems languishing while other students move ahead. One of the most striking aspects of this debate is the inability of good, sound research to sort out which of these claims are accurate and which are not, an ambiguity that makes the California and Massachusetts advisories, and their success in getting schools to follow them, all the more surprising.

In terms of state policy, the antitracking side triumphed in California and Massachusetts. My study describes the political movement against tracking and then investigates what happened after the states began pushing schools to detrack. It represents one of the first attempts to assess whether the antitracking movement of the 1980s had an impact on increasing the number of untracked schools. The book chronicles how schools wrestled with their states' endorsements of detracking.

The study presented here casts doubt on the bedrock assumptions of tracking's opponents. Specifically, by documenting the multitude of factors going into schools' tracking decisions, the book's data directly refute the prevailing explanation for tracking's existence, that the practice of grouping students by ability is and always has been about race, class, and inequality—that when everything else is stripped away, maintaining special privileges for some students and denying them to others is the dominant theme of all tracking decisions.

Arguments about race and class are not absent from local tracking controversies (in many communities they are front and center) but the tracking debate is much more complicated than that. The debate unfolds within an environment that structures policy decisions. Tracking policy is a function of individual policymaking environments, consisting of each school's institutional and organizational characteristics, political influences on policy, and the technical challenge of reform. This study hypothesizes that it is these environments that lead some schools to embrace detracking and others to reject it. The study models influences on policymaking using data from a number of sources, including surveys of schools in California and Massachusetts and interviews with some 250 educators at twenty-nine school sites in those two states.

Results from the study show that local environments do indeed drive policy adoption, that tracking is not solely a matter of stratifying privilege by race and class, and that state policy is a factor, but by no means the most important one, when schools settle the issue. Reform of tracking entails risks, and a troubling pattern emerges from the study. Because advocates of detracking argue that it promotes social equity (although little empirical evidence exists to either verify or reject the claim), the schools that have embraced the reform serve predominantly poor and low-achieving students. Consequently, if the hopes of tracking reformers are not realized, detracking may wind up hurting the very students it is intended to help.

I became interested in the tracking controversy while pursuing doctoral studies at the University of Chicago in the late 1980s. Having taught for nine years in public schools in California, in both special education and in a rapid learner program, a program providing gifted students with an accelerated curriculum two to three years above grade level, I was skeptical of the wisdom of untracking. I remain skeptical to this day. At the time the research began, however, I was also skeptical that local policymakers would follow a recommendation on which the best evidence and the most informed, fair-minded experts were so evenly divided, and I could not imagine that schools would turn away from a practice that enjoys widespread popular support.

On that score, I was profoundly wrong. The study documents hundreds of schools that have diminished their use of tracking. Ultimately, of course, the success of an educational reform lies in the attainment of better educational results. This book is concerned with a more immediate question, whether educators embrace a reform so that it becomes part of their actual day-to-day practice and is thus given a chance to improve outcomes. Implementation studies like this one stem from the commonsense notion that winning policy debates in education are hollow accomplishments if schools ignore the policies they are urged to follow.

When implementation research came into its own, in an explosion of studies investigating the education reforms of the Great Society and later federal initiatives of the early to mid-1970s, the reforms were not faring very well where it counts—in the schools. These early studies focused on a specific type of reform, those establishing programs—with funding, regulations, and bureaucracies organized around politically negotiated objectives. At the federal level, Title I, bilingual education, Head Start, and special education programs were created and implemented in the schools, with a trailing army of state and district officials lined up behind programmatic endeavors. These initiatives, known as categorical programs, identified special populations (or "categories") of students and provided a battery of services to help with their education. Implementation researchers found—and this is an admitted oversimplification—that schools undermined these programs' original goals by molding them to fit what local educators either were already doing or wanted to do. The categorical student was being served within the limits of local aims and local conventions, but beyond that nothing much had really changed.[3]

The second type of program investigated by the early implementation studies was reform promoting innovative curricula and instructional approaches. The findings were as disheartening as those from categorical programs. Once the routines of teaching chewed up and digested the creative new elements of such initiatives as Man: A Course of Study (a social science program), the New Math, or the numerous science programs backed by the National Science Foundation, the new content being taught was virtually indistinguishable from what had been taught earlier. Teachers clung to tried-and-true instructional methods, and within a single decade after such programs debuted, investigators were fortunate even to locate the expensive new materials that had been developed and disseminated by university labs. When found, they were not found in classrooms. They were found in storage closets.[4]

A depressing view spread among academic researchers: schools cannot change. This belief still lingers, and though it is an unwarranted generalization, the early implementation research on which it is based squares with my own experiences. As one who began teacher training at the time of that research, I can testify that these programs, sent into the schools from Washington, Albany, or Sacramento, were largely left to the mercy of school personnel. In countless schools, educators buried these programs without a funeral. In some, they buried them without checking for a pulse.

My quarrel is with the caricature of local decisionmaking that has grown out of these failures. Studies of program implementation frequently employ predetermined objectives—the aims of the program under examination—as the yardstick by which change is measured. The approach starts with a policy and then assesses how faithfully schools have replicated its prescriptions. The other objectives of schools are seen as background noise, or even worse, as impediments to the pursuit of policy objectives. The language skills of non–English-speaking youngsters might be the most important priority of federal bilingual programs, and the demonstration of lively scientific experiments may be the most important aim of the National Science Foundation, but they are only two among many concerns of teachers and local school officials. Measured against the singular purposes of federal and state policy, it is no wonder that schools end up looking backward and obstinate.[5]

The fundamental problem with this view of policy implementation, then, is that it inevitably defines what schools are about in artificial terms. It conceives of schools as implementation sites for education policy instead of places where dozens, hundreds, perhaps even thousands, of educational endeavors transpire daily, some of which are governed by policy—and many that are not. It also incorrectly characterizes the relationship of schools and governments. Schools are wild horses. They existed long before they were roped and lassoed into a public system of governance, saddled by formal regulations, bridled by bureaucracies, and corralled into serving the purposes of politically negotiated policy. And like wild horses, when these elements of their domestication become too difficult to deal with, schools have a tendency, quite simply, to do what they damned well please.

Given this legacy of nonimplementation, the California and Massachusetts tracking reforms, like any state reform, clearly started from a severely disadvantaged position. In addition, the two states merely issued documents recommending tracking reform. They did not mandate that schools detrack, offer huge amounts of money for implementing reform, or threaten schools with dire consequences for keeping their conventional tracking policies. No dazzling new technologies were provided to untracked schools, no cutting-edge managerial plans for grouping students of heterogeneous ability, no powerful new bureaucracies to see to it that schools followed the states' wishes. At best, the reforms were a long shot.

So the success of these states in getting schools to move away from tracking is a surprise. Moreover, the example that detracking provides is important because this reform is strikingly different from the curricular and categorical reforms of past eras. It entails government officials proclaiming best practices without an attendant program to put them into effect. And considering the tight budgets and shrinking bureaucracies of governments at all levels, not to mention the increasing zest with which policymakers try to dictate classroom instruction, it is likely to resemble reforms of the future.

This study begins from a local starting point, from the perspective of schools—their policies and their policymaking—recognizing that implementing reform will be bounded by local phenomena. By itself, the approach is not unique. Numerous implementation researchers now place schools at the center of their work. The dismal findings of the early implementation studies spurred efforts to specify what happens to state and federal reforms in local settings. The countless state education reforms adopted after the release of *A Nation at Risk* in 1983 fueled a new wave of implementation studies that extended into the 1990s. Much of this research elaborated on a discovery of the earlier studies. Through a process known as mutual adaptation, reforms designed from above and handed down to implementers are molded to fit local conditions, while at the same time, local conditions also change in response to reform. Compromises are struck between the objectives of reform and immovable elements in the local status quo.

What contributes to real, substantive change emerging from this process? Can reform occur without its most crucial objectives being adapted to the point that they are unrecognizable? Or, to paraphrase Linda Darling-Hammond, how can state reforms effectively deal with "the power of the bottom over the top"?[6]

One branch of the research on the 1980s reforms focused on the instruments states used to prod local authorities toward change: mandates, regulations, incentives, sanctions, and the like. Results were mixed. Mandates that raised high school graduation requirements gained broad public support and were quickly implemented. By providing funds, states pushed districts to lengthen the school day, boost starting teachers' salaries, and implement mentor teacher programs. Inducements were also usually paired with measures increasing accountability, in the form of state curriculum frameworks, a tightening of teacher certification standards, and state testing programs. Other policies ran into trouble. Career ladders for teachers died in Georgia, Florida, and Texas; state takeovers of underperforming school districts did not produce noticeable achievement gains in California or New Jersey; and tightening up teacher licensing failed to substantially improve the quality of teachers, mainly because states continued to issue emergency credentials in the event of teacher shortages, circumventing the reform.[7]

Another branch of studies focused on local implementers and proceeded from the idea that the will and capacity of local educators affect the implementation of reform. David Cohen and Deborah Ball studied a group of math teachers responding to California's ambitious 1985 curriculum framework and found that the teachers had changed their instruction, but not as much as reformers had hoped. Teachers interpreted the recommended approaches in light of their own mathematical knowledge and previous training. Even those who were eager to innovate only did so partway.

James Spillane explored an interesting slant on the same idea when he investigated school districts' role in implementing state instructional reform. He describes two administrators in the same district who used reading reforms to pursue different ends. One was deeply committed to revamping traditional reading instruction in favor of a whole-language approach. She favored mandates to force change. Another believed in the reforms, but felt instructional choices were rooted in both an understanding of one's students and a solid grounding in research. She favored a series of workshops that allowed teachers to construct their own instructional styles.[8]

In general, the studies of the 1980s and 1990s produced more optimistic findings than the studies of the 1960s and 1970s. State-initiated reforms could effect change. Compiling student portfolios for assessment became part of the Vermont teacher's repertoire; Kentucky school districts overhauled the way they governed schools; textbooks stressing problem solving entered California's math classrooms. But researchers also reaffirmed the limits of state action. State departments of education, struck by personnel and budgetary cutbacks during the 1990–91 recession, lacked capacity themselves. Studies like Cohen and Ball's and Spillane's made clear that change would only come incrementally and at the discretion of local officials. A series of studies conducted by the Consortium for Policy Research in Education (CPRE) concluded that a decade of nonstop state initiatives had transpired without seriously affecting the independence of local educators. Policy activity was not zero sum. Ambitious reforms and centralization of state authority were often matched by equally ambitious reforms and centralization of district authority in local arenas. Richard Elmore and other CPRE researchers observed that some districts anticipated state reforms by taking action before the state, some used state reforms to justify what they were already doing, and others exceeded the minimal efforts of the state to tackle bold new programs.[9]

The interest in local will and capacity has opened several new avenues for implementation research. The concept is unassailable. For educational reform to take place, local educators must be willing to change. They must also have in hand the resources necessary for abandoning the old and embracing the new. But a downside is apparent when reading research other than the exemplary studies I have cited here. Unfortunately, many researchers are infatuated with the reforms they are studying. As Thomas Corcoran and Margaret Goertz observe, "Discussions of capacity are often framed by advocates of particular reforms and their beliefs about what is essential to implementing their ideas."[10] The same narrow conclusions come barreling through—that we should applaud those courageous, trailblazing educators who are altering the traditions of schooling and view with a touch of pity, maybe even disdain, those teachers and principals who resist reforms. Frequently, resistance is attributed to a lack of training, the fear of change, insufficient child-centeredness, or some other deficiency, anything, in fact, except the possibility that the proposed reform is simply a bad idea. Too often, schools wind up looking as passive as ever, and these researchers mournfully conclude that a heavy dose of professional development will convince resistant educators to do what they currently, and most emphatically, do not want to do.

The problem lies with how will and capacity are conceptualized. Modeled as psychological phenomena, "will" and "capacity" are susceptible to circular reasoning. They can easily be viewed as open minds and abundant skills respectively in the case of a reform's supporters and as obstinacy and ignorance in the case of a reform's resisters. The researcher's task then becomes a self-fulfilling prophecy, locating and describing two archetypes and ultimately arriving at the predictable conclusions described above.

I conducted this study with the assumption that local educators hold diverse opinions on tracking reform and possess varying capacities to function under different policies. But, significantly, by also assuming that educators' willingness and ability to detrack are constrained by local circumstances, I shift the study's focus onto forces external to the decisionmaker.

An advantage of this strategy is that the variables of primary interest—at least in the analysis of survey data—are relatively objective and protected from investigator bias. My own skepticism about tracking reform, for example, cannot influence a school's student population, one of the organizational properties of schools that, it turns out, strongly affects tracking policy. Another researcher going into California and Massachusetts might interpret the data differently than I have, but we should come up with the same numbers for many of the variables.

Another advantage is that I do not have to plumb the depths of implementers' psychologies or render a verdict on their motives. Contemporary research on tracking is teeming with heroes and villains. I assume that bigotry, tolerance, ignorance, wisdom, traditionalism, and openness to change are plentiful in schools, but, to cite the example of school population again, they are probably randomly distributed among large, small, and medium-size schools. The fact that tracking varies by school size suggests that tracking and untracking involve more than the clash of vile and noble intentions.

Focusing on the implementation environment produces one additional advantage. Researchers who are interested in other educational reforms or in other policy fields may find lessons here that are relevant to their own interests. Chapter 4 details how tracking policy is shaped by various forces: *institutional* (the demographic characteristics constituting a school's institutional identity); *organizational* (in this case, student population and the grade levels the schools serve); *political* (influence exerted on tracking policy by important actors, including state policymakers but also parents); and *technical* (the logistics of instructing students of widely varying achievement levels in the same classroom, the main problem principals and teachers wrestle with in untracked schools).

As I have described them here, these forces are particular to the tracking controversy. Education is only one policy field, tracking is only one education policy, and natural limitations of the study's design and data reduce the ability to generalize its findings. But it would not take much to imagine similar influences affecting the implementation of other reforms in education or reform in other fields. One could reasonably hypothesize, for example, that implementing measures to improve the delivery of urban health care would be affected by hospitals' and community clinics' institutional identities and their varying organizational forms, by the competing claims of local political actors, and by an array of technical challenges. Broadly conceived, the phenomena that this study examines are not unique to schools or to education policy.

How have the tracking wars been resolved in California and Massachusetts? What happens when state reform meets school policy? The short answer is that the battle shifted to local schools in both states—fought publicly in front of school boards in some communities, negotiated quietly behind closed doors in others. Hundreds of schools agreed with their state's recommendation and began to detrack. Hundreds of others ignored state policy and went on tracking as usual. The long answer fills the pages of this book.

The project is presented in the seven chapters that follow. Chapter 2 summarizes the research on tracking and offers an explanation for why tracking reform rose to the top of the policy agenda in the 1980s. The publication of *Keeping Track* by Jeannie Oakes in 1985 galvanized the anti-tracking movement. The book argued that tracking's origins are rooted in racism and the protection of class privilege. I critically review the historical evidence on this charge and trace its course from scholarship to policy, from its emergence as the theme of *Keeping Track* to its position as the rationale for policy in California and Massachusetts.

Chapter 3 provides the study's conceptual framework. I describe the structure of local policy environments. The survey and case study data are explained, the study's limitations are discussed, and a snapshot is provided of current and past tracking practices in the two states' middle schools. Chapter 4 investigates influences on tracking policy, why some schools track and other schools detrack. The study's survey data are analyzed to uncover the forces shaping tracking policy.

Chapter 5 explores governance issues. The distribution of authority over the tracking issue is examined, again using survey data. I also present case studies of two schools. Both actively opposed upper-level authorities on the tracking issue. One school fought the state to protect its tracked system, the other fought its local district to preserve heterogeneously grouped classes.

Chapter 6 goes inside schools to examine the relationship of tracking and subject areas, especially as manifested at the departmental level. Another case study is offered, a school where the math department's initial resistance to detracking foreshadowed the reform's eventual demise.

Chapter 7 goes another step deeper into schools, focusing on teachers and the classroom. The impact of tracking policy on instruction, the strategies teachers deploy in detracked settings, and schools' professional development activities are all described. I present a case study school in which detracking has gained acceptance and support from both faculty and community members.

Chapter 8 summarizes the book's major findings and discusses implications of the research. The bottom line is this: If we want to know why tracking reform is accepted by some schools and rejected by others, we must understand why schools make the decisions they do. The undulations of local policymaking must be explored, mapped, and built into any robust explanation of school reform. This book tries to accomplish just that.

2

The Origins of Tracking Reform

IN 1987 THE CALIFORNIA STATE Department of Education released *Caught in the Middle,* a document laying out a set of ambitious policies for reforming middle schools. In 1993 the Commonwealth of Massachusetts issued *Magic in the Middle,* a document similar to California's in tone and content. The two states deplored middle-level education's longtime habit of imitating the characteristics of high schools, urging instead that all schools serving young adolescents— middle, intermediate, and junior high schools, referred to as "middle schools" in the aggregate—forge a unique identity featuring their own pedagogy, curriculum, and organization. One practice in particular drew fire—tracking, the sorting of students by ability or prior achievement between classes. In the span of six years, the states issued several documents discouraging the use of tracking and exhorting middle schools to heterogeneously group students as much as possible.[1]

Why did California and Massachusetts do this? Why did they turn against a practice so deeply embedded in the culture, traditions, and curricular structures of secondary education in the United States? This chapter focuses on the intellectual foundations of the antitracking movement, especially on the dramatic charge that tracking thwarts equal educational opportunity. Empirical research has failed to resolve the most important questions about tracking, but the argument that tracking is fundamentally unfair and socially reprehensible permeates the politics of the issue, running like a steel rod from Jeannie Oakes's seminal book, *Keeping Track,* through the rise of the detracking movement in the late 1980s, to the explicit and authoritative endorsements of detracking that the policies of California and Massachusetts represent.

Conflicting Orientations

The matching of students and curriculum is a vexing educational problem because schools are not merely settings for gathering information—like libraries or computer terminals—but places for students to learn content that is designated, authoritatively, by someone else. We call this content "the curriculum"; when bundled together into units of instruction, "courses"; and when collected into several years of study in the major subjects, the old-fashioned "course of study" or "program."

In a publicly financed and publicly governed school system, matching students with curriculum involves reconciling what a legitimate party has decided students should learn with the characteristics of students. One or more of the following student characteristics might be relevant to the match: the student's ability, performance level, previously completed courses, age, interests, work habits, and career path. A good match is simpler when it involves a single student, as might be found in the training of Buddhist monks or when a parent teaches a child how to ride a bicycle, because the instructor can then readily adjust the difficulty of the lesson to the individual. But for most public school students, the curriculum experienced in school is experienced simultaneously by other students sitting in the same room. Instruction is fitted to group characteristics, and adjustments to a particular group level, even if calibrated with the greatest precision, may yield a poor match for some individuals.

Note the three-part challenge in designing an instructional system: deciding what students should know (content), deciding what they are capable of learning (ability), and finally, reconciling the content with students' ability to learn it. Also note that the differentiation of curriculum and the differentiation of students are two separate tasks. Differentiating curriculum organizes content into hierarchies of courses. Much of what we learn can be sorted, even if crudely, into different levels—primary and secondary, basic and advanced, undergraduate and graduate, concrete and abstract, simple and complex—an assumption undergirding curricula from prekindergarten to the great universities. When this idea is combined with the assumption that progress through the curriculum is dependent on one's previous learning, which varies from person to person, the justification for ability grouping is created.

Middle school is generally the first place students experience tracking. Around sixth or seventh grade, students who have not yet mastered basic decoding skills may attend a remedial reading class for English. Readers who gobble up sophisticated literature far beyond their age mates, on the other hand, may be grouped into an accelerated English class featuring more challenging materials. In mathematics, about 24 percent of middle school students take algebra in eighth grade, another 27 percent take pre-algebra, and the remainder take regular or remedial math, with both of these latter courses focusing on arithmetic and basic skills. Sadly, outside of algebra classes, only a scant amount of the eighth grade math curriculum contains fresh topics introduced since fifth grade; basic operations with whole numbers, fractions, decimals, and percents are repeated year after year.[2]

One perspective on tracking, the social orientation, holds that ability grouping invites bias into schooling. It charges that ability is often defined and measured in a way that discriminates by race and class.[3] As a result, when students are assigned to ability groups by their measured ability or prior achievement, white and wealthier students are often disproportionately represented in high groups and poor and minority students in low groups. Even when the procedures for assigning students to tracks are technically valid, tracking may still have a segregative effect, the social orientation argues, because of the depressed achievement of disadvantaged students. By exposing students to different curricula, tracking stratifies learning by race and class and reinforces social inequality.[4]

Another perspective on tracking, the functional orientation, argues that tracking is useful for grouping students to receive appropriate instruction. Those who defend tracking assume that schooling is just as much a waste of time for students who already know the content to be taught as it is for students who are incapable of learning the material in the first place. They also believe that instruction is more efficiently delivered if teachers can pitch the material at a level apprehended by most of the students in a class. Placing students in courses in which they will flounder, the functional orientation argues, does not advance the cause of equity.[5]

What Is the Evidence?

What is known about tracking's effects? Does it treat minority or economically disadvantaged students unfairly? What about detracking? What are the effects of heterogeneously grouping students by ability?

Because hundreds of studies have investigated tracking during the last century, several volumes could be devoted to these questions. I will summarize a small portion of the literature for the purpose of sketching the broad outline of the tracking debate, but the reader should keep in mind that in doing so I am plucking declarative statements from a sea of nuances, conditions, contingencies, and qualifiers. The bottom line is this: few, if any, of the questions about tracking's effects are settled, and research is ambiguous on the policy direction that schools should pursue. The ambiguity centers around three pivotal questions.

What Is the Effect of Tracking on Achievement?

This question is typically investigated by comparing the mean achievement of grouped and ungrouped students. A number of researchers have conducted comprehensive reviews and meta-analyses of tracking's achievement effects. A meta-analysis is, in effect, a study of studies. Data from all of the high-quality studies that address a common question are combined to draw conclusions about what they say as a body of research. Frederick Mosteller, Richard J. Light, and Jason A. Sachs reviewed fifteen experimental studies, with random assignment of students to experimental and control groups, and concluded that there is "little evidence that skill grouping has a major impact, either positive or negative, on students' cognitive learning." [6] This is in line with Adam Gamoran and Mark Berends's review of survey and ethnographic research. They conclude that when appropriate controls for prior achievement are incorporated most of tracking's influence on academic achievement evaporates, theorizing that the weak effects are because track differences in instruction are small. [7]

James A. and Chen-Lin C. Kulik and Robert Slavin have conducted meta-analyses of studies of ability grouping at both the elementary level, where it is typically limited to the formation of within-class groups for reading instruction (and occasionally mathematics), and the secondary level, where the formation of between-class ability groups in most, if not all, academic subjects is common. They find ability grouping in elementary schools associated with achievement gains. Slavin detects the strongest gains for schools using the Joplin Plan, a cross-grade-level strategy for grouping students in reading. [8]

These researchers part ways when it comes to tracking in secondary schools. Slavin finds no significant achievement gain for tracking and argues that educators should shun the practice because by stratifying students unnecessarily it violates the institution's responsibility for modeling democratic principles. [9] Kulik and Kulik, on the other hand, point out that Slavin's review is dominated by studies in which the different tracks studied an identical curriculum. They detect consistent achievement gains when the curriculum is adjusted to track level, especially for students in gifted pro-grams. Slavin excludes studies of gifted programs and special education from his review.[10]

The Kuliks are correct that contemporary tracking is unthinkable with-out curriculum adjustment, but the point identifies a deeper problem. Al-most all of the studies in both meta-analyses were conducted before 1975, leaving out the many significant changes that have occurred in tracking since then. As I mentioned in chapter 1, assigning students to tracks us-ing IQ tests or other omnibus tests of ability is now rare. Today's schools typically group students on a subject-by-subject basis, rather than placing students into rigid tracks that dictate all of one's academic courses. And mobility exists. Students move up or down in track depending upon their performance in class. To be blunt, the tracking evaluated in the Slavin and Kulik meta-analyses bears little resemblance to tracking in today's schools.[11]

What Is the Effect of Tracking on Equity?

Instead of the general effect of tracking on achievement, this question focuses on tracking's impact on the distribution of achievement. Studies have usually tackled this question by comparing the achievement of stu-dents in different tracks and then extrapolating these findings to groups that are over- or underrepresented in high and low tracks. Qualitative research stresses how tracking denies low-ability students challenging curricular op-portunities and stigmatizes them with demoralizing labels.[12] Quantitative research has documented achievement advantages associated with high-track membership and disadvantages associated with low-track member-ship. Adam Gamoran, for example, found that the achievement gap be-tween students in academic and vocational high school tracks is greater than the gap between students who stay in school and those who drop out. In the same study, however, low-ability students reap no clear benefit from advanced coursework, and Gamoran warns, "one cannot simply thrust all students into advanced courses and expect their achievement to rise." [13]

The low-track disadvantage works against the achievement of poor and minority students because they are disproportionately enrolled in classes for low-achieving students. The suspicion that schools unfairly assign poor or minority students to low groups has been refuted, however. Their over-representation in low tracks apparently stems from low grades and test scores, not from any systematic discrimination in track placement.[14]

Nothing is settled in the equity research, but assume for a moment that high-track students enjoy a net gain and low-track students suffer a net loss as a result of tracking. If both outcomes were true, these offsetting effects would be consistent with the zero overall effect noted above. Simply put, if three students alike in every respect—including ability—were assigned to high, medium, and low tracks, the low-track student would achieve the least, the middle-track student would achieve more than the low-track student, and the high-track student would achieve the most of all. Of course, very few schools would be clamoring to differentiate the coursework of three students alike in every respect, so this imaginary situation does not help much in deciding what to do in real schools, where students may differ in hundreds of ways.

It also does not mean that low-ability students will benefit by simply abolishing low tracks and reassigning them to middle or high tracks. If all low-achieving students were so reassigned, the upper tracks would be vastly different places from the upper tracks producing the advantage in the first place. Moreover, we also know that tracking differs from subject to subject and from school to school. The high track in a low-achieving school may resemble, in both student composition and curriculum, the low track of a high-achieving school.

Information is sparse on the curriculum and instruction employed by different tracks or whether students of all abilities benefit from the same curricular and instructional exposure. In short, although the evidence suggests that achievement is hampered by placement in low tracks, we are not sure of the precise mechanisms producing the low-track disadvantage, whether low tracks can be reformed to make them more productive places of learning, or what are the alternative grouping arrangements that would correct low tracks' deficiencies.[15]

What Happens to Achievement and Equity at Untracked Schools?

Should tracking be abolished? As implied by the answer to the last two questions, the answer to this one is unclear. Until quite recently, tracking has been such a universal feature of high schools that there have not been enough untracked schools to assess their effectiveness. And untracking is often ambiguously defined in research. Consider the subtitle of the book *Constructing School Success: The Consequences of Untracking Low-Achieving Students.* The book reports on a program in San Diego that moves a select group of low-track high school students into high tracks and gives them intensive academic support—all the while keeping the schools' track system intact. Contrary to the subtitle, no students were untracked.

Identifying students who can benefit from a more rigorous curriculum and moving them into high tracks seems like a good idea, but studies like this one are not very helpful in gauging what happens if schools abolish tracking and randomly assign students to heterogeneous classes.

Another problem plagues the "heterogeneous" classes that pop up in large national databases such as High School and Beyond (HSB) and the National Education Longitudinal Study (NELS). It is difficult to determine how schools in these databases actually created their classes. School policies are not measured in HSB or NELS; heterogeneous classes are those labeled as "mixed ability" or classes that teachers think have a large spread in achievement. An unknown number of these heterogeneous classes are situated within schools that continue to peel off high- and low-achieving youngsters into separate classes before heterogeneously grouping the students that remain. Heterogeneous classes that coexist at the same school with special education classes and advanced placement classes are not as heterogeneous as the school's overall composition. To compound the research problem, schools frequently consider mixed-ability classes experimental, staffing them with volunteer teachers and filling them with volunteer students. They bear no resemblance to the heterogeneous classes that would be formed if all remedial, special needs, bilingual, honors, gifted, and advanced placement classes were abolished.

Despite these restrictions, a few researchers have taken a stab at evaluating untracked settings with the existing data. Analyzing HSB data, Valerie Lee and Anthony Bryk find that schools with less tracking foster more equitable distributions of achievement without a loss in mean achievement. But Lee and Bryk deemphasize the impact of tracking per se and attribute the effect to the fostering of a strong academic culture, one that encourages students to take more academically rigorous courses.[16]

Using NELS data, Laura M. Argys, Daniel I. Rees, and Dominic J. Brewer investigate what happens to achievement in detracked classes. They conclude that detracking is not a costless reform, that the benefit reaped by low-track students from heterogeneously grouped classes is exceeded by the achievement loss of high- and middle-track students in those same classes.[17] Again, however, keep in mind the profound difficulty, when it comes to tracking, of extracting sound policy recommendations from studies based on HSB and NELS data. This research labors under a fundamental handicap, relying on data from what ostensibly are heterogeneous classes without being able to identify whether these classes are, in fact, situated within untracked schools. The one finding from NELS avoiding this handicap—that racial gaps in achievement are fully formed by eighth grade and stay unchanged during the high school years, when student exposure to tracking is most intense—suggests that tracking has little effect on racial achievement inequalities.[18]

When the California and Massachusetts policies supporting detracking were adopted, no large-scale evaluations of untracked schools had ever been conducted. As the finishing touches were being put on the book you are now reading, such studies still had not been conducted. With the evidence supporting detracking fraught with ambiguity, how could California and Massachusetts policymakers give it such a thumping endorsement? Why would they urge schools to embark on what amounts to a grand experiment involving the achievement of hundreds of thousands of middle school youngsters? This question gets at the heart of the argument woven through the remainder of this chapter, that scientific findings (and the lack of them) played an inconsequential role in developing the two states' tracking policies. In pursuing this line of argument, I would now like to lay the groundwork for understanding more generally how public issues enter the realm of public policy.

Agenda Setting

In the 1980s, the forces that drive the public agenda came together fortuitously for tracking's opponents. John Kingdon (1983) presents a detailed model for explaining how issues advance to the front burner of the decision agenda where they are seriously considered by policymakers. Issues gain a place on the agenda because three processes, or "streams," are linked: problems, policies, and politics. Kingdon's framework cannot tell us why one policy is adopted instead of another, nor does it shed light on questions arising from policy implementation, so I will rely on its insights in this chapter alone. It is ideal for explaining how tracking reform shot to the top of the national reform agenda in the 1980s.

Kingdon's problem stream refers to the public recognition that a persistent social condition is significant enough to warrant governmental attention.[19] Conditions can come to be seen as problems through the ingenious framing of issues by policy entrepreneurs, activists who labor to sway the policy process. Public concern also grows in response to shifts in widely followed indicators or because of focusing events, incidents that rivet attention on a particular problem. The launching of *Sputnik* in 1958 and the release of *A Nation at Risk* in 1983 convinced two different generations that educational crises demanded immediate action.[20]

The policy stream refers to the ebb and flow of proposals, how potential solutions may sit on the shelf for years and years before they are strategically linked to particular problems and pushed to the fore. The academic community often serves as a spawning ground for new policies. The programs of the Great Society relied on ideas percolating among social scientists for years. Kingdon presents the example of the Carter administration's proposals for deregulating aviation, trucking, and railroads, policies typifying the Chicago School of Economics and its influential critique of governmental regulation that had commenced roughly two decades earlier.

The political stream encompasses the rise and fall of political actors and political movements that can attract the public's attention to a given issue. An electoral sweep of Congress by the Democratic party in 1964 and the ongoing civil rights movement gave President Johnson the power he needed to pass a host of bold domestic programs in 1965. The Republicans' surprise capture of both the House and Senate in 1994 led, in almost a straight line, to President Clinton's 1996 State of the Union statement that "the era of big government is over," words that would have been an apostasy for any Democrat only a few years earlier. The point is that democracy still works; political tides influence the actions of governments.

The genius of Kingdon's formulation is that it gives structure to events easily mistaken for happenstance. There are reasons why certain issues suddenly become "hot" while others sit unnoticed. When the problem, policy, and political streams are joined around one issue, that issue grabs the attention of policymakers and rises to the top of the decision agenda, the queue of issues demanding action. Moreover, changes in the problem or political streams may be enough to open a "policy window," allowing entrepreneurs an opportunity to push the issue forward by linking it to a ready and waiting solution.

In stressing the near independence of the three streams, Kingdon diverges from linear formulations of policymaking. One implication is counterintuitive, that policy solutions may precede the problems they are intended to solve. Also called into question is the idea that governments develop policy after a rational process of initially identifying and prioritizing several problems, conducting an inventory of all possible solutions, testing alternatives under experimental protocols, gathering evidence on costs and benefits, and so on. Contrast such an idealization with the unruly process Kingdon describes:

> The probability of an item rising on the decision agenda is dramatically increased if all three streams—problems, policies, and politics—are joined. An alternative floating in the policy stream, for

instance, becomes coupled either to a prominent problem or to events in the political stream in order to be considered seriously in a context broader than the community of specialists. If an alternative is coupled to a problem as a solution, then that combination also finds support in the political stream. Similarly, if an alternative is seized upon by politicians, it is justified as a solution to a real problem. None of the streams are sufficient by themselves to place a problem firmly on the decision agenda.[21]

The linking of streams frequently is the project of a singularly important actor, the policy entrepreneur, an influential individual who pushes a favorite cause. In 1985, education's movers and shakers began focusing on criticism of tracking. The abolition of tracking moved boldly onto the decision agenda. New scientific substantiation of detracking's benefits had not surfaced to warrant the attention. A single book was largely responsible for its happening.

Keeping Track

Jeannie Oakes's *Keeping Track: How Schools Structure Inequality* was published in 1985. The book reported on data from a study of twenty-five junior and senior high schools scattered across the country. The multiyear project, housed at UCLA and known as A Study of Schooling, was conducted in the late 1970s and examined the general conditions of schools in America. Tracking was just one topic of many investigated by the project. Led by John Goodlad, Oakes's mentor at UCLA, the study also produced Goodlad's popular book *A Place Called School* (1984) and Kenneth Tye's *The Junior High School* (1985).[22]

A critique of *Keeping Track* should begin by noting some of the book's strengths. Oakes actually went inside schools and meticulously documented what happens in classrooms. A central assertion of *Keeping Track,* that many low-track classes are deadening, noneducational environments, has been verified again and again, especially by qualitative research. The book is well written and an engaging read, and *Keeping Track* has had an influence on educational thought and policy that few works of social science ever achieve.

The policy importance of *Keeping Track* is twofold. The book packs a powerful political appeal, as exhibited in its ability to rally opposition to tracking. It has also been tremendously influential with scholars. In a cursory search of the online version of the *Social Science Citation Index,* I could find only two education-related texts with more citations than *Keeping Track* for the ten-year period from January 1988 to December 1997: Howard Gardner's *Frames of Mind* (cited 673 times) and Allan Bloom's *Closing of the American Mind* (641). *Keeping Track*'s 415 citations places it at the head of a group that includes E. D. Hirsch's *Cultural Literacy* (382), Jonathan Kozol's *Savage Inequalities* (320), Christopher Jencks's *Inequality* (313), and Dan Lortie's *Schoolteacher* (299).[23]

In Kingdon's terms, *Keeping Track* is a near perfect specimen of policy entrepreneurship. It linked tracking to what it argued was a persistent problem of inequality in American schooling: the gaps between white and nonwhite students and between rich and poor students, disparities stubbornly resisting the ameliorative efforts of compensatory education programs. It framed the tracking debate as an argument over whether schools should persist with a practice founded on racist intentions and continuing to produce racist results. It presented the abolition of tracking as a policy move that would benefit economically disadvantaged students and students of color. And it married the antitracking cause to a national surge of interest in education reform that was cresting about the same time.

To invoke Kingdon's terminology, *Keeping Track* defined a problem, provided a solution, and tapped into powerful political currents to pry open a policy window. An extended excerpt from the book's first few pages illustrates how it frames the tracking issue:

> Educational equality is an idea that has fallen from favor. In the eighties we have decided that excellence is what we want, and that somehow excellence and equality are incompatible.
>
> What happened to educational equality? Perhaps, in the decades following *Brown v. Board of Education,* we were naive enough to think that wanting schools to make things right was enough. It was not. . . . Programs failed. Children in Head Start didn't catch up. Remedial and compensatory classes didn't seem to remediate or compensate. Children making long bus rides seemed to gain nothing but bus rides. Millions were spent; achievement gaps between the haves and the have-nots remained. . . . our focus was almost exclusively on the characteristics of the children themselves. We looked for sources of educational failure in their homes, their neighborhoods, their languages, their cultures, even in their genes. In all our searching, we almost entirely overlooked the possibility that what happens within schools might contribute to unequal educational opportunities and outcomes. We neglected to examine the content and processes of

Table 2-1. NAEP Reading Scores (Age Thirteen), 1971–96

Year	White (W)	Black (B)	B-W gap	Hispanic (H)	H-W gap
1971	261	222	−39	n.a.	n.a.
1975	262	226	−36	232	−30
1980	264	233	−31	237	−27
1984	263	236	−27	240	−23
1988	261	243	−18	240	−21
1990	262	242	−20	238	−24
1992	266	238	−28	239	−27
1994	265	234	−31	235	−30
1996	267	236	−31	240	−27

Source: National Assessment of Educational Progress (NAEP), reported in table 107, *Digest of Educational Statistics, 1997,* U.S. Department of Education, National Center for Educational Statistics.
n.a. Not available.

schooling itself for ways they may contribute to school failure. . . . [It is] my hope that this inquiry into school tracking and its relationship to issues of equality and excellence will attract some of the attention generated by the current schooling crisis to this fundamental feature of schooling and that it will make clear how tracking may inhibit the learning of many of our country's teenagers—especially those who are poor and nonwhite.[24]

The Problem of Inequality

Keeping Track correctly identifies inequality as a leading problem in education. Educational opportunities and educational outcomes were not equally distributed before 1985, nor have they been equally distributed since then. But the passage above implies something more, that inequality remained unchanged in the decades leading up to the 1980s and that tracking was a prime obstacle to progress. Is this accurate?

The first part of this assertion can be tested with data that are routinely collected on various educational outcomes. Contrary to the impression left by *Keeping Track*'s introduction, by most measures the attainments of poor and nonwhite students steadily improved up until the mid-1980s. Specifically, the outcome gaps between white students and other racial groups shrank considerably in the ten- to fifteen-year period before the book's publication in 1985.

Tables 2-1 to 2-4 present data on educational outcomes for white, black, and Hispanic students. Tables 2-1 and 2-2 display scores from the National Assessment of Educational Progress (NAEP). Table 2-3 reports Scholastic

Table 2-2. NAEP Math Scores (Age Thirteen), 1973–96

Year	White (W)	Black (B)	B-W gap	Hispanic (H)	H-W gap
1973	274	228	−46	239	−35
1978	272	230	−42	238	−34
1982	274	240	−34	252	−22
1986	274	249	−25	254	−20
1990	276	249	−27	255	−21
1992	279	250	−29	259	−20
1994	281	252	−29	256	−25
1996	281	252	−29	256	−25

Source: National Assessment of Educational Progress (NAEP), reported in table 118, *Digest of Educational Statistics, 1997.*

Aptitude Test (SAT) scores of blacks and whites from 1976 to 1994, and table 2-4 shows the high school dropout rates for whites, blacks, and Hispanics in the period 1967–96. Figures 2-1 and 2-2 highlight major trends in the gaps between white and minority students. The four tables and two figures provide a quick but comprehensive review of educational progress for white and nonwhite students over the last three decades.

Let's look at the gap between white and nonwhite students on these indicators, paying close attention to where the gap stood about the time that *Keeping Track* came out in 1985. The black-white and Hispanic-white gaps in reading and math achievement contracted dramatically until the mid-1980s (see tables 2-1 and 2-2). The reading gap for blacks and whites shrank by about one-third from 1971 to 1984 before declining even fur-

Table 2-3. SAT Scores, by Race, 1976–94

Year	White (W)	Black (B)	B-W gap
1976	944	686	−258
1978	931	686	−245
1980	930	690	−240
1982	927	707	−220
1984	932	715	−217
1987	936	728	−208
1988	935	737	−198
1990	933	737	−196
1992	933	737	−196
1994	938	740	−198

Source: College Entrance Examination Board, as reported in table 126, *Digest of Educational Statistics, 1996,* U.S. Department of Education, National Center for Educational Statistics.

Table 2-4. High School Dropouts among Persons Sixteen to Twenty-four Years, 1967-96 [a]

Percent

Year	All persons	Race and Ethnicity		
		White	Black	Hispanic
1967	17.0	15.4	28.6	n.a.
1970	15.0	13.2	27.9	n.a.
1975	13.9	11.4	22.8	29.2
1980	14.1	11.3	19.2	35.2
1981	13.9	11.4	18.4	33.2
1982	13.9	11.4	18.4	31.7
1983	13.7	11.2	18.0	31.6
1984	13.1	11.0	15.5	29.8
1985	12.6	10.4	15.2	27.6
1986	12.2	9.7	14.1	30.1
1987	12.7	10.4	14.2	28.6
1988	12.9	9.6	14.3	35.8
1989	12.6	9.4	13.9	33.0
1990	12.1	9.0	13.2	32.4
1991	12.5	8.9	13.6	35.3
1992 [b]	11.0	7.7	13.7	29.4
1993 [b]	11.0	7.9	13.6	27.5
1994 [b]	11.5	7.7	12.6	30.0
1995 [b]	12.0	8.6	12.1	30.0
1996 [b]	11.1	7.3	13.0	29.4

Source: Table 101, *Digest of Educational Statistics, 1995*, U.S. Department of Education, National Center for Educational Statistics; table A23, *Dropout Rates in the United States, 1996*, U.S. Department of Education, National Center for Educational Statistics.

n.a. Not available.

a. The table reports "status" dropouts, persons who are not enrolled in school and who are not high school graduates.

b. Because of changes in data collection procedures, data may not be comparable to figures for earlier years.

ther in 1988 (see figure 2-1). The math gap contracted by a little less than 50 percent (from 46 to 25) in the period 1973 to 1986. The Hispanic-white gap fell by about 25 percent in reading from 1971 to 1984 and by just less than 50 percent in math from 1973 to 1986.[25]

The SAT gap between blacks and whites declined from 258 points in 1976 to 217 points in 1984, a decline of about 15 percent (see table 2-3). And the dropout rate improved for both whites and blacks, but it improved more impressively among blacks (see table 2-4). The black rate in 1967 (28.6 percent) was about 1.86 times the white rate, but by 1984 the multiple had dropped to 1.41 (see figure 2-2). Hispanic rates do not show the same improvement, remaining stubbornly high over the 1970s, 1980s, and

Figure 2-1. Race/Ethnicity Gaps in NAEP Reading Scores (1971–96)

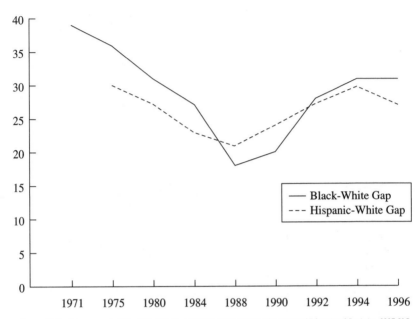

Source: National Assessment of Educational Progress (NAEP), based on table 107, *Digest of Educational Statistics, 1997*, U.S. Department of Education, National Center for Educational Statistics.

1990s. This statistic is notoriously difficult to interpret, however, because of noise introduced by immigration. New arrivals to the United States ages sixteen to twenty-four who do not have a high school diploma and who are not enrolled in school are counted in the dropout numbers even though they never "dropped in." [26]

These tables contradict the perception of widening inequality leading up to 1985. The best indicators we have of educational progress—reading and math achievement scores, SAT scores, and school dropout rates—demonstrate that nonwhite students were doing much better in the mid-1980s than they were one or two decades earlier. Curiously, the progress of these same students slowed markedly after 1985. With the benefit of hindsight, a reader of *Keeping Track* in the 1990s would notice that the patterns before and after 1985 are exactly the opposite of what one would expect. Outcomes were more equitable in 1985 than they were before 1985, and they made little progress on the equity front after that, even as the antitracking movement gathered steam and schools across the country embraced heterogeneous grouping.

Figure 2-2. Race Gap in Dropout Rate (1967–96)

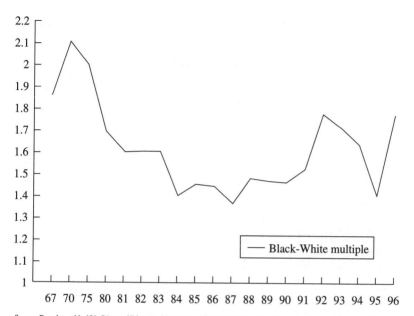

Source: Based on table 101, *Digest of Educatinal Statistics, 1995,* U.S. Department of Education, National Center for Educational Statistics; table A23, *Dropout Rates in the United States, 1996,* U.S. Department of Education, National Center for Educational Statistics.

The History of Tracking

Keeping Track furnishes a coherent narrative linking the origins of tracking to educational inequity. The chapter called "Unlocking the Tradition" presents historical evidence showing that tracking grew out of malignant social intentions, as part of an effort to deny immigrants, the urban poor, and students of color equal educational opportunities. Viewing the past through the lens of what is known as critical revisionism, the book's critique epitomizes the social orientation that condemns curricular differentiation.

But this history warrants close scrutiny. Critical revisionism often provides simple explanations for complex events: the long arm of capitalism penetrates and controls nearly every social phenomenon, from the struggles of mass movements down to the most personal of interactions; social change is driven by racial discrimination and class oppression; racism, class privilege, and economic exploitation conspire to thwart equality and justice. The story travels along a single plot line, and causality falls neatly into place.

Too neatly. Paul Peterson, Diane Ravitch, and other scholars have shown that although the history of American education is indeed marred by the cruelties of race and class discrimination, the school system also evolved from less sinister intentions. Practitioners and policymakers labored under more complicated circumstances than the revisionists acknowledge.[27]

Keeping Track establishes a timeline fixing tracking's creation at the dawn of the twentieth century. It claims that "the earliest free public high schools were established in New England in the 1860s"; that students in the schools of the 1800s "were not grouped for instruction until late in the nineteenth century and then only by ages and grades"; and that in the 1890 high school "individual differences were not an educational concern, and grouping was not an educational practice." [28] In this telling, tracking arose contemporaneously with the rapid societal changes just beginning to stir in 1890, particularly the influx of large numbers of dark-skinned, southern and eastern European immigrants into impoverished urban communities. These developments placed extraordinary pressures on schools.

> The solution ultimately settled upon was the comprehensive high school—a new secondary school that promised something for everyone, but, and this was important, that did not promise the *same* thing for everyone. Gone was the nineteenth-century notion of the need for common learnings to build a cohesive nation. In its place was curriculum differentiation—tracking and ability grouping—with markedly different learnings for what were seen as markedly different groups of students. (italics in original)[29]

This explanation anachronistically dates the origins of both the public high school and curriculum differentiation. The earliest free public high schools were established in New England in the 1820s, not the 1860s, and from the very beginning, according to William Reese, their champions argued for "a sequenced, graded curriculum." [30] In fact, the grading of curriculum, which insisted that school subjects contain a rational, hierarchical order, preceded the grading of students.[31] Even so, David Tyack reports that as early as 1838, Henry Barnard had argued "a classroom containing students of varying ages and attainment was not only inefficient but also inhumane," and John Philbrick, the principal of the new Quincy School, declared on its opening in 1848 that the students "should be divided by their tested proficiency." [32]

Keeping Track recognizes that nineteenth-century students were grouped by ages and grades but fails to acknowledge that this effectively stratified the same two aspects of schooling as tracking in the twentieth century—students by ability and curriculum by level of difficulty. The grading of curriculum was a common practice by 1860. The grading of students was achieved through high schools first granting admission and then basing year-to-year promotions on examination scores. Although marginal students were not shunted off into vocational courses or placed in remedial programs inside high schools, as with tracking, stiff entrance exams barred them from entering in the first place, or promotional exams washed them out once they began to flounder. The exclusive status of high schools was further secured when advanced curriculum was removed from the lower grades and made the exclusive domain of secondary education. As Reese describes these mid-nineteenth-century events:

> Removing the advanced studies from the lower grades was controversial. As the system evolved, the curricula became better coordinated, and the primary, grammar, and high school grades came to resemble a ladder of opportunity that narrowed at the top. But the elimination of advanced subjects below the high school meant lost opportunities for pupils unable to advance. Most high school pupils were from the middle and upper classes; thus removing advanced subjects from grammar schools restricted chances for talented but less advantaged youth to taste the higher learning. Angry Democrats in particular saw the "reform" as discriminating against the poor.[33]

The "common learnings" of the nineteenth century that *Keeping Track* tells us fell victim to tracking in the next century were hardly models of egalitarianism. In many respects, the nineteenth century's system of sorting was far more ruthless than later tracking systems. The people's college, as high schools were known, epitomized an unwavering meritocracy, one that did not grant special dispensation to the student who had to work but would rather study. Opponents of publicly funded high schools accused them of teaching impractical knowledge and abstract topics of little use to working people. These resentments were evident when the town of Beverly, Massachusetts, voted 249 to 143 to close its high school in 1860.[34]

The emergence of distinct curricular tracks within the high school also predates *Keeping Track*'s timeline. Significantly, tracking was a common feature of high schools before attendance rolls were populated by immigrants or the poor. In an early history of the high school curriculum, Harold Rugg reports that subject area conferences leading up to the 1893 Committee of Ten report "condemned the *general custom* in American high schools of preparing 'separate courses of study for pupils of supposedly different destination' " (italics are mine).[35]

Approximately 6.7 percent of teens attended high school in 1890, more in areas such as New England than others. When high school enrollments then boomed, curriculum differentiation spread, of course, but it spread along with all other elements of secondary education, not simply as a reaction to immigration or other demographic trends. The new students flocking into high schools were primarily from middle class families, not differing much in class origins from the students who had attended in earlier years. David Angus compared data on the fathers' occupations represented in urban midwestern high schools from 1858 to 1895 with George Counts's study of occupational representation in four cities' high schools in 1922. He concluded that the social class of high school students changed very little over the entire period, contradicting the notion that tracking's increased popularity at the turn of the century was primarily a strategy for segregating the poor.[36]

The Committee of Ten report of 1893 is one of two documents historians frequently call upon to bracket this period's development of high school into a mass institution. The Cardinal Principles of Secondary Education, an influential document supporting differentiation issued by the National Education Association in 1918, is the other benchmark. The two documents are also frequently used to represent opposing positions on curriculum differentiation, with the Committee of Ten supporting a point of view that was overthrown twenty-five years later by the Cardinal Principles. This portrayal accurately reflects philosophical differences between the two elite commissions issuing these reports, but it cannot be stretched to represent the views of the research community in general, teachers and other education practitioners, or the American public.

The Committee of Ten recommended four courses of study and insisted that colleges accept completion of any of them for admission. Today, the four courses would be considered academically oriented. Moreover, the Committee argued that a firm grounding in academic knowledge was as appropriate for students who would leave school after grade nine as for students who would go on to attend college. The report was responding to two forms of fragmentation in the high school curriculum: between schools because of varying programs of college preparation (to meet the varying admission requirements of different colleges) and, as reported by Harold Rugg, inside schools as distinct curricular tracks.[37] The report did not recommend one curriculum for all; it did recommend that the different curricula should all contain rigorous, substantive subject matter.

In his longitudinal study of Philadelphia's Central High School, David Labaree reports that the school adopted a two-level tracking system in 1889—one track for the college-bound student and one for the non-college-bound. Labaree cites a mix of reasons for the policy. After seeing the credentials of its practical education devalued in the local labor market, mainly by its competitors' similar curricula, the school decided to differentiate its courses and to strengthen its preparation of students for college. In addition, a majority of the faculty now came from the university, and they were more amenable than their high school–educated colleagues to a stratified curriculum organized by departmentalized subject areas, reforms recently embraced in higher education. Though it is true that Central High's curriculum was differentiated in response to environmental demands, these influences were mainly local and pragmatic.[38]

Keeping Track tells a different story of tracking's popularity, one where the democratic principles and unifying themes of the Committee of Ten were subverted by a rising tide of bigotry and racism. Social Darwinism— the idea that Darwin's theories of biological selection could explain society's winners and losers—is identified as the germinating intellectual force for tracking. The social Darwinists frequently defended racist or ethnocentric practices on the basis of "the survival of the fittest," justifying as a matter of biological fate the terrible conditions in which so many non-whites and immigrants lived. The book cites deplorable statements by G. Stanley Hall, a leading psychologist of the child study movement, Ellwood P. Cubberly, a prominent educational historian, and Lewis Terman, one of the founders of the IQ testing movement in the United States. Oakes asserts, "social Darwinism provided the 'scientific' justification for the schools to treat the children of various groups differently," and concludes that "curricular differentiation was made possible only by the genuine belief—arising from social Darwinism—that children of various social classes, those from native-born and long-established families and those of recent immigrants, differed greatly in fundamental ways."[39]

Tarred with social Darwinism, tracking's origins are rendered an artifact of prejudice. This history gives the impression that the social Darwinists were the leading advocates of tracking at the turn of the century. Not discussed are the tolerant, sober-minded educational progressives who supported curricular differentiation. They supported it along functional lines, arguing, at a time when most citizens completed only eight years of schooling, that curriculum differentiation would help alleviate the shocking rates of "retardation," the term for retaining students in grade, and "elimination," the term for dropping out of school. An outpouring of studies released from 1900 to 1920 documented that schools were losing students in droves. A 1911 report estimated that "the public schools lost one-half of their students between the ages of thirteen and fifteen." [40]

The substance and structure of the curriculum were hotly debated topics at the dawn of the twentieth century. These deliberations involved scholars and policymakers with widely diverse views, including nativists who feared the waves of immigrants landing on our shores. However, the idea of providing different curricula to different students was also investigated, analyzed, and debated by turn-of-the-century scholars with other concerns. They raised questions that cut to the very purpose of education, questions that existed long before the advent of tracking—and still exist today. These questions defy easy answers. One of differentiation's significant consequences, for example, was to reduce schooling's focus on academic training and to insist that what is taught vary according to students' real-world experiences and practical interests. In this regard, the early-twentieth-century progressives who promoted tracking have a lot in common with the end-of-century progressives who condemn it. [41]

This brings us back to the prestigious bookends of this period, the Committee of Ten report of 1893 and the Cardinal Principles of 1918. The core belief of the Committee of Ten that was overthrown by the latter document was not a distaste for tracking. What perished was the preeminence of academic learning in the school's mission. The Cardinal Principles relegated the intellect to one among many facets of the student—vocational, social, personal—that schools should develop. Cultivating students' intellectual powers was seen as essential only for the few students who would go to college.

Thus, *Keeping Track*'s characterization of the Cardinal Principles as a set of elitist recommendations contradicting the egalitarian sentiments of the Committee of Ten report is ironic. Early progressives defended the Cardinal Principles as the culmination of several years' rebellion in the field. Teachers who saw education primarily as the servicing of students' needs considered the academic curriculum of the Committee of Ten an elitist imposition of private college presidents on public high schools. In Harold Ruggs's words, the Cardinal Principles "based its discussions and recommendation upon the facts of classroom practice. . . . it was written from the needs of high-school pupils, not from that of college entrance." [42]

Important interest groups also weighed in on the side of a differentiated curriculum. Labor unions provide an interesting example. Jeffrey Mirel points out that *Labor News,* a liberal newsletter in Detroit, editorialized in favor of a differentiated curriculum in 1918, citing the belief that tracking promoted equity. Going back further in time, an 1886 survey showed that rank-and-file members of New York labor organizations supported manual training in the curriculum and a public system of trade schools by a two-to-one margin. Although union leaders of the time staunchly opposed vocational training, they were ultimately brought on board. By 1893, the machinists union in Chicago was petitioning the school board to include manual training in the schools. Why did labor unions reverse course? It was not because they had been duped into supporting class privilege. A growing network of private sector trade schools threatened to siphon off students from public schools. Workers were fighting to protect the institutional viability of the public schools, which they saw as their children's best hope for social and economic advancement.[43]

The press for differentiation was not strictly an urban phenomenon. The historian Lawrence Cremin warns that the conventional story of the birth of vocational education, on which consensus was won when labor reluctantly gave its support, "virtually ignores the telling support that derived from a half-century of agrarian protest and innovation," support expressed in textbooks and newsletters and through political lobbying by powerful farm groups. Farmers, labor unions, college presidents—they would all have their say in fashioning the high school curriculum. No single group or ideology reigned supreme. Pluralism, not capitalism or social Darwinism, was the dynamic driving school politics in the early years of the twentieth century.[44]

Tracking was only one plank in a campaign to refashion schools around students' varying interests and abilities. David Tyack and Larry Cuban explain the functionalist rationale:

> Something must be terribly wrong, thought reformers, if half the students don't even reach eighth grade and if the high school remains an elitist institution. The rigidity and narrow academic emphasis of the educational structure was a major cause of this problem, reformers asserted. All children were expected to ascend the ladder of the graded classrooms, studying the same subjects in the same ways and taking exams for promotion from rung to rung.[45]

Was tracking used by some to further bigotry and intolerance? Yes, regrettably it was. Like other educational activities that make distinctions among students—awarding letter grades, meting out discipline, promoting and retaining students—tracking has been used both fairly and unfairly. But racism, ethnocentrism, and class bias were only part, not the whole, of tracking's history. To again cite Labaree's case study, when Philadelphia's Central High adopted tracking in 1889, years before IQ tests, the school was overwhelmingly made up of white, middle class students. Immigration and race and class segregation were simply not factors.[46]

Let us sum up *Keeping Track*'s impact on two of Kingdon's agenda-setting streams—problems and policies. First, a problem is identified as readers are told of racial achievement gaps stubbornly resisting the efforts of compensatory programs. We are urged to look inside schools for causes, and tracking is identified as a prime suspect. A history of tracking is presented that locates the practice's origins at the beginning of the twentieth century, a period of tremendous immigration and wrenching social change, and a period when widely disseminated theories justified race and class inequalities. By linking tracking to social Darwinism and the worst elements of the IQ testing movement, the book names tracking as an institutionalized source of inequality.

From start to finish, *Keeping Track*'s history of tracking is the story of privilege winning out over equal opportunity. Oakes succinctly summarizes the argument in the foreword to another author's book: "The matching of students to different tracks carried with it racial, ethnic, and social-class overtones *from the very beginning* . . . and today most educators and policy makers are deeply troubled by the fact that sorting students into 'high' and 'low' tracks severely limits the educational and occupational futures of low-income, African-American and Latino students" (italics in original).[47] These words were written at a time of great pessimism among students of education policy. Researchers were declaring it almost impossible for any education policy to achieve its intended objectives. Here was a policy still achieving its shameful objectives after eighty years.

That raises Kingdon's third stream, politics. The opponents of tracking heard and responded to *Keeping Track*'s powerful message.

Antitracking Politics and Detracking Policies

As indicated in the passage from *Keeping Track*'s preface, the book's publication coincided with an immense surge of concern about the functioning of the educational system as a whole. After the release of *A Nation at Risk* in 1983, commission after commission deplored the sorry state of American education, and international tests showed U.S. students near the bottom in math and science achievement. A flurry of press accounts documented the growing crisis in education, opinion polls registered the public's concern about education, and politicians campaigned for office on the promise of fixing the broken-down school system.[48]

The first batch of reforms instigated by *A Nation at Risk* tightened up high school graduation requirements, implemented new tests and standards for licensing prospective teachers, and generally raised the bar for both students and educators. While the politics of education tends to scramble and render worthless ideological labels such as "liberal" and "conservative," it is not misleading to say that the first post–*Nation at Risk* reforms were enthusiastically supported by educational conservatives. But liberals were wary. They feared that get-tough reforms would negatively affect minority students and the poor. They also wanted to maintain the hard-fought policy momentum they had won in the 1970s toward equalizing resources between schools in wealthy and disadvantaged communities.

As Joseph Murphy puts it, "No sooner had the ink dried on these early reform measures than they came under attack." [49] Observers were announcing that the get-tough reforms had failed and that a second wave of reform had commenced, one directed at the internal operations of schools. Wave II of the reform movement was about "restructuring" schools, overhauling the organization and management of local systems, altering power relations in schools, and changing the essential nature of teaching and learning. Improving urban schools and the chances of students at risk of failure were restored to primacy among policy analysts. Sturdy old planks of progressivism, including tracking reform, were pushed forward as solutions to American education's deepening problems.

This period also marked the reemergence of middle school reform as a serious topic among educational opinion makers. The historical struggle by middle grade educators to gain institutional autonomy from the high school is embodied in a set of principles known as the middle school philosophy. It attempts to revitalize connections with elementary education by discouraging such secondary school practices as tracking and departmentalization by subject area.[50] In the 1960s middle school reformers had changed the grade structures of junior highs by moving ninth graders in many communities back to high schools, but this failed to diminish either departmentalization or tracking in middle schools. A 1981 survey of middle school principals, the 1988 Johns Hopkins Education in the Middle Grades Survey, and a survey of middle school practices conducted in 1989 by the Association for Supervision and Curriculum Development (ASCD) reported frequent use of tracking in mathematics and English–language arts, though the ASCD report noted, "Recognizing the adverse effects of such grouping on student achievement, many leaders are attempting to move away from the practice."[51] One of the researchers of the Johns Hopkins study, Jomills Henry Braddock II, concluded that the practice of tracking students contradicts the mission of middle schools:

> Learning opportunities in the middle grades remain highly stratified— despite a middle school philosophy that encourages heterogeneous classes, despite various calls for school reform and restructuring to develop critical thinking skills among the nation's youth, and despite exhortations to insure that all children are provided equal access to learning opportunities.[52]

The antitracking and middle school movements joined forces during the 1980s. Heterogeneous grouping could serve as an organizational feature separating middle schools from high schools. Detracking frequently anchored efforts to restructure schools around student-centered practices. Once detracked, schools needed new curricula, new instructional approaches, and new ways of organizing students and teachers. Within a few short years of *Keeping Track*'s publication, the NAACP Legal Defense Fund, the American Civil Liberties Union (ACLU), the Children's Defense Fund, National Governors' Association, the College Board, and the National Education Association all issued proclamations against tracking. Condemnations also surfaced in the popular press. A 1988 article in *Better Homes and Gardens* asked, "Is Your Child Being Tracked for Failure?" In 1989 *Psychology Today* published "Tracked to Fail," and "The Label That Sticks" appeared in *U.S. News and World Report*.[53]

The decade ended with the prestigious 1989 report from the Carnegie Council on Adolescent Development, *Turning Points: Preparing American Youth for the Twenty-first Century,* which explicitly linked untracking to effective middle school reform. The report called for middle schools to create learning communities more responsive to the unique needs of adolescents and condemned tracking as "one of the most divisive and damaging school practices in existence."[54]

Kingdon's agenda-setting streams came together for tracking reformers in the 1980s. Jeannie Oakes's *Keeping Track* was extremely influential, as evidenced in its citation by scholarly works, articles in popular magazines, and important position papers. The book provided a clear indictment of tracking around which a reform movement could gather. Reformers were able to define inequality as a problem long exacerbated by tracking, to propose heterogeneously grouped classes as a feasible alternative, to tap growing disenchantment with the public schools, and to rally the middle school movement and important political organizations to their cause.

Recall that Kingdon described a chain of events: "An alternative floating in the policy stream . . . becomes coupled either to a prominent problem or to events in the political stream. . . . If an alternative is coupled to a problem as a solution, then that combination also finds support in the political stream. . . . if an alternative is seized upon by politicians, it is justified as a solution to a real problem." [55] All of these events had transpired, and tracking was a hot issue.

As I turn to the policies in California and Massachusetts, let me be clear about the limits of the following discussion. I did not research the behind-the-scenes politicking and the deliberations of state policymakers that led to the tracking proclamations. To do so adequately would have required at least one more full-scale study. I will show, however, that the essence of the indictment scrutinized throughout this chapter—that tracking is socially reprehensible—found local allies in both states. I will also review objections made by defenders of tracking after the policy was adopted in California, while it was in the initial stages of implementation. In domains of public policy as localized as education, national movements wither and die unless local advocates flock to the cause. [56]

In California, Oakes's book and the other antitracking books coming out of UCLA's A Study of Schooling had homegrown appeal. In addition, the California League of Middle Schools, a professional organization of middle school educators, issued position papers sharply critical of tracking. In one of its 1988 monographs, *Equal Access to Education: Alternatives to Tracking and Ability Grouping,* Jeannie Oakes receives fifteen of thirty-four citations. [57] In Massachusetts, Anne Wheelock, an analyst at the Massachusetts Advocacy Center and the author of *Crossing the Tracks: How "Untracking" Can Save America's Schools* (Oakes's foreword to the book is quoted above), advised officials in the Boston Public Schools as they mulled over the tracking issue. She also served as the project director for the 1990 report from the Massachusetts Advocacy Center, *Locked In/ Locked Out: Tracking and Placement in Boston Public Schools,* which, unlike most indictments of tracking, included special education and bilingual classes in its condemnation. [58]

Representing the culmination of hearings and research by State Superintendent of Public Instruction Bill Honig's Middle Grade Task Force, California's *Caught in the Middle* was released in 1987. It expresses the desire to move middle schools away from tracking and toward heterogeneous grouping. Echoing the language of *Keeping Track,* the report states:

Heterogeneous grouping practices should be normative in middle grade classrooms. If permanent or semipermanent "ability" grouping or tracking occurs for all or most of a student's school day, substantial harm can result. Researchers are invariably consistent in their conclusion that large numbers of poor and minority students, in particular, are precluded from realizing the true meaning of equal access when tracking occurs.[59]

The document cites the need for schools to provide all students equal access to curriculum through the creation of untracked structures and urges middle schools to make themselves institutionally distinct from high schools. As summarized by the cochairpersons of the task force, "The uniqueness of middle grade education is emphasized." [60]

The antitracking stance of *Caught in the Middle* subsequently found its way into the curriculum frameworks released by the State Department of Education (for example, *English–Language Arts Framework,* 1987; *Mathematics Framework,* 1992). After citing Oakes's research, the math framework baldly declares, "This *Framework* calls for heterogeneous grouping and untracking as a goal and recommends against attempting to group students by ability." [61] Detracking also surfaced in the state's criteria for Program Quality Reviews (PQRs), state-sanctioned reviews conducted by teams of local educators. Couched in the flexible language typical of such documents, the PQR criteria issued in 1988 reflected the state's concern with tracking, stating in the section describing exemplary instructional practices: "Heterogeneous grouping is a feature of the school. Ability grouping and tracking are not the only grouping strategies of the classroom or the school organization." [62]

In Massachusetts, the first official proclamation against tracking came in 1990, when the Massachusetts Department of Education issued *Structuring Schools for Student Success: A Focus on Ability Grouping.* The document urged schools to consider reductions in tracking, a recommendation made specific to middle schools in 1993 with the publication of *Magic in the Middle.*

Research delineating the harm of rigid ability grouping and tracking on student achievement, student self-esteem and self-efficacy, and school climate is now well established. Most critically, as students are grouped, they experience increasingly distinct levels of access to valued knowledge. Because the effects of tracking are cumulative and because ability grouping in the elementary grades is widespread, differences in achievement may appear dramatic by the middle grades and may seem to justify grouping whole classes by perceived ability.[63]

Later the document recites the claim that disparities in racial achievement can be traced to tracking: "The decline in overall achievement and the widening of test score gaps between white students and their African-American and Latino peers suggest that middle grade students are not equally exposed to the enriched, meaningful curriculum and instruction that will develop the knowledge and skills that they need to succeed." [64]

The superintendents of Boston and Springfield moved quickly to reform tracking in their urban systems. In awarding new funds to programs targeting at-risk students, Massachusetts officials began granting preferences to schools engaged in schoolwide detracking efforts. But beyond this modest inducement, the Massachusetts Department of Education encouraged tracking reform without wielding much leverage over local schools and districts. State curriculum frameworks would not appear on the scene until the mid- to late 1990s, and the very idea of getting the state involved with evaluating local schools' operations, as in the California PQR process, runs against the grain of Massachusetts's political culture (see chapter 5).

In California's tracking debate, the critics of tracking were clear winners. No organized opposition appeared to denounce the policy when it was adopted by the state. But the losers soon became apparent. In 1989, a group of parents and educators representing gifted children, the California Association for the Gifted (CAG), attacked the state's support of detracking. In response to *Caught in the Middle,* many middle schools had moved to eliminate honors courses, triggering howls of protest from CAG.

In April 1989 Superintendent Honig met with representatives of CAG, which had supported him in his campaigns for office. Honig then sent an open letter to every middle school principal in the state explaining that state policy did not recommend the elimination of honors programs, but adding, "Even as I say this, I urge you, also, to refrain from the abusive tracking practices that place a child early in his or her school years into tracks from which the child cannot emerge and in which he or she is not adequately challenged." The organization watched and waited but soon grew disappointed. Representatives of CAG met with Honig again eight months later to complain, "The issue of advanced classes is still posing problems throughout the state, as middle schools implement what they perceive to be the State direction to eliminate tracking. We need to discuss with Mr. Honig the actual and threatened elimination of honors classes in many districts." [65]

The CAG representatives were never able to get more than memorandums out of Honig urging that bright students remain challenged by the curriculum. The state's arsenal of policy instruments—curriculum frameworks, PQRs, workshops and colloquiums supporting *Caught in the Middle*—echoed the call to detrack. But such calls are not mandates; whether schools hear them, for the most part, is up to schools themselves.

Summary and Conclusion

Massachusetts and California have urged their middle schools to abandon the longstanding practice of tracking. This chapter has traced the philosophical, historical, and political origins of these policies.

Two opposing orientations are in conflict in the tracking controversy: a social orientation that values educational practices for their social impact, especially their impact on social equality, and a functionalist orientation that values practices for making schooling more efficient. Empirical evidence on the debate's key questions is inconclusive, and research fails to give clear policy direction on the tracking issue. The governmental agenda is not forged from scientific evidence, however. Instead, conforming to John Kingdon's theory of agenda setting, the confluence of problem, policy, and political streams pushed tracking to the fore in the mid-1980s.

Keeping Track by Jeannie Oakes was instrumental in gaining the attention of policymakers and igniting a national movement to abolish tracking. The book supplied all of the ingredients necessary for a policy entrepreneur to shape the public agenda. It argued that an unacceptably wide racial gap in school outcomes persisted despite years of equity efforts, and tracking was identified as the major culprit. A history of tracking was presented that depicted the practice as the product of class and ethnic bigotry, heterogeneous grouping was endorsed as an alternative policy, and powerful political allies were rallied to the cause.

A national movement arose dedicated to the abolition of tracking. Policymakers in California and Massachusetts responded to the outcries for reform, and the education departments of both states issued policy proclamations urging middle schools to reform their tracking policies. The edicts were issued as policy recommendations, however, not as directives, so whether schools would actually follow the states' advice would be decided by local authorities.

And not a soul knew what the schools would do.

3

The Schools Respond

D ID MIDDLE SCHOOLS IN CALIFORNIA and Massachusetts follow the recommendations of their state
education departments and reduce tracking? Or did they keep on grouping
students by ability as they always had? This chapter reports what happened
to tracking reform and also examines opposing explanations for why some
schools track and other schools do not, setting the stage for chapter 4's
exploration of the forces driving tracking policy.

Data

Before presenting statistics on tracking policies, I must explain how the
study's data were collected. Three surveys were administered by mail. The
first was conducted in California in the fall of 1990, the second in California in the spring of 1994, and the third in Massachusetts in the spring of
1995. The surveys asked school principals questions pertaining to the development and implementation of tracking policy. I will refer to the first
California survey using the shorthand "CA 91," since June 1991 was the
final month of the academic year in which the survey was administered.
The second California survey is called "CA 94" and the Massachusetts
survey "MA 95."

The data do not escape problems associated with information from self-
selected participants. Since it is impossible to know why principals did or
did not return surveys, interpretation of results must be offered cautiously.
This would be a significant problem if the study's objective were to precisely estimate the amount of tracking and untracking in schools. The
study's primary goal of explaining why some schools track and others detrack makes it more important that a wide variety of tracking policies are
represented in the data and in numbers sufficient for analyzing the different

conditions surrounding different practices. These criteria are met by the three samples.

The surveys were supplemented by extensive fieldwork. In 1991 I visited twenty-three schools in California and conducted interviews with 175 teachers and principals. The schools were chosen to represent a cross-section of California middle schools. After completing the first phase of the study in 1992, I selected six of these schools to continue following, and in addition to occasional phone conversations, I revisited all six schools in 1995 and 1996. Six Massachusetts schools were added to the case study sample in 1996, and I visited these schools in 1996 and 1997. The second phase of fieldwork included eighty-nine interviews.

In sum, the study spanned the years from 1990 to 1997; two surveys were conducted in California and one in Massachusetts; the three surveys report on the tracking policies of 589 schools; and a total of 264 interviews were held with teachers and principals at twenty-nine school sites. I discuss the study's methods, data, and limitations in greater depth in Appendix A.

Untracking in the Schools

I asked principals to report the number of ability levels in which their school grouped eighth graders for academic classes. I also asked if this system had changed during the previous five years and how many levels existed in the prior system, which in the case of CA 91 and MA 95, probes back before the release of California's *Caught in the Middle* and Massachusetts's *Magic in the Middle*.

As shown in tables 3-1 and 3-2, California schools sharply reduced tracking after the release of the state advisory. Math remained the most-tracked subject, but it also experienced substantial reform. In CA 91, principals reported that their prior systems offered three to four separate levels of ability-grouped classes in math (mean of 3.58), but this dropped to fewer than three levels in 1991 (mean of 2.88). By 1994, students were ability grouped into only two to three levels of math classes (mean of 2.34). The same steady trend toward detracking is apparent in the other subjects. Tracking in English fell by nearly one full level (2.40 to 1.75 to 1.50), history by about one-half level (1.85 to 1.41 to 1.37), and science by one-third level (1.58 to 1.28 to 1.28). There is noticeable slowing in history and science tracking as they approach a single level of heterogeneously grouped classes.

Reductions in tracking are also evident in Massachusetts, but they appear more uniform across subject areas (see table 3-3). Tracking also

Table 3-1. CA 91, Mean Number of Levels in Eighth Grade Subjects, Prior and Current System
$(N = 373)$ [a]

Subject	Prior	1991	Change
Math	3.58	2.88	−0.70
	(1.56)	(1.37)	
English	2.40	1.75	−0.65
	(1.19)	(0.97)	
History	1.85	1.41	−0.44
	(1.05)	(0.64)	
Science	1.58	1.28	−0.30
	(0.91)	(0.56)	

a. Standard deviation indicated in parentheses.

Table 3-2. CA 94, Mean Number of Levels in Eighth Grade Subjects, Prior and Current System
$(N = 166)$ [a]

Subject	Prior	1994	Change
Math	2.77	2.34	−0.43
	(1.23)	(0.97)	
English	1.79	1.50	−0.29
	(0.87)	(0.67)	
History	1.57	1.37	−0.20
	(0.79)	(0.62)	
Science	1.43	1.28	−0.15
	(0.73)	(0.61)	

a. Standard deviation indicated in parentheses.

Table 3-3. MA 95, Mean Number of Levels in Eighth Grade Subjects, Prior and Current System
$(N = 134)$ [a]

Subject	Prior	1995	Change
Math	3.00	2.59	−0.41
	(1.23)	(1.01)	
English	2.38	1.86	−0.52
	(1.45)	(1.10)	
History	2.12	1.66	−0.46
	(1.47)	(1.08)	
Science	2.14	1.72	−0.42
	(1.44)	(1.07)	

a. Standard deviation indicated in parentheses.

Table 3-4. Tracks Eliminated[a]
Percent

Action taken	CA 94	MA 95
No tracks eliminated	55.2	60.0
Remedial	31.9	20.8
General	6.1	21.6
Honors	19.0	15.2

a. Totals exceed 100 percent because schools may eliminate more than one level.

appears more pronounced in Massachusetts than in California. Levels of tracking in English (mean of 1.86), history (mean of 1.66), and science (mean of 1.72) in 1995 exceeded those found in California in 1991. Like California, the average school in Massachusetts offered between two to three levels of eighth grade math (mean of 2.59). Subject area differences in tracking, and, in particular, the question of why mathematics is the academic subject most conducive to tracking receive extended attention in chapter 6.

The two states exhibit interesting differences in the tracks that were eliminated (see table 3-4). Massachusetts's schools seem to have reduced tracking across the whole system without targeting one track or another for elimination. The general track was abolished by 21.6 percent of schools. In contrast, the general track was abolished by only 6.1 percent of California schools. In fact, most of the schools engaged in detracking in California focused their efforts on the remedial track. Eliminating the honors track, a move that frequently sparks bitter controversy, was part of detracking 19 percent of the schools in California and 15.2 percent in Massachusetts.

The remainder of this book investigates the differences between schools embracing reform and schools rejecting it. To do this, each school's tracking policy must be modeled comprehensively (in a way that faithfully represents the whole of a school's tracking system) and meaningfully (in a way that distinguishes schools that are truly doing something different from schools continuing with conventional practices). Very little information is lost by focusing on tracking in math and English alone since these subjects constitute the core of the academic curriculum, but tracking in mathematics poses a problem. Schools with fully detracked math programs are still rare, less than 20 percent in either state. I decided to define "untracked" schools as those with only a single level (in other words, with only heterogeneous grouping) in eighth grade English but up to two ability levels of eighth grade math. All other schools are categorized as "tracked," that is, those

Figure 3-1. Percent of Schools Untracked[a]

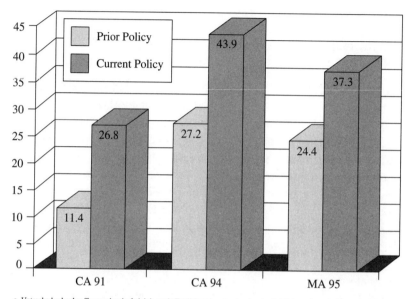

a. Untracked schools offer one level of eighth grade English and one or two levels of eighth grade math. Tracked schools offer more than one level of English or more than two levels of math.

with more than two levels of mathematics or with any tracking whatsoever in English.

Using these definitions, figure 3-1 exhibits the policies reported in the three surveys. The progress of tracking reform is evident here, with 26.8 percent of schools in CA 91, 43.9 percent of schools in CA 94, and 37.3 percent of the schools in MA 95 showing reformed systems. Note that in 1991 only 11.4 percent of California schools reported that their prior system was untracked. Untracked schools nearly quadrupled by 1994, with almost 44 percent reporting detracked systems.

I categorize schools' tracking policies using these definitions for the remainder of the book. Readers should keep in mind that most of the untracked schools, with their two levels of mathematics, have not in the strictest sense adopted heterogeneous grouping. They are, however, taking significant steps toward detracking by meeting preliminary targets of reform. Offering two levels in math and one level in English represents a significant break from past tracking practices. This definition captures some dramatic policy changes that occurred after the two states launched their tracking reforms. Why did some schools, but not all, follow the states' recommendations?

Why Some Schools Track and Others Detrack:
The UCLA Project's Explanation

In the 1990s, Jeannie Oakes and Amy Stuart Wells led a team of UCLA researchers conducting a three-year study of detracking at ten racially mixed secondary schools: four junior highs and six high schools. Their findings on tracking reform's implementation reinforce Oakes's earlier work on tracking's history and effects. In the UCLA researchers' telling, tracking exists to guarantee the unfair distribution of privilege. White and wealthy students benefit from access to high-status knowledge that low-income students and students of color are denied. Writing as advocates of reform, the UCLA team argues that tracking can only be dismantled if three factors are altered: the technical and organizational structures supporting curriculum differentiation, the schools' cultural norms, and the distribution of political power at schools.[1]

Structural aspects of schooling include such details as the schedule that matches students and teachers, the school calendar, and the availability of interdisciplinary curricula. The UCLA project reports that untracked schools use teaming, in which teachers from different subject disciplines work together in teams; block scheduling, which combines class periods into single course blocks of time; the creation of tutorial periods in which struggling students may receive remedial help; year-round scheduling, with three-week intersessions that permit students to retake courses they have failed; and "double dose" scheduling, which allows, say, students who are inadequately prepared for algebra to take two periods of the course daily. These innovations are designed to make the task of untracking easier to accomplish.

The UCLA researchers believe several aspects of school culture underpin tracking. They argue that notions of intelligence and ability are socially constructed, defined over time so as to legitimize the distribution—or, more accurately, the maldistribution—of power in society. They contend that intelligence and ability have come to be accepted as socially stratified by race and class in America, that academic ability, for example, is commonly believed more prevalent among upper income, white populations and less prevalent among African Americans, Hispanics, and the poor. They also assert that many people believe these are innate characteristics.

In what the UCLA researchers call the "conventional view" of intelligence, ability is seen as stable, unidimensional, easy to measure, and difficult to change through schooling. They argue that achievement tests buttress this view by assessing cultural capital rather than academic learning. They further argue that the distribution of scores on achievement tests, in a normal (bell-shaped) curve, misleads the public into thinking that the social distribution of achievement reflects the unfolding of natural events, the inevitable outcome of an educational system based on merit.

The UCLA team sees curriculum differentiation as an ugly manifestation of this blatantly unfair "ideology of intelligence." [2] Tracking is "a hierarchical structure supported by a culture that values the knowledge and life experiences of some students more than others." It is a system that creates college-prep, high-ability tracks allowing "White and wealthy parents to maintain separate classrooms for their children and any lower-income or non-White students who 'act white and wealthy,' which means they buy into the dominant culture's view of the educational system as fair and meritocratic." [3]

In terms of tracking's politics, the UCLA researchers are most concerned about the opponents of detracking in local schools. Observe how one school's technical structure, culture, and politics converge in a war over tracking reform:

Inside the school, two factions within the faculty struggled bitterly for control. The most active members of the Idea Team—white, highly-experienced female teachers in their forties—worked diligently and quietly through a newly established set of study groups to change tracking at Central High. Meanwhile, the Good Old Boys—a group of entrenched male teachers, most of whom had been athletic coaches at one time—loudly and staunchly defended the school's status quo.

The gulf between the Idea Team's conviction that all students can learn given the right opportunities and the Good Old Boys' adherence to a conventional view of intelligence was strikingly revealed by the comment of veteran Good Old Boy science teacher Walter Brown: "Some of that may be simple intellectual ability. Some kids are just born with it. . . . Some kids have got it and some kids don't."

The Good Old Boys knew that giving way to new conceptions of intelligence would mean losing their comfortable and familiar teaching routines, as well as the power they had traditionally held in their paternalistic, sports-minded school community. The Idea Team knew that their lowest achieving students, many of whom were Latino and low-income from migrant farmworker backgrounds, could not afford for the Good Old Boys and the set of beliefs they represented to prevail.[4]

Those who oppose detracking are not looked upon very kindly in this study. Tracking reformers are described in heroic terms. The assistant principal at a suburban school, an avid detracking advocate, is described as on "a crusade." She works "to make middle-class suburbia more responsive to the needs of its least politically powerful constituents" and struggles to change the community's "dominant paradigm" that says "some students cannot achieve."[5] The UCLA study argues that white middle-class and wealthy parents fight hard to maintain the privileges that tracking confers.

Most salient was the pressure placed on schools by savvy parents whose children had been clearly advantaged under the more competitive and highly selective tracking system. Although this form of parental opposition was generally cloaked in a discussion of educational merit and opportunity, these parents were often equally concerned about losing the high status tracking conferred on the families of gifted or honors students. In addition, more blatant racist and classist attitudes sometimes emerged from white and usually middle to upper-class parents who expressed their discomfort with the notion of mixing their children with students from very different backgrounds and thus different past experiences in the educational system.[6]

Stripped of their unabashed advocacy and bias, some of the UCLA project's descriptions are consistent with the observations of mainstream implementation research. The characteristics of students do in fact make a difference in the innovations that educators attempt, and, at least since the Great Society, these characteristics have included the racial composition, socioeconomic status, and achievement level of a particular school's students. Any significant reform spawns local supporters and opponents, found both inside and outside of schools. It is true that resistant parents can slam the door on school reform, and it is also true that parents of gifted and high-achieving students vehemently oppose detracking. And researchers agree that schools' organizational structures play a consequential role in shaping how policy is implemented.

I would like to step back and consider these observations from a different perspective, one that focuses on the local institutional settings in which educational reforms are decided. I present an alternative to the UCLA proj-oect's conceptual framework. Some of its components resemble the UCLA scheme; others are very different. This framework generates a set of hy-pothesized influences that will be tested empirically in chapter 4.

An Alternative Framework

I expect any school's position on a particular reform proposal to be shaped by four factors—a school's institutional characteristics, its organi-zational characteristics, the technical challenges posed by reform, and po-litical influences on policy. Keep in mind that as applied to tracking policy these factors cut both ways. They encourage the adoption of tracking re-form in some schools; in others, they hinder its adoption.

Institutional Characteristics

Schools possess institutional identities. Local knowledge of a school's identity is expressed through informal labels: "the football school," "a good school for the college bound," "a school for free spirits," "a tough school." More remote judgments about schools' identities are made from traits that can be quantified, reported, and analyzed. A school's demo-graphic characteristics, especially as they reflect its surrounding commu-nity and student body, may indicate whether a particular reform is appro-priate or not. Some governmental programs are designed for a certain type of school, for example, those serving large numbers of economically dis-advantaged, homeless, non–English-speaking, or migrant students. As dis-cussed in chapter 2, several reforms in the latter half of the 1980s attempted to focus national attention on the needs of disadvantaged students. In a survey administered in conjunction with the National Assessment of Edu-cational Progress (NAEP) in 1988, schools located in urban areas or exhib-iting high levels of student poverty were more likely to be engaged in sig-nificant reform than other schools.[7]

Educational institutions may use reform to shore up legitimacy. Put cynically, schools that are perceived as failing may embrace reforms to convince their various constituencies—taxpayers, central office adminis-trators, the state, parents, the business community, voters—that they are on the road to improvement. Churning through reform proposals, constantly throwing out the old and embracing the new, is an effective way for insti-tutions to convince internal and external constituencies of two things: that they remain sympathetic to powerful interests (by adopting reforms advocated by one group or another) and that they are positioned on the "cutting edge" of educational trends. These reforms are frequently more symbolic than real. As David Tyack puts it, "educators have often embraced innovation in protective symbolic ways to satisfy the reformers and the public and to advance their own reputations while leaving the core of instruction in the classroom relatively undisturbed." [8]

Advocates, researchers, and policymakers construct and hone the symbolic dimensions of policy when state policy is crafted. The significance of this symbolism carries over into the local arena. Tracking reformers argue that the race gap is exacerbated by tracking and that detracking promotes educational equity. I expect urban schools and schools with large numbers of students from low-income families to respond favorably to the states' antitracking policies. Local policymakers may embrace detracking because "it is intended for schools like us," because it reinforces local goals, and because it signals constituencies that significant steps toward improvement are being taken. As Paul Berman has stated, "the decision to adopt an innovation, to seek funds to innovate, and all associated activities define what a school district intends to do and communicates these intentions to various audiences, both external and internal to the district." [9] States signal local educators to adopt particular reforms; schools use these reforms to signal local constituencies. [10]

The Technical Challenge

Technical challenges refer to factors impinging on the delivery of instruction by teachers in classrooms, the school's core operation. Both critics and defenders of tracking agree that teachers must teach differently in tracked and untracked settings (one of the major topics of chapter 7). The best evidence we have that the composition of instructional groups affects teaching comes from studies of within-class ability grouping systems, with the same teacher teaching all groups. Rebecca Barr and Robert Dreeben's study of first grade reading found that teachers formed reading groups in response to the distribution of ability within a classroom. Once groups were created, if a critical mass of nonreaders or poor readers was present within a particular group, the pace of instruction for that group slowed significantly. [11]

Keep in mind that classrooms and schools represent different aggregations of students. Schools first face the task of creating classes from a pool of students whose membership is dictated by attendance areas, parent choice, or other criteria. The classic defense of tracking asserts that it is a valuable tool for facilitating instruction. By narrowing the spread of achievement in the classroom, the argument goes, tracking reduces the number of students requiring special help and maximizes the number of students who can readily grasp concepts in any given lesson, thereby increasing instructional efficiency.

Barr and Dreeben's finding may not apply to whole schools. Maureen Hallinan's study of middle school tracking found no relationship between the spread of achievement at schools and the number of tracks they employ. Although track size varied somewhat by achievement heterogeneity, several organizational factors—for example, district policy on the size of classes, course prerequisites, qualifications for honors classes, and scheduling—determined the number of tracks that schools created. Brian De-Lany makes this point more bluntly, describing a process in which schools first patch together course schedules, dictated primarily by resource constraints, and then sort students into the slots available.[12]

Any effect of achievement heterogeneity on school policy will probably be generated from the classroom. Let me describe this in real terms. On a standard, off-the-shelf achievement test, a typical class of thirty eighth graders performs as follows: one or two students score somewhere around the third or fourth grade reading level, one or two at the twelfth grade level, and the rest of the class is scattered in between. If this class is in a school dominated by low-achieving students, as many as ten readers might labor along several years below grade level, unable to read their textbooks in any subject. Creative teachers attempt numerous ways to involve poor readers in class activities, of course, but even the best teachers complain that extreme heterogeneity is deadly for effective teaching.[13]

A Texas study of heterogeneous classes concluded:

> If, in consideration of the social psychologists' case against homogeneous ability grouping and tracking, school systems feel impelled to abandon ability grouping and "special" classes for some students, then they must recognize that the extremely heterogeneous classes that result are indeed also "special." They place extraordinary demands on teachers' time, attention, and classroom management skills. Our study indicates that skilled classroom managers can make many of the adjustments that are necessary in heterogeneous classes, but less skilled managers cannot. Even in the hands of skilled classroom managers, extremely heterogeneous classes appear to be less than ideal learning environments.[14]

I expect schools that are more homogeneous to be more receptive to detracking than heterogeneous schools. Schools with wide spans of achievement, on the other hand, will probably resist the reform.

Organizational Characteristics

Many of a school's most significant organizational features are decided by superior authorities, usually district officials. These include schools' attendance boundaries (or in the case of magnet schools and charter schools the procedures for admission), the grade levels schools serve, and the number of students who enroll. In addition to fixing the size of the teaching staff, site administration, and auxiliary staff, district officials usually decide who fills these positions. It is not surprising, considering all of the cross-cutting layers of organization and authority, that a proposed reform involving teachers, students, or curriculum may impinge on one or more existing organizational arrangements.[15]

Which organizational characteristics of schools can be expected to come into play as local educators consider tracking reform? Grade levels probably make a difference. The Johns Hopkins and ASCD studies reported that schools containing a ninth grade (that is, schools serving grades 7–9) were especially likely to track. Schools ending in eighth grade (for example, serving grades 5–8) were less likely to track. This rings true for a couple of reasons. Ninth grade courses carry high school credit, and tracking is still very popular at high schools. Teacher licensing probably also plays a part. Teachers with single-subject credentials, those trained to teach one subject all day—math, English, history, and so forth—are more likely found in junior high schools (grades 7–9) than in the other grade configurations. Multiple-subject teachers, who are trained to teach in elementary schools, are common in middle schools (grades 6–8), where interdisciplinary courses tap their expertise. Both the Johns Hopkins and ASCD researchers identified detracking as a central element of middle school reform.

The middle school movement, which first stirred in the 1960s, reshuffled grade levels by stripping middle-level education of the ninth grade—and its high school curriculum—and pushing the middle school entry grade down to the sixth or even fifth grade. When it regained momentum in the 1980s, the middle school movement urged schools to embrace a philosophy stressing how different the institution is from a high school. Schools changed their names from "junior high" to "middle school," a switch laden with symbolism, refocused curriculum toward younger adolescents, embraced elementary school instructional practices, and, important to this investigation, began raising serious doubts about whether tracking was in the best interest of young adolescents.[16] I expect that grade 5–8 and 6–8 middle schools will react more warmly to tracking reform than grade 7–8 and 7–9 schools.

Studies conducted in the 1980s suggest that school size also affects tracking. The number of students correlates across education's organizational units. Large classes are usually found in large schools located in large districts. In small schools, administrators have little latitude in scheduling students and teachers into each instructional period, and in some schools, there simply are not enough students to justify two distinct levels in any subject. In large schools, students in the same grade must be divided up into separate classes anyway, and by using ability or past performance as a criterion for doing so, schools are able to create specialized advanced and remedial courses for the students who may need them.[17]

Researchers have done an about-face on the issue of school size. After World War II, James Conant led a contingent of advocates for the large school, arguing that bigger schools allowed for a varied curriculum, more extracurricular activities, better student services, and the efficient use of administrators.[18] State and local officials picked up the call, and thousands of districts and schools disappeared through consolidation. A remarkable indicator of this campaign's accomplishments is the fact that the average public *school* in the United States held approximately 490 students by 1980, far more than the 300 students held by the average *district* in 1950. It bears repeating: The average school of 1980 was 63 percent larger than the average district of 1950. As schools have grown larger, practices like tracking may have become more deeply entrenched and difficult to give up.[19]

Environmental conditions may also induce heavily populated schools to resist change. Big schools are frequently tough places to work, especially in urban areas. Employing an ill-defined technology, attempting to produce uncertain outcomes, and operating in a stressful atmosphere, the large urban school is what James Q. Wilson calls a "coping agency." Discretion over core activities often flows to the frontline workers of coping agencies. It has been observed that principals of urban schools engage in "creative insubordination" to avoid central office interference with the routines they have honed over years of practice. Schools with huge numbers of students may also develop deeply institutionalized rules for conducting business and a thick layer of on-site administration. These are all inertial forces. Small schools may be less likely to experience these pressures for maintaining the status quo.[20]

Political Influences

Political interests are expressed through the influence that competing groups, both internal and external to the school system, bring to bear on education policy. District and school decisionmakers are the targets of these activities. A 1960 study of big city government, *Governing New York City* by Wallace S. Sayre and Herbert Kaufman, offers a concise way of thinking about local politics. Sayre and Kaufman show that city policy emerges from the interplay of key actors (called "core groups") and supporting players (called "satellite groups"). Core actors either hold formal power over policy or are close to power. Satellite actors are not decisionmakers themselves. They seek to influence policy by convincing a core actor of a particular course of action. Core actors may become satellite actors if the authority to create policy is vested in another level of the bureaucracy.[21]

The school principal and teachers are the core actors at local schools, except when policies that the district has centralized are decided. At the district level, central office administrators make routine policy decisions, but when issues are controversial, the school board acts. State recommendations are only one factor in these decisions. The state functions as a satellite actor in local arenas.

The UCLA project identifies parents as a major player in local tracking decisions. In several California communities, local policymakers have witnessed a replay of the state-level wrangling: detracking advocates pitted against parents defending honors courses and other classes for high-achieving youngsters. The UCLA researchers report that four strategies are used by parents who defend the high tracks (with the researchers' original terms in parentheses): threatening to leave the school ("elite flight"); appealing a decision to abolish tracking to higher authorities ("co-opting institutional elites"); mobilizing coalitions of parents to fight detracking ("Not-Quite Elites" buying in to the opposition); and striking bargains with reformers (receiving "detracking bribes").[22]

However, the prospect of parents in general opposing tracking reform, not just parents of high-achieving students, should not be discounted. The Public Agenda Foundation's 1994 study *First Things First: What Americans Expect from the Public Schools* summarizes the public's attitude:

Only 34% of Americans think that mixing students of different achievement levels together in classes—"heterogeneous grouping"—will help increase student learning. People remain skeptical about this strategy even when presented with arguments in favor of it. Eighty-seven percent of those opposing heterogeneous grouping remain doubtful even when told that one benefit of heterogeneous grouping is that more accomplished students serve as role models for underachievers. Focus groups on heterogeneous grouping conducted for another Public Agenda research project suggest that other arguments in favor of the idea—such as academic research indicating its benefits or the need to avoid stigmatizing students—are equally unconvincing to most people.[23]

I hypothesize that parents involved in tracking policy will resist reform. In all kinds of communities, school and district officials are reluctant to alienate parents. Even when parents' objections are infrequent, they remain powerful. As Sam D. Sieber reports:

When Berman and Pauley (1975: 40–43) asked teachers to identify problems that arose in the course of implementation from a list of 12 items, only 8 percent selected "parental or community opposition." But in spite of being infrequently mentioned, this factor was considered *most decisive* in teachers' perceptions of project difficulties. Thus, parental or community opposition yielded the highest correlation with perceptions of difficulty of any of the 12 items on the list, which included planning deficiencies and troublesome attributes of the innovation.[24] (italics in original)

Summary and Conclusion

California and Massachusetts have succeeded in convincing hundreds of middle schools to begin the difficult task of detracking their curricular structures. Hundreds of other schools are ignoring state policy and continue to group students into classes on the basis of ability. What determines these different responses to tracking reform? Are there differences between tracked and untracked schools that may explain the contrasting policies? Researchers from UCLA believe that conceptions of intelligence favoring white and wealthy students over poor students and students of color and the skewed distribution of cultural and political power interlock to thwart tracking reform. Their research, consistent with Jeannie Oakes's earlier work on tracking, boils down to the conviction that good schools detrack and bad schools track, that the decision to track or detrack reflects a school's commitment to social justice and basic fairness.

Table 3-5. Description of Variables

Variable	Description
Institutional	
Community (urban, suburban)	Reported on survey of school principals and entered as dummy variable for urban and suburban schools, with rural the omitted category.
Socioeconomic status of school	SES—Index computed by state, aggregated from student level data describing parents' level of education.
Percent nonwhite	Percentage of total school enrollment that is nonwhite.
Math score	School math achievement as measured by California Assessment Program (CAP, 1990 test) for CA 91; California Learning Assessment System (CLAS, 1994 test) for CA 94; and Massachusetts Educational Assessment Program (MEAP, 1996 test) for MA 95.
Technical	
Spread in achievement	Measure of heterogeneity of achievement in schools.
Organizational	
Eighth grade population	Natural log of eighth grade student population.
Grade levels	Grade configuration of school. Entered as three-level categorical variable for CA samples because of policy falling linearly across levels (1 = grades 6–8, 2 = grades 7–8, 3 = grades 7–9). For MA 95, modeled as dichotomy: 1 = grades 7–8, 0 = not grades 7–8.
Political	
State	Influence of state policymakers on tracking policy as reported on survey of school principals.
District	Influence of district policymakers on tracking policy as reported on survey of school principals.
Principal	Influence of school administration on tracking policy as reported on survey of school principals.
Teachers	Influence of teachers on tracking policy as reported on survey of school principals.
Parents	Influence of parents on tracking policy as reported on survey of school principals.
Community groups	Influence of community groups on tracking policy as reported on survey of school principals.
School board discussion	Indicates whether school board or school committee discussed tracking policy (0 = no discussion, 1 = issue discussed).

I present an alternative framework, one combining knowledge about schools' institutional settings with the recent findings of national surveys about tracking's use. It differs from the UCLA project in assumptions and approach. My study focuses on the local policymaking environment, instead of trying to discern the motives of advocates on the issue. The UCLA researchers believe that people who defend tracking are driven by self-interest, racism, and class bigotry—tracking reformers by tolerance and altruism. The political conflict at each school is seen as the reenactment of a larger social struggle, the battle to rid U.S. society of inequality. From this perspective, explaining why schools track or untrack is primarily a project of unmasking the psychology behind each actor's position on the issue, especially of uncovering the motives of tracking's defenders.

I assume that virtue is found in equal amounts in tracking's defenders and critics. Tracking is not a moral litmus test; both tracking and detracking are morally legitimate. This study analyzes how schools' organizational properties and other characteristics structure local policymaking, promoting tracking reform in some schools and inhibiting it in others. This is not to deny that racism and other evils exist or to argue that motives are irrelevant to understanding public policy. That would be naive. It is to claim that, regardless of motives, people are constrained by the settings in which they make decisions. Jeannie Oakes and her followers agree with this, but the constraints they are most concerned about emanate from society's political and social structures. I focus on the more immediate environment. If the study's conceptual framework is valid, then patterns should emerge along the lines outlined in this chapter—large schools should adopt different policies than small schools, schools in poorer communities should favor detracking more than schools in wealthier communities, and so on. These patterns emerge because decisionmakers respond similarly to similar situations. If the framework is wrong, then policy should look random on these variables. The variables are presented in table 3–5.

The next chapter investigates the empirical evidence on why some schools continue tracking and other schools support reform.

4

Influences on Tracking Policy

HOW DO MIDDLE SCHOOLS make decisions about curricular tracking? What is behind the policies reported in chapter 3? What explains the dramatic reductions in tracking that occurred in the 1990s? Why have some schools reformed their tracking policies, completely eliminating ability grouping in English classes and sharply reducing it in math classes, while others are staying with highly tracked systems?

I begin with an overview comparing characteristics of tracked and untracked schools. This first cut at the data shows the simple, bivariate relationships between tracking policy and each of the factors that may influence policy. Some of these relationships overlap, especially those either directly measuring or strongly correlated with social conditions—for example, urbanicity, socioeconomic status (SES), and achievement scores. I will employ statistical models later in the chapter to tease these elements apart and pinpoint what is driving tracking policy in local schools. But first a look at the big picture.

Comparing Tracked and Untracked Schools

A school's demographic profile is related to different tracking policies, but urban schools do not stand out as unique in any of the samples (see figure 4-1). In the California samples, urban and suburban schools look very similar in their policies. Both departed from their earlier heavy use of tracking (only 6 percent were untracked in the "prior systems" reported in the 1991 survey, not shown here). Detracked schools in urban and suburban communities subsequently rose to over 20 percent in 1991 and jumped to more than 35 percent in 1994. Rural schools are the unique group in California. They were already hospitable to heterogeneous grouping before the

Figure 4-1. Percent of Schools Untracked, by Community

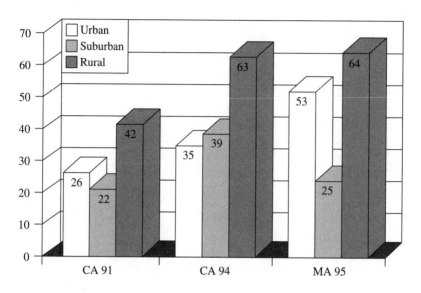

push to reform, and they continued to be responsive in 1994, when almost two-thirds reported detracked systems. In Massachusetts, suburban schools are unique. Only 25 percent of suburban schools in MA 95, but over 50 percent of urban schools and almost two-thirds of rural schools, report reformed tracking policies.

The issue of race permeates the tracking debate. In addition to the debate over tracking's effect on students, there is an implementation question. Critics claim that students of color are likely to attend schools where tracking channels them into dull curricula and unproductive learning environments. In the late 1980s a Johns Hopkins study found that schools with more than 20 percent of enrollment Hispanic and African American were more likely to track than those with fewer students of color. As summarized by one of the researchers, "The use of between-class grouping is especially common in middle grade schools with high concentrations of Hispanic and African-American students." [1] But tracking reform's big push occurred after the Johns Hopkins survey. In the present study's surveys, racial composition either appears irrelevant to the development of tracking policy or runs counter to the pattern discovered by the Johns Hopkins researchers (see table 4-1). In CA 94, predominantly white schools, those with 0 to 25 percent nonwhite students, are the least likely to have embraced reform (35.7 percent untracked). Predominantly minority schools do not exhibit

Table 4-1. Schools Untracked, by Nonwhite Enrollment
Percent

Nonwhite	CA 91	CA 94	MA 95
0–25	27.5	35.7	32.3
26–50	22.6	54.3	33.3
51–75	27.8	39.0	50.0
76–100	32.9	45.0	80.0
Summary statistics			
Chi square	2.6	2.7	9.5
Degrees of freedom	3	3	3
p value	.460	.437	< .05

peculiar policies, nor do racially mixed schools, those with 25 percent to 75 percent students of color. In MA 95, racial composition is related to policy, but in an intriguing way. Schools with high minority enrollments are moving decisively away from tracking. Ten schools with nonwhite enrollment of more than 75 percent responded to the MA 95 survey, and eight were detracked.

Critics charge that tracking harms poor students. In this study, SES is strongly associated with tracking policy, but not in the direction suggested by the tracking critique (see table 4-2). I standardized state measures of school SES (mean of 0 and SD of 1) and ran analyses of variance. Reform is reaching schools with disadvantaged populations. Students attending untracked schools were of lower SES than those attending tracked schools in all three samples, with the gap in mean SES's ranging from 0.30 to 0.45 standard deviations, statistically significant differences. The larger absolute values of the untracked schools indicate that the effect primarily stems from low-SES schools having embraced detracking. In MA 95, for example, the SES index of untracked schools averages about 0.3 standard deviations below that of the average Massachusetts middle school.

Table 4-2. School Socioeconomic Status and Tracking Policy, ANOVA
Standardized indexes of SES

Policy	CA 91	CA 94	MA 95
Tracked	.114	.164	.154
Untracked	−.306	−.186	−.301
Summary statistics			
F Statistic	$F_{1,353} = 12.6$	$F_{1,153} = 4.8$	$F_{1,124} = 6.2$
p value	< .001	< .05	< .05

Figure 4-2. Percent of Schools Untracked, by Achievement Quartile

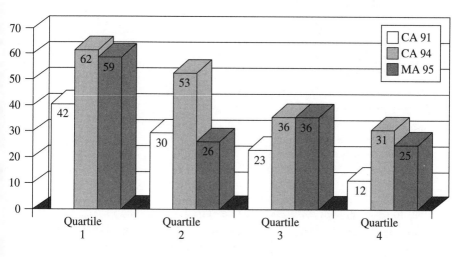

School achievement differs by tracking policy. Low-achieving schools are significantly more likely to detrack than high-achieving schools, not surprising, perhaps, considering detracking's appeal among urban schools and low-SES schools. Figure 4-2 illustrates how much detracking has occurred at schools performing at different levels on state math tests. Examining the CA 94 quartiles from left to right, the proportion of detracked schools declines from 62 percent in quartile 1, the schools with the lowest achievement, to 31 percent in quartile 4, the highest-achieving schools. In MA 95, the lowest-achieving schools also stand out in support of detracking, but the other three quartiles look fairly similar in resisting the reform.

The technical challenge of achievement heterogeneity also appears related to policy (see table 4-3). The exception is CA 91, but heterogeneity

Table 4-3. Achievement Heterogeneity and Tracking Policy, ANOVA
Standardized indexes of spread

Policy	CA 91	CA 94	MA 95
Tracked	−.004	.232	.146
Untracked	−.047	−.271	−.326
Summary statistics			
F Statistic	$F_{1,353} = 0.13$	$F_{1,143} = 9.68$	$F_{1,124} = 7.25$
p value	> .05	< .01	< .01

Table 4-4. Schools Untracked, by Eighth Grade Population
Percent

Eighth graders	CA 91	CA 94	MA 95
1–199	45.2	63.3	50.8
200–299	23.9	50.9	27.5
300–399	19.4	23.7	20.0
400+	22.5	41.0	0.0
Summary statistics			
Chi square	13.6	12.1	12.2
Degrees of freedom	3	3	3
p value	< .01	< .01	< .01

had to be computed differently for this group (explained in Appendix B). Once again, achievement in math was used in the analysis. Both CA 94 and MA 95 lean in the expected direction, with tracked schools exhibiting greater variance in student achievement than untracked schools. This bias is consistent with the belief that schools use tracking as a technical tool to accommodate students' academic differences. However, measures of mean achievement and spread of achievement are frequently correlated. Schools with extremely high scores, for example, usually have very few low achievers and a tighter band of achievement than schools nearer the mean. Schools with extremely low scores exhibit a similar tendency by having few high achievers. The question arises whether level and spread both influence policy as indicated by table 4-3 and figure 4-2, or if only one of them has an effect. I will address this issue in the multivariate analysis.

The organizational characteristics that I theorized would sway tracking are significant. Tracking policies correspond to school population differences (see table 4-4). Large schools track; small schools do not. And grade configuration also makes a difference, with the grade 6–8 school leading the pack on reform in both states (see table 4-5). In MA 95, the grade 7–8 and 7–9 schools stand out as resistant to tracking reform. Only 10 percent of the 7–8 schools in MA 95 have detracked their systems, and not one of the 7–9 schools. In California, grade 7–8 schools show a reluctance to detrack, but they engaged in modest reform between 1991 and 1994. In CA 94, the similarity of the grade 7–8 and grade 7–9 policies softens the chi-square test of equal proportions ($p = .11$). Testing grade 6–8 versus the other two configurations, however, yields a value of $p < .03$. In all three surveys, then, the grade 6–8 schools' willingness to detrack is significantly greater than schools with other grade levels.

Table 4-5. Schools Untracked, by Grade Configuration
Percent

Grade levels	CA 91	CA 94	MA 95
Grades 5–8	n.a.	n.a.	40.7
Grades 6–8	34.6	51.7	49.3
Grades 7–8	22.0	35.5	10.3
Grades 7–9	14.0	33.3	0.0
Summary statistics			
Chi square	10.4	4.5	15.0
Degrees of freedom	2	2	3
p value	< .01	.11	< .01

n.a. Not available.

Political influences appear important in tracked and untracked settings. In table 4-6, two patterns emerge from the power that competing parties exert on tracking decisions. Parents are the only actor with a consistently differentiating effect on policy, meeting thresholds of statistical significance in the two California surveys ($p = .13$ in MA 95). In all three surveys, schools with tracked systems report higher levels of parent influence than those with detracked systems. It also appears, however, that tracking is mainly "school business," with educators at the core of the enterprise—

Table 4-6. Tracking Policy and the Influence of Actors
Ratings based on (1) no influence, (2) moderate influence, (3) considerable influence, and (4) great influence.[a]

Actor	CA 91		CA 94		MA 95	
	Untracked	Tracked	Untracked	Tracked	Untracked	Tracked
Principal	3.22	3.21	3.35	3.24	3.30	3.20
	(0.80)	(0.77)	(0.87)	(0.80)	(0.78)	(0.81)
Teachers	3.17	3.18	3.13	3.12	2.94	3.04
	(0.75)	(0.79)	(0.95)	(0.80)	(0.94)	(0.85)
District	2.71	2.79	2.65	2.79	2.45	2.48
	(0.80)	(0.92)	(0.99)	(0.91)	(1.10)	(0.99)
Parents	2.16*	2.41*	2.17*	2.52*	2.26	2.49
	(0.74)	(0.82)	(0.82)	(0.90)	(0.87)	(0.83)
State	2.39	2.31	2.45	2.32	1.91	1.73
	(0.81)	(0.98)	(1.06)	(0.96)	(0.88)	(0.83)
Community	1.51	1.62	1.47	1.68	1.43	1.56
groups	(0.66)	(0.79)	(0.76)	(0.83)	(0.74)	(0.75)

*$p < .05$ for t statistic.
a. Standard deviation indicated in parentheses.

principals and teachers—exercising the most power. The other local actors—parents, district officials, and community groups—are less influential. And like countless studies of implementation have shown before, the state's influence over school affairs appears remote.

Modeling the Influences on Tracking Policy

The bivariate analyses of the data indicate that schools' institutional and organizational characteristics, as well as achievement heterogeneity and the influence of important actors, all have an effect on tracking policies. I now report on statistical treatments that remove overlapping influence and isolate each factor's individual strength. Using school tracking policy as the dependent variable, I ran logistic regression equations to determine the best-fitting model for each of the three surveys' data, the model providing the most parsimonious representation of the data's underlying structure. The variables were described in chapter 3. Coefficients for the full and best-fitting models are presented in table 4-7 (pp. 66–67). Additional details on the chapter's statistical treatments can be found in Appendix B.

A discussion centering on regression coefficients would be burdened by abstractions, so to simplify the analysis and to express the effects on policy in concrete terms, I have converted the best-fitting models' statistically significant coefficients to odds ratios and applied them to a mythical sample of 100 schools. I have rigged this "coin-flip" sample so that the initial probability of tracking or detracking is equal. In other words, before anything else occurs, this imaginary sample is set so that fifty schools are tracked and fifty schools are untracked. The magnitude of an effect is revealed in how this 50-50 distribution changes when only one variable is altered, holding constant the other variables in the model. I will draw on the case study interviews to flesh out each factor's impact on tracking.

Institutional Characteristics of Schools

Tracking's critics have argued for decades that tracking hurts students who do not do well in school, and its defenders have answered that tracking's abolition would hurt students who achieve at high levels. Achievement, racial composition, SES, and urbanicity form a bundle of school characteristics that are central to the tracking controversy. Tracking has been portrayed as a purveyor of educational inequality, and its defenders as at least selfish, perhaps even racist. With state-level policies on tracking stated as recommendations, not mandates, and with the state's powers of

Figure 4-3. Effect of Community on "Coin-Flip" Sample, MA 95

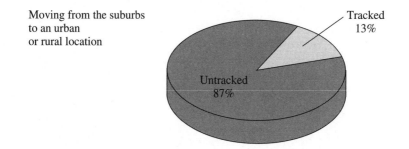

Moving from the suburbs
to an urban
or rural location

Tracked
13%

Untracked
87%

implementation notoriously weak, it looks as if local constituencies on both sides of the policy have responded to the cues transmitted by the public combatants on the issue.

The Massachusetts experience dramatizes what these battle lines mean for the distribution of tracking among schools. In the best-fitting model for MA 95, knowing just two things about a school, whether it is located in the suburbs and whether it serves grades 7–8, allows one to predict tracking policies with greater than 70 percent accuracy. Community generates most of the effect. Urban and rural schools are far more likely to detrack than suburban schools. Figure 4-3 asks us to ponder the following: if the mythical coin-flip sample of 100 Massachusetts schools were located in the suburbs, and we could somehow jack up their foundations and fly them to an urban or rural area, the 50-50 division would be transformed into an amazing eighty-seven untracked schools and only thirteen tracked schools.

Now, neither this exercise in imagination, nor the MA 95 community effect, should be taken too seriously. Schools' institutional characteristics are so tightly interwoven that it is impossible to tease them completely apart. As a practical matter, the institutional factors identified as significant in the regressions, the suburban effect in MA 95 and the achievement effect in the two California samples, are essentially tapping the same construct, reflecting differences in the social conditions of tracked and untracked schools. Those who condemn tracking present an indictment appealing to schools with certain institutional characteristics: urban schools with poorer, lower-achieving students. This indictment has little appeal for suburban schools with wealthier, higher-achieving students. It is almost as if the tracking debate of the 1980s is able to reach forward in time and steer policy implementation in the 1990s.

Urban schools' receptivity to tracking reform has been building for

Table 4-7. Logit Models of Tracking Policy[a]

	CA 91		CA 94		MA 95	
Clusters and factors	Full model	Best fit	Full model	Best fit	Full model	Best fit
Institutional						
Urban	-1.028*	...	.376	...	.293	...
	(.563)	...	(.778)	...	(1.185)	...
Suburban	-.347	...	.273	...	-1.481*	-1.900***
	(.468)	...	(.669)	...	(.874)	(.514)
SES	.543	...	-.172	...	.946	...
	(.542)	...	(.704)	...	(.727)	...
Percent nonwhite	.001	...	-.036**	-.026***	.020	...
	(.011)	...	(.015)	(.009)	(.020)	...
Math score	-.023***	-.012***	-.110**	-.102***	-.028	...
	(.008)	(.003)	(.045)	(.029)	(.091)	...
Technical						
Spread in achievement	-.042	...	-.003	...	-.002	...
	(.380)	...	(.002)	...	(.003)	...
Organizational						
Eighth grade population	-.488	-.850***	-1.544***	-1.482***	-.805	...
	(.313)	(.242)	(.582)	(.467)	(.782)	...
Grade levels	-.365	-.445**	-.557	...	-2.658***	-2.547***
	(.258)	(.219)	(.441)	...	(.984)	(.747)

Political

	(1)	(2)	(3)	(4)	(5)	(6)
State	.042	⋮	.403	⋮	.720	⋮
	(.198)		(.284)		(.387)	
District	.166	⋮	−.276	⋮	−.088	⋮
	(.215)		(.315)		(.319)	
Principal	−.067	⋮	.501	⋮	.428	⋮
	(.229)		(.348)		(.423)	
Teachers	.223	⋮	.295	⋮	.083	⋮
	(.259)		(.377)		(.384)	
Parents	−.473*	−.444**	−.633*	−.635***	−.732*	−.485*
	(.243)	(.175)	(.342)	(.242)	(.407)	(.283)
Community groups	−.358	⋮	−.281	⋮	−.021	⋮
	(.276)		(.335)		(.438)	
School board discussion	−.379	⋮	.453	⋮	−.849	⋮
	(.327)		(.496)		(.604)	
Constant	8.172	8.633	12.174	12.163	.998	2.165
	(2.862)	(1.699)	(4.127)	(3.026)	(5.724)	(.836)
Summary statistics						
Chi square	37.84	43.43	46.96	32.15	39.68	28.51
Degrees of freedom	15	4	15	4	15	3
p value	<.001	<.001	<.001	<.001	<.001	<.001
Correctly predicted policies (percent)	76.4	77.2	76.6	71.7	77.8	74.3

*$p < .10$, **$p < .05$, ***$p < .01$.
a. Positive values favor detracked schools. Standard error indicated in parentheses.

years. The push to untrack Massachusetts urban schools was well under way by the time of the 1995 survey. Springfield schools began detracking in 1990. A panel appointed by the superintendent of the Boston Public Schools recommended tracking's abolition in 1991. In 1993, the school district in Amherst agreed to review its tracking practices as part of the settlement of a lawsuit brought by the NAACP. To facilitate the review, Jeannie Oakes and Anne Wheelock were brought in to speak to educators about tracking. Also in 1993, a Cambridge school panel recommended the elimination of tracking at all middle and high schools. In July 1990 the *Boston Globe* reported that the detracking initiative was one reason the Massachusetts Department of Education "has come to be considered a national leader in urban reform." [2]

The bivariate analyses suggested that schools' racial compositions were not significant in deciding tracking policy. And in MA 95, black, Hispanic, and Asian students were more likely to attend untracked than tracked schools. But the regression output for CA 94 makes the opposite case. With other factors controlled, the percentage of nonwhite students is positively associated with tracking at a statistically significant level (shown in table 4-7). Increasing a school's proportion of students of color increases the likelihood of tracking. Does this support the argument that tracking is used to channel students of color into a stratified curriculum and preordain their fate in the labor market?

No. In fact, the finding may provide additional evidence that the tracking debate has cultivated local constituencies both for and against the reform. African Americans attend the average tracked and untracked school in CA 94 in equal numbers, and more Hispanics are found in the typical untracked school than tracked school (see table 4-8). After modeling each race statistic separately, I discovered that the other variables in the regression equation make Asian enrollment the controlling component of the nonwhite variable. Asians are significantly more likely to attend tracked schools in CA 94. This may be connected to the tracking debate. Asian students are usually omitted from the list of tracking's victims, no doubt because they tend to do well in school. This omission probably dilutes the appeal of the tracking indictment at schools with substantial Asian populations.[3]

This finding on race does not address, let alone refute, the charge that tracking segregates students by assigning different races to different tracks. The distribution of students among tracks within schools must be known to answer that question. But it does contradict the belief that tracking is more prevalent in minority communities. In other words, students of color

Table 4-8. Racial and Ethnic Composition of Tracked and Untracked Schools, CA 94 and MA 95
Percent

	CA 94		MA 95	
Race	Tracked	Untracked	Tracked	Untracked
Black	8.3	8.4	5.5**	12.9
Asian	17.0***	10.2	3.3	4.4
Hispanic	30.9	37.9	6.4*	11.3
White	43.2	42.8	84.6**	71.2
Other	0.6	0.7	0.2	0.2

*p < .10, **p < .05, ***p < .01.

might still be affected differentially by tracking, but not because they attend schools where decisionmakers adjust policies to reflect the racial composition of the school as a whole.

The racial composition of school faculties casts more doubt on the charge that tracking is an example of institutionalized racism. If tracking were systematically shunting students of color into dead-end classes, one would expect black and Hispanic teachers to support its abolition. After a period of time, the racial characteristics of staffs should diverge in tracked and untracked schools. I was able to obtain descriptive data on teachers and administrators in the CA 94 schools (see table 4-9). The only significant personnel difference between tracked and untracked schools is that tracked schools have more administrators and teachers, a result of the schools'

Table 4-9. Certificated Personnel of Tracked and Untracked Schools, CA 94
Percent, unless otherwise indicated

Personnel	Tracked	Untracked
Administrators (number)	4.4**	1.8
Teachers (number)	47.4*	24.0
Age (years)	44.2	44.8
African American	13.8	16.4
Asian	6.6	6.3
Hispanic	6.5	6.2
White	72.5	70.4
Female	76.8	78.6
Male	23.3	21.4

*p < .10, **p <.05.

larger size. The racial composition of the teaching staff is comparable at tracked and untracked schools, underscoring the doubtful link between tracking and school-level measures of race and ethnicity.

Achievement is important to schools' institutional stature. In reference to test scores, the principal of one of the lowest-scoring case study schools told me, "Rightly or wrongly, that's a neon sign that the community sees, and if they see high scores, they think, 'good school.' " Past studies of school reform have shown that low-achieving schools are attracted to new programs promising to boost student performance. High-achieving schools, on the other hand, are hesitant to alter practices that they regard as successful, making a skeptical audience for reform efforts.[4]

Recall that in CA 94 the achievement metric is the percentage of high-achieving students at each school. At the average school in CA 94, about 11 percent of students met this definition of high-achiever status on the math portion of California Learning Assessment System (CLAS) test. As illustrated in figure 4-4, a five-percentage-point increase in high achievers, holding other factors constant, changes the distribution of policy in the imaginary coin-flip sample from the original 50-50 division to sixty-three tracked schools and thirty-seven untracked schools. A ten-percentage-point increase results in a 75-25 distribution, and a twenty-percentage-point increase yields a whopping 90-10 distribution in favor of tracking. Reducing the number of high achievers by like amounts would tip the distribution of policy equally toward untracking.

Why do high-achieving schools endorse tracking while low-achieving schools support reform? Institutional prestige certainly plays a part. The academic attainments of a school's students burnishes its institutional reputation. Since parent influence is already accounted for in the models, the influence reported here is above and beyond the pressure exerted by parents of high-achieving youngsters. The presence of large numbers of high achievers apparently compels schools to add honors courses whether parents ask for them or not. Offering honors-level courses may enhance a school's standing in the community and impress the high school to which it feeds students. And the opposite is probably true too. Lower-achieving schools may support detracking because they are reluctant to offer classes labeled "remedial," thereby drawing attention to the academic deficiencies of the schools' students.

To sum up this section's findings, tracking policy is related to a school's institutional characteristics, but not in the way tracking's critics found in the 1980s. There is substantial evidence that the reform movement has succeeded in altering the distribution of tracking among schools with different

Figure 4-4. Effect of Achievement on "Coin-Flip" Sample, CA 94[a]

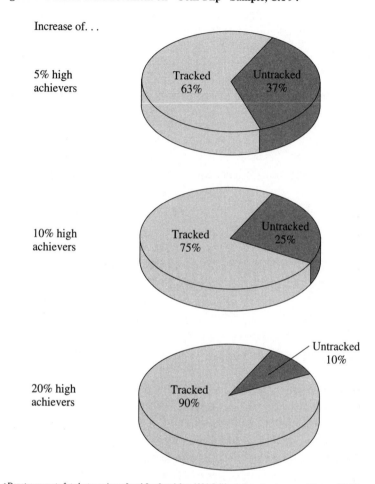

Increase of...

5% high
achievers

10% high
achievers

20% high
achievers

[a] Denotes percent of students scoring at Level 5 or Level 6 on 1994 California Learning Assessment System (CLAS) test. Mean = 11.1 percent, SD = 9.5 percent.

characteristics. California and Massachusetts policymakers responded to the antitracking movement's searing indictment by endorsing tracking's abolition, and local policymakers have detracked schools serving some of the very youngsters that tracking supposedly harms. The most-tracked schools in this study are found in suburban neighborhoods, not in cities. Schools with poor students have heeded the call to detrack, while schools attended by wealthier students continue the practice. The racial composition of California schools appears unrelated to their policies. In California tracking is no more prevalent in schools where nonwhite students constitute a majority of enrollment than in white-majority schools. In Massachusetts, the typical untracked school is attended by more black, Hispanic, and Asian students than the typical tracked school.

The Technical Challenge of Heterogeneity

The effect of achievement heterogeneity washes out in the multivariate analyses. Could this be right? Heterogeneous schools face the daunting tasks of teaching Shakespeare to students who cannot decode *The Cat in the Hat* and challenging students who are ready for algebra while simultaneously instructing students who have not mastered the multiplication tables. Surely, these schools find it difficult to abandon a differentiated curriculum.[5]

Teachers are in the best position to assess the technical implications of detracking. Here, teachers at two untracked schools describe the challenges of teaching heterogeneous classes well:

> It's very hard, and I question whether or not I'm doing it. I'm concerned that the low ones are being left behind. You cannot teach three different things at one time.   —*Teacher, English*

> I teach the pre-algebra concepts to the highest. Now, the others have no background when I begin to talk about these things. And I have certain basic concepts that I must cover in pre-algebra in order for them to be successful in Algebra I, which would be the next step. How do you teach those basic concepts, say, in a pre-algebra group when a kid back here doesn't even know his multiplication tables? I mean, we're talking about a different level. He doesn't know how to subtract. That's where we are with these kids.   —*Teacher, Math*

The problem of achievement heterogeneity is particularly acute when other constraints on teaching are tightened, such as when large classes are made even larger. Remedial classes are traditionally staffed at lower pupil-teacher ratios than regular or honors classes. Eliminating tracking moves remedial students into mixed-ability classes that are larger. Supporters of detracking recognize this challenge but argue that teachers must employ different teaching strategies to handle classes that are diverse in abilities. A principal and a teacher offer observations on opposite sides of the issue:

I would say that the biggest resistance [to detracking] is the concern about meeting the diverse needs and that you will only be teaching to the middle and, therefore, your top kids will be lost and your bottom kids won't know what to do and, therefore, they'll fall further behind. To me that reflects their lack of awareness of the different instructional strategies that can be used to meet diverse needs; and that is truly a staff development issue.   —*Principal*

There are a lot of people who . . . feel like it's a step backwards to do this, that we're being asked to not only take on more difficult classes but at the same time, because of budget, we're going to be asked to take on larger classes. We won't be able to meet the kids' needs.
                                       —*Teacher, Social Studies–Language Arts*

This argument comes up again and again in schools that are detracking. Reformers argue that heterogeneous classes are difficult but manageable with sufficient training on alternative instructional strategies. Teachers who are resistant to detracking see their effectiveness severely hobbled in meeting students' needs and doubt that training will solve the problem. The impact of detracking on instruction is explored in greater depth in chapter 7.

The Organizational Characteristics of Schools

This chapter's first graphic (figure 4-1) showed rural schools to be receptive to tracking reform. The apparent popularity of detracking in rural communities is related to something else—school size. Rural schools tend to be smaller schools, and smaller schools tend to have smaller classes.[6] A reduced student population, rather than anything intrinsic to rural schooling, allows schools to detrack. However, as a teacher at a rapidly growing school sitting in the middle of three brand-new subdivisions remarked, "If you had 400 kids versus now 650, it stands to reason that [tracking] would grow."

As I have defined them, a school's institutional and organizational characteristics differ in that the latter are manipulable. Officials cannot change a school's community or the socioeconomic characteristics of its students, but they can adjust attendance boundaries and build new schools to alter school enrollments. Figure 4-5 illustrates the impact of decreasing a school's eighth grade population by multiples of thirty students, the equiva-

Figure 4-5. Effect of Eighth Grade Population on "Coin-Flip" Sample, CA 94[a]

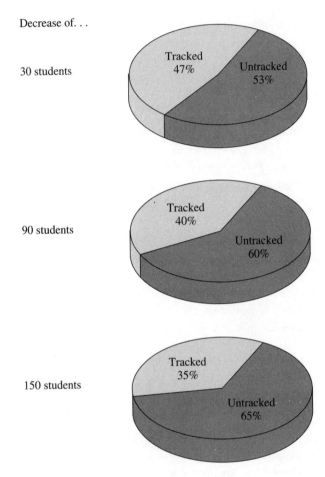

Decrease of. . .

30 students

90 students

150 students

a. Mean = 312, SD = 136.

lent of about one class or section. Subtracting thirty students from schools in the mythical sample for CA 94 produces a 53-47 split favoring detracked schools. When enrollment is lowered by 150 students, the same as reducing the number of eighth graders at the average CA 94 school by half, the original 50-50 distribution becomes 65-35 in favor of detracking.

Untracked structures are most evident in schools serving 200 eighth graders or less. The significance of the number 200 makes sense from the standpoint of organizing faculty and student time. When 200 students are scheduled into six or seven different subjects and classrooms for a single instructional period, there are not enough students in any one subject to make ability grouping feasible. If only thirty students take history during third period, for example, then only one teacher will be supplied to teach them. Held to an allotted number of faculty by central office, schools impose minimum enrollments on new class offerings. A long-running complaint about small schools is that students falling outside the mainstream, either those extraordinarily advanced or those in need of remedial help, are not adequately served. Small schools cannot track even if they want to do so.[7]

Organizational theory and research long ago established a connection between organizational size and internal complexity.[8] As schools get larger, the propensity for tracking also increases. Recall from the bivariate analysis in table 4-4 that not a single MA 95 school with 400 or more eighth graders (there are six such schools) and only two of the sample's nine schools with 300–399 students are untracked. The pattern is linear in MA 95, but the two California samples exhibit a curious pattern. As the California schools get larger, untracking decreases as expected and then oddly increases again among the very largest schools. Extremely large schools, those with 400 or more eighth graders, seem to be supporting tracking reform, with the proportion of untracked schools almost doubling from 1991 to 1994 (23.7 percent to 41.0 percent). The effect of school size obviously is not so straightforward in California. What is going on?

The most compelling explanation can be traced to two historical phenomena: changes in popular sentiment on the efficacy of large schools and development of strategies to cope with enrollment booms. In the 1970s and 1980s, researchers began suspecting that large schools foster unhealthy school climates, that they are difficult to manage, promote an impersonal, factorylike setting for teacher-student interactions, deplete any sense of community or coherent academic purpose, invite violence into classrooms and hallways, and depress academic achievement.[9] California experienced a surge in enrollments at about the same time these doubts were reaching a crescendo. By 1990, schools were bursting at the seams. State and local governments, hamstrung by the state's most severe economic recession since World War II and the revenue-raising limitations of Proposition 13, lacked the financial resources for the massive school construction program needed to alleviate the strain. Educators began employing their own coping strategies.

Two of the case study schools amplify how these strategies can affect tracking. The first school adopted a year-round schedule, an innovation receiving modest financial support from the state. With the school's four-track schedule (these "tracks" do not refer to ability groups), one-fourth of the students are on break at any one time (one track off, three tracks on). The student body is effectively disaggregated into four equal groupings for the purpose of scheduling classes. Any tracking system must operate within these year-round groupings, meaning that the tracking policies for this school's 600 eighth graders are actually policies developed for four sub-units of 150 students each. It is no surprise, then, that this school acts more like a small school than its enrollment indicates, and it has found detracking easier than one would expect. Since the school's principal wanted to detrack anyway, there was now a ready-made excuse to offer recalcitrant parents. The principal explains:

> The GATE [gifted and talented education] parents objected to the whole teaming [and detracking] idea—we had GATE classes at that time—but when you go year-round, that has a tremendous influence. When you take the population of the school and divide it into four segments you don't have enough kids to fill those classes. I've also had parents in the last two years, upset, who had their children in re-mediation for reading, in a low reading group in elementary school—not special ed. They got that through sixth grade and got to seventh grade and find they're in a mainstream and, boom, there's nothing available and "everybody will read and comprehend."   —*Principal*

Large schools may also subdivide into interdisciplinary "teams" without altering the academic calendar. This innovation was employed by several schools in the study as part of a general endorsement of the middle school philosophy, discussed below. But it is also intended to relieve the stress of overpopulation. One school organizes its faculty into instructional teams consisting of English, math, history, and science teachers, a teacher serving one of the special needs populations (for example, special ed or bilingual), and a guidance counselor. Students are assigned to one of the teams, and all students are scheduled into core classes by team. At this big school, too, tracking policies are made for smaller organizational units than total enrollment figures can reveal. In 1993 a California State Department of Education survey found that about 25 percent of the state's middle schools were using schoolwide interdisciplinary teaming.[10]

The larger the school, the more likely it will track. But tracking is not the only way schools group students. To alleviate the stress of overpopulation, some schools have subdivided into smaller operational units, simultaneously reducing the need for differentiated classes. These coping strategies

Figure 4-6. Effect of School Grade Levels on "Coin-Flip" Sample, MA 95

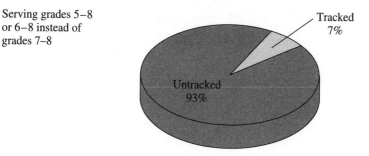

Serving grades 5–8
or 6–8 instead of
grades 7–8

Tracked
7%

Untracked
93%

underscore how tracking functions within the overall school organization, how it is only one component of a larger structure that organizes students for instruction.

The grade levels a school serves also influences tracking. Detracking is rapidly becoming an integral characteristic of schools with a middle school grade configuration. In MA 95, for example, changing the mythical coin-flip sample from grade 7–8 schools to grades 5–8 or 6–8 would yield an overwhelming ninety-three untracked schools and only seven tracked schools (see figure 4-6). The abolition of tracking is now a prominent plank in the middle school movement's reform agenda. This movement is especially powerful at middle schools that begin with grades five or six. Schools serving grades 7–8 and 7–9, on the other hand, operate more like traditional junior highs, and tracking remains popular there.[11]

Remember that the tracking policies examined here are for eighth grade, a grade level that, although embedded in different grade configurations, is common to all of these schools. When deciding how stratified the eighth grade curriculum will be, educators appear to respond to the grade levels served by their entire school instead of following a general rule defining the appropriate policy for eighth graders. Like school size, grade configuration is also manipulatable. A grade change may be merely cosmetic, of course, but where school administrators are able to overhaul staff and curriculum, they often succeed in injecting practices into schooling that are more conducive to detracking.

Educational philosophy or ideology undoubtedly has a hand in this. In districts offering more than one graded form of school, principals and teachers undoubtedly gravitate toward the type of school that reflects their own educational beliefs. In educational shorthand, grade 6–8 schools today represent "progressive" practices and grade 7–8 and 7–9 schools represent traditional ways of conducting business. Listen to counselors at two schools that were launching detracking initiatives at the same time that their schools changed to a 6–8 configuration:

> This has been couched in the middle school changeover.
>
> —*Counselor*

> It started with the state and the *Caught in the Middle* book, and what they feel is right for kids at this age. And then, of course, it's come out of this middle school movement. . . . It hasn't really taken hold. But we have some teachers who have been to conferences, who are very much involved with the middle school movement and are trying to move this school in that direction.   —*Counselor*

State certification laws allow teachers with elementary licenses to teach multidisciplinary courses, which are usually found in 6–8 middle schools, but single-subject courses, which dominate grade 7–8 and 7–9 schools, require teachers with secondary licenses.[12] The distinction between an elementary and secondary outlook on schooling is very real, what researchers often describe as contrasting "pupil" and "subject matter" orientations.[13] Middle schools encompass these separate worlds of elementary and secondary education, often with adherents of both perspectives on the same staff. Distinctive cultures form within schools. A principal describes his school's faculty:

> We are really moving towards being a 6–7–8 middle school. The school has been predominantly secondary credentials—people who saw themselves as, maybe someplace down the road, teaching in the high school—classes taught very much like high school. Now, as we see where we're going, our vision is driving what we're doing in hiring new teachers. The other teachers will be gone a few years from now; they'll be at a high school.   —*Principal*

The appeal to diminish tracking finds a sympathetic ear at 6–8 schools, with their cultures more attuned to the undifferentiated curricula and holistic instructional approaches of elementary education. Junior highs, especially those offering high school courses in the ninth grade, look more like high schools, with sequential course offerings and hierarchical instructional arrangements that are hostile to heterogeneous grouping. Thus, although alike in teaching eighth graders, the manner in which these schools

Figure 4-7. Effect of Parent Influence on "Coin-Flip" Sample, CA 91[a]

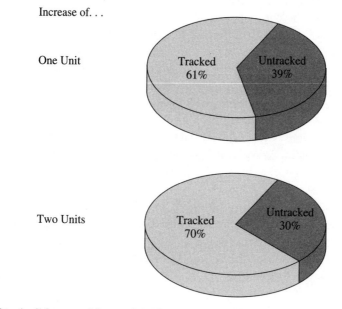

Increase of. . .

One Unit

Tracked 61%

Untracked 39%

Two Units

Tracked 70%

Untracked 30%

a. Categories of influence are no influence, moderate influence, considerable influence, and great influence.

organize eighth grade students and eighth grade curriculum greatly depends on the overall grade structure of the school.

Political Influences

It makes sense that a school's grade levels and student population affect tracking policy since these two characteristics mark the organizational structure in which policies are developed and implemented. But structures are empty without people inhabiting them, and school policy is neither developed nor implemented by institutional traits. It takes actors.

As shown in the ratings of actor influence, generally speaking, parents are overshadowed by school people when tracking policy is decided. However, when parents choose to step forward on the issue, their influence is potent—and decisively in support of tracking. Figure 4-7 shows the predicted policies of the mythical CA 91 sample after a one-unit change in parent influence. If parent influence on tracking policy is increased, for example, from "no influence" to "moderate influence," and no other variable is altered, the 50-50 distribution of the coin-flip sample changes dramatically. Now thirty-nine of the schools are untracked and sixty-one of the schools are tracked. A two-unit increase in parent influence results in 70 percent of the coin-flip schools being tracked. Reducing parent influence by equal amounts would produce exactly the opposite effects. A two-unit decrease in parent influence, for example, would create a new distribution favoring untracked schools by an identical 70-30 margin.

Parents of high-achieving students passionately defend honors classes threatened by tracking reform. Schools with a growing population of gifted and talented students resist detracking, and some schools have even added new honors courses to their curriculum. Teachers at schools that plan to eliminate tracking worry about the reaction of parents of high-achieving students.

> They know school board members; they know administrators; they are the most vocal. They are the ones that are on the site council, that volunteer. We have some that work in the office, you know, volunteer. They have access to the counselors and to the principal, and they don't hesitate to speak up.   —*Teacher, History*

> It's going to be the GATE parents complaining, which is probably why we're going to stick with GATE.   —*Teacher, Science*

> Somewhere along the line, we are going to have to give those parents the opportunity—we have to get it all out before you can move on. Somewhere, we're going to have to face it. Whether the anxieties are valid or not, they need to voice them and get it out. It needs to be talked out. I really don't think we have opened it up to the parents. And that may be a mistake.   —*Teacher, English*

Currently, tracking's critics offer the most prominent explanation for parents' intransigence, that it is driven by race and class privilege. The survey data do not support this charge. Parent activism favors tracking with school urbanicity, racial composition, and SES controlled. In all kinds of schools, when parents were active in policymaking, tracking was likely to occur. In terms of race, this finding echoes the conclusion of the most extensive study heretofore conducted on parents' attitudes toward tracking reform, the Public Agenda Foundation report:

> Some proponents of heterogeneous grouping, professional educators and others, have suggested that parental opposition to it is a camou-

flage for racial prejudice—the fear of white parents that their children will be put in classes with "underachieving" African-American students, but opposition to heterogeneous grouping is as strong among African-American parents as among white parents, and support for it is generally weak.[14]

If the contention that white, wealthy parents use tracking to separate their children from children of color and to maintain social privilege is not a good explanation of parents' differentiating effect on policy, then what is?

A persuasive explanation is found by contrasting the collective interests of schools and the particular interests of parents.[15] Think of all the ways that schools serve groups. Schools create policies for collectivities, for all of the students, parents, faculty, and assorted parties who operate within the educational enterprise or otherwise come in contact with it. As democratically governed institutions, public schools represent society's collective investment in education, interests that are, in Talcott Parsons's terms, universal rather than particularistic.[16] Ideally, laws pertaining to student attendance, discipline, and graduation are enforced both uniformly and fairly. Socially acceptable definitions of valued knowledge mold the curriculum that students are taught. The teacher's mission is seen in terms of universal goals, and experts on the profession frequently remark on teachers' ready acceptance of consensus values and the egalitarianism permeating teachers' sense of themselves and their work.[17] All of these elements bias schools against ubiquitous forms of differentiation.

Parents' interests, on the other hand, are anything but universal, focused instead on protecting the interests of specific children: their children.

In the case of academic matters, parents may express apprehension that the class is moving too quickly, thereby leaving a struggling student behind, or that it is not moving fast enough, boring a student who has already mastered material and is ready to move on. Good teachers, of course, reassure parents that they will do whatever is humanly possible to bring struggling students up to speed or to challenge the most advanced student. Good parents are always willing to work at home to reinforce the school's efforts. But these good intentions and mutual efforts are sometimes directed toward smoothing over what ultimately develops into an unresolvable conflict between the needs of an individual and the needs of a classroom. In a class of thirty to thirty-five, a single student represents only 3 percent of the whole, and although individualized learning techniques or cooperative learning groups may help for a time, often schools are simply unable to accommodate an individual student's needs to a parent's satisfaction. When this happens with a critical mass of parents, policymakers are soon asked to fix the situation. Calls for differentiation rise up, loudly, and redress is sought from teachers, administrators, and sometimes even school boards. Thus far, evidently, tracking reform has been unable to alter this dynamic or to diminish its political consequences.

Parents are the political actors with a differentiating influence on tracking policy, but principals wield the most power overall in deciding policy. I am not relying on the study's survey responses, which are principals' evaluations of their own power, to arrive at this conclusion. In the case study interviews, teachers and counselors reported that schools were eliminating tracking because of the principal's initiative, compromising on tracking as a result of the principal's skill at negotiation and bargaining, or defiantly resisting pressures to untrack in support of the principal's convictions about educational practice. In schools where parents were up in arms over tracking policy, they were either confronting the school principal or counting him or her among their staunchest allies, and in schools where anxious parents reluctantly acquiesced to the reform, school principals were instrumental in convincing them to give it a try.

In several schools, principals initiated the move away from tracking. He or she served as a lightning rod for the multitude of forces encouraging reform: policy documents from the state education department, the national middle school movement, district reform initiatives, and teachers who wanted to do things differently. In the comments of the teachers below, notice the various influences they see expressed through their principal's position on tracking:

> It was [the principal]'s idea, moving more towards the middle school concept of mainstreaming everybody. She's a firm believer in heterogeneous grouping.   —*Teacher, English*

> We have a principal who wants to switch from a junior high to a middle school. And according to *Caught in the Middle* and the new framework, the classes should be heterogeneous, and it's going in that direction. He wants heterogeneous grouping.   —*Teacher, Math*

> He's allowing it to happen. There has been a core of probably five to ten teachers who have been interested in it, two or three more pushy about it than others, I guess you could say. And we have not been able to get anybody moving on it prior to this principal. We now have somebody who will tell people, "You will do this. You will do that.

If it's best for the kids, this is what we're going to do." Our past
principals didn't want to rock the boat.   *—Teacher, Science*

Central office started—well, what triggered it was about four years
ago, the whole middle school movement started, *Caught in the
Middle* was published. And so they formed a task force here—and as
a result of that, it was found that heterogeneous grouping was recommended. But central office, I do believe, did impress upon the
principal that we should start moving in that direction.
                                                    —Teacher, English

The site administrator is an advocate of heterogeneous grouping;
that's where the push is coming from.
                                    —Teacher, History–Language Arts

Like any controversial issue, tracking reform may force changes in a
principal's leadership style. A principal who has spent considerable time
coaxing reluctant faculty members to accept untracking explains:

What has had to happen as part of this whole process is just sort of a
leadership issue. My style is to try to come to consensus and to facilitate and necessarily be directive. And with all the changes that
we're having to do and the level of readiness of people, I figured out
last year that there's certain things I cannot use collaboration on in
the same way that I have in the past; because I would try to please
and make sure everybody felt good about whatever. But when it came
to heterogeneous grouping, it was such a diversity of opinion that I
needed to make an educational judgment, which I did, and came out
in October with, "this is what we're going to do." And then after
response to that—I have allowed dialogue—but it hasn't changed my
mind. Because I already made up my mind.   *—Principal*

One can hear in these words a school leader grappling with the task of
bringing teachers around to a point of view many of them distrust and, in
some cases, strenuously oppose. A similar challenge arises when parents
question the wisdom of detracking. Schools that manage to reform without
too much internal rancor or public turmoil are invariably led by strong
principals who reach out to persuade others of the reform's virtues. Among
the most effective strategies: appointing a task force to investigate the
pros and cons of tracking, holding evening informational meetings for the

school community, or promising reluctant parties that the school will first experiment with reform before plowing ahead with schoolwide change. In a few schools, principals initially introduced heterogeneously grouped classes made up of student and faculty volunteers, collected data on these classes' performance, and then slowly expanded the practice within the school.

School principals can also block tracking reform. They can simply ignore state documents on the policy or actively undermine district efforts to detrack. Just as principals can advance detracking by slowly introducing it into their schools, anti-reform principals can weaken the push for detracking by isolating it within one subject or interdisciplinary team or by experimenting with it in situations where failure is almost guaranteed.

Political influences on tracking are reflected in three general patterns of activity. First, actors close to schools, such as teachers and school principals, exercise the most influence over policy, and actors distant from school settings, such as the state, wield little or no influence. Second, of the school insiders, principals are instrumental in steering proposals through rough waters and seeing to it that detracking is given a chance or in rallying opposition to reform and insisting that curriculum differentiation remain a hallmark of their school. And third, parents are generally secondary players in developing policy, but when their influence is expressed, it has a strong, differentiating effect. Parents are powerful opponents of tracking reform, and the parents of high-achieving students are particularly hesitant to abandon tracking.

Summary and Conclusion

California and Massachusetts middle schools are moving away from the age-old practice of curricular tracking. This chapter has shed light on the reasons why some schools continue tracking while other schools reform their curricular systems. The local policymaking environment is structured so that in some schools tracking is maintained and in others reform is favored.

When local policymakers decide the tracking question, they are influenced by the institutional characteristics of schools. Urban schools, schools serving poorer students, and low-achieving schools are more likely to detrack than suburban schools, high-achieving schools, and schools serving wealthier students. In both states, the debate that preceded policy adoption featured allegations that tracking is detrimental to low-achieving, poor, and minority youth, students who dominate the enrollments of urban public schools. Defenders of tracking, on the other hand, argued that high-achieving students would be held back by tracking's abolition, that hetero-geneously grouped classes are inhospitable to the curricular acceleration that takes place in high-track classes. Detracking advocates criticized this defense as the thinly veiled attempt of middle class white parents to hang on to privileges they enjoy from curricular stratification. The debate thus succeeded in drawing bright lines defining the winners and losers under either policy, and coupled with tracking reform's endorsement by a bur-geoning middle school movement, the die was cast for detracking's imple-mentation. The institutional pattern uncovered here, the acceptance and rejection of tracking reform by schools exhibiting contrasting institutional characteristics, reflects deep divisions in the tracking debate. Absent any strong mechanisms to enforce state policies on tracking, schools attend to the steady stream of cues from the debate to guide them in policy.

Technical considerations may come into play when tracking policy is decided, but the survey data do not confirm school achievement heteroge-neity as an important factor. Interviews with educators, on the other hand, suggest that spread in achievement makes a difference in classrooms. Or-ganizational structures consistently shape tracking. A school's total en-rollment drives the size of its classes. Tracking's critics and defenders agree that heterogeneously grouped classes are difficult to teach when they hold more students. Large schools have been reluctant to detrack, while small schools frequently exhibit heterogeneously grouped course offerings. These small schools may also be facing their own constraints on policy since many of them do not have enough students to warrant curriculum differentiation.

Tracking also varies by the grade levels schools serve, supporting the idea that policies are favored when compatible with schools' organizational arrangements. Middle schools can be found in various forms, usually be-ginning with the fifth, sixth, or seventh grade and ending with the eighth or ninth grade. These configurations attract teachers with different preparation and skills, shaping the school culture and predisposing it for or against particular practices. Grade 6–8 and 7–9 schools provide the sharpest con-trast. The 6–8 schools are more sympathetic to the middle school move-ment's push to become less like high schools and more like elementary schools. They have moved away from tracking. The grade 7–9 schools, on the other hand, are linked to high schools by the ninth grade curriculum, which offers courses carrying high school credit, and by the presence of teachers trained in single subject areas. They continue to track.

Actors in the local environment are not quiet when tracking reform is discussed. Parents are unambiguous in their support for tracking, and differentiation flourishes where parental preferences are incorporated into policymaking. This phenomenon surfaces in schools of all shapes and sizes, from the lowest achieving to the highest achieving, in the poorest and wealthiest of neighborhoods. Schools that are detracking may shield policymaking from the political power of parents, strike compromises that detrack some but not all of a school's curriculum, or persuade resistant groups of parents to give untracking a try. School principals are the key figures in managing the political interactions of parents and tracking policy.

Tracking is not a simple matter. Contrary to the most prominent explanation of tracking's use, it is not formulated simply to mirror social inequalities of race and class or any other single dimension of the policy environment. Instead, a constellation of factors produces tracking policies: institutional, technical, organizational, and political. These influences are exerted within a system of educational governance, the topic of the next chapter.

5

Governing Reform

THIS CHAPTER USES the Massachusetts and California experiences with tracking reform as a road map for exploring key relationships in the educational system: the sharing of power between state and local educators and, at the local level, between district and school officials. It concludes with an up close description of how the tracking wars affected life at two schools.

Educational Governance in the Two States: A Brief History

California's constitutional convention in 1849 crafted the basic architecture of the state's system of public schools. With an eye toward joining the union the following year, California's founders established a system funded by revenues from the sale of public lands, with a school year of no less than three months and an elected state superintendent of public instruction.[1] The state's public land holdings were so extensive, estimated at 5 million acres by the first state school superintendent, John G. Marvin, that the legislature was in no rush to provide additional school funding. Several years passed before public lands were surveyed, let alone sold. In 1852, the legislature allotted $50,000 to the state's schools, and though a modest sum, it was quite an improvement over the $70 in public revenues spent by California schools in 1850.[2]

Pinching pennies is not the story here. The state's founders had created a school system, but it was almost completely vacant (see table 5-1). In all of California, the 1850 census counted only eight schools, seven teachers—two schools apparently shared a teacher—and 219 students. When one considers the Gold Rush pioneers who had flocked to California, the numbers are not so surprising. The state's population was dominated by adult males. Only about 10 percent of residents were children five to nine-

Table 5-1. Schooling in California and Massachusetts, 1850 and 1870

State and year	Total state population	Population aged 5–19	Schools (N)	Teachers (N)	Pupils (N)	Total income (dollars)	Income public funds (dollars)
CA 1850	92,597	9,610	8	7	219	17,870	70
MA 1850	994,514	306,562	4,066	5,049	190,292	1,424,873	977,630
CA 1870	560,247	153,354	1,548	2,444	85,507	2,946,308	1,669,464
MA 1870	1,457,351	430,351	5,726	7,561	269,337	4,817,939	3,183,794

Source: Lawrence A. Cremin, *American Education, The National Experience, 1783–1876* (Harper & Row, 1980), pp. 182–85.

teen years of age, compared to 37 percent nationally, and these youngsters were more likely found working in mines or in businesses servicing miners' needs than attending school. When the Gold Rush faded, however, and safe and reliable transportation from the East had become commonplace, the number of school children in California soared. By 1870, the state's total population had jumped more than fivefold to just over 560,000, including 150,000 children. California now boasted 1,548 schools with 85,000 pupils and 2,444 teachers. A vast school system had been built in less than two decades, and, for the most part, it had been constructed from the top down. The state constitution and the state bureaucracy encouraged communities to create schools and organize them into local districts, and communities responded by doing just that.[3]

The Massachusetts school system, in sharp contrast, was already deeply institutionalized and intimately grounded in local levels of governance by the mid-nineteenth century. From the earliest days of colonial New England, three institutions—the school, the town meeting, and the church—formed the nucleus of civic life. The Massachusetts Act of 1647 required every town of at least 50 families to hire a schoolmaster for teaching children how to read and write. Towns of 100 families or more were commanded to provide a grammar school to prepare students for advanced training.[4] Although most communities ducked the grammar school requirement, by the time Horace Mann was appointed the first secretary to the state board of education in 1837, the state was populated with thousands of schools. These were local schools, beholden to their towns, not to the state. Mann's office held weak statutory powers, but he relentlessly campaigned for a state system of education, one that he promised would respect local-

Table 5-2. State Centralization Scores within Specified Intervals[a]

Interval	States
5.00	Hawaii (6.00)
4.50–4.99	Oklahoma (4.91), Alabama, South Carolina
4.00–4.49	Washington (4.37), Oregon, Florida, Minnesota
3.75–3.99	West Virginia (3.94), Mississippi, Indiana, Kentucky, Virginia, New Jersey, Michigan, Nebraska, Iowa, North Carolina, Colorado, New Mexico, Pennsylvania
3.50–3.74	**California** (3.65), Ohio, New York, Wisconsin, Arkansas, Maryland
3.25–3.49	Tennessee (3.48), Montana, Utah, Kansas, Alaska, Illinois, Idaho
3.00–3.24	Georgia (3.24), Rhode Island, Louisiana, Vermont, Delaware, New Hampshire, Maine, South Dakota
2.50–2.99	Arizona (2.91), North Dakota, Texas, Missouri, Nevada, **Massachusetts** (2.73), Connecticut
Under 2.50	Wyoming (1.86)

Source: Frederick M. Wirt, "School Policy Culture and State Decentralization," in Jay D. Scribner, ed., *The Politics of Education*, part 2 (University of Chicago Press, 1977), p. 173.
a. Mean = 3.59, SD = 0.56.

ism while simultaneously bringing the schools under a common structure. During Mann's illustrious career, he was never able to dampen the mystique of localism or the suspicion of state control that ran throughout the commonwealth.[5]

Unlike those of California, Massachusetts's schools predated the state's active role in education and did so by nearly two centuries. State government in California spurred the development of a school system where no schools had existed before, and with the promise of financial support, persuaded local communities to cooperate with the state's educational endeavors.

These early histories established a remarkably resilient pattern in state-local relations. Today, the two states evidence radically different political cultures on matters of education policy. Whether it is selecting textbooks or providing tax revenues, the state's role is stronger in California than in Massachusetts. To cite one index of these differences, Fred Wirt created a numerical scale in 1977 measuring the centralization of education policy in the states (see table 5-2).[6] Wirt's formula finds Massachusetts the third-least centralized state in the nation, while California sits in the middle of the pack on the division of state and local authority. Wirt makes the case, "There is much inertia in policy operations, those 'standard operating procedures' that carry a policy system through crises as well as routines. Therefore, what we see today of policy may be the tip of the historical iceberg."[7]

Table 5-3. Levels of Actor Influence on Tracking Policy[a]
Mean ratings (standard error)

CA 91		CA 94		MA 95	
Principals	3.20 (.04)	Principals	3.29 (.04)	Principals	3.23 (.07)
Teachers	3.18 (.04)	Teachers	3.12 (.07)		
				Teachers	2.98 (.08)
Dist. Admins.	2.77 (.05)	Dist. Admins.	2.71 (.08)		
Parents	2.35 (.04)	Parents	2.36 (.07)	Dist. Admins.	2.49 (.09)
State Admins.	2.33 (.05)	State Admins.	2.36 (.08)	Parents	2.41 (.07)
				State Admins.	1.81 (.07)
Comm. Groups	1.60 (.04)	Comm. Groups	1.58 (.06)	Comm. Groups	1.52 (.06)

a. Differences between adjacent vertical cells are statistically significant (t-test).

Let us turn to the tracking reforms of the 1980s and 1990s and see if the tip of this historical iceberg remains in view.

The State Role in Tracking Policy

In table 5-3, I have reproduced data from chapter 4 in a slightly different form. The table displays the influence of different actors on tracking policy. I am drawing once again on three separate surveys of school principals, the first conducted in California in 1991 (CA 91), the second in California in 1994 (CA 94), and the third in Massachusetts in 1995 (MA 95). In answering questions about influences on tracking policy, the principals responded to a four-category scale, indicating that actors had "no influence," "some influence," "considerable influence," or "great influence."

The California surveys exhibit almost identical patterns. The school is the center of policymaking, and ratings of influential actors come in bunches that roughly correspond to the actors' distance from the center. Principals and teachers are the most influential actors, followed by district policymakers, then parents and the state, and finally community groups. School-site educators are the core actors on tracking policies, and influences from outside the system and from further up the system's hierarchy are weaker.

In Massachusetts, the influence ratings are more spread out. Massachusetts principals possess singular influence on tracking policies—they stand alone. Teachers are the second-most influential actor in Massachusetts, but they wield less influence than California teachers. District and state policymakers exert much less influence in Massachusetts than in California, and parents and community groups are about the same in the two states.

The most striking difference between the states is in the ratings for state officials. In California, state administrators rank about even with parents (2.36 in 1994), but in Massachusetts they get a significantly weaker rating (1.81). Figures for individual categories of influence (not shown in table) are illuminating. Massachusetts's state policymakers were more often described as having "no influence" (42 percent vs. 23 percent in California), and their influence was less often described as "considerable" or "great" (18 percent vs. 44 percent).

Why are state officials in California perceived as more influential than their Massachusetts counterparts? Administrators in the California State Department of Education possess a number of tools for conveying state policy to local districts and schools. California is one of the nation's twenty-two textbook adoption states. For K–8 classrooms, districts purchase books that appear on a state-approved list, a law in effect since 1884.[8] Massachusetts districts are free to purchase texts of their own liking. California's curriculum frameworks, originating in the 1940s and written for most academic subjects since the 1960s, guide textbook selection and define the broad content of academic subjects. Starting in the early 1980s, frameworks also began describing teaching activities that the state considers effective. In 1995, Massachusetts issued the draft copy of a curriculum framework for mathematics, its very first.

Every three years, California schools are visited by a team of state-sanctioned evaluators in a process known as the Program Quality Review (or PQR). The teams comprise local educators from districts outside the school under review, but they operate under the auspices of the state and follow state-generated criteria in rendering their judgments.[9] Massachusetts has no parallel process of state-sanctioned review.

All of California's state powers have been called on to promote its detracking initiative. State officials in Massachusetts, on the other hand, lack these instruments for forcefully conveying state policy to local schools. As reported in chapter 4, this study's surveys showed that even in California state policy is not very influential in local tracking decisions. But the analysis below demonstrates that this is not the final word on the subject.

Districts and Schools Sharing Authority

Either schools develop their own tracking policies or districts adopt policies for them. In the case of schools, reform-minded teachers may want

Figure 5-1. Source of Tracking Policy

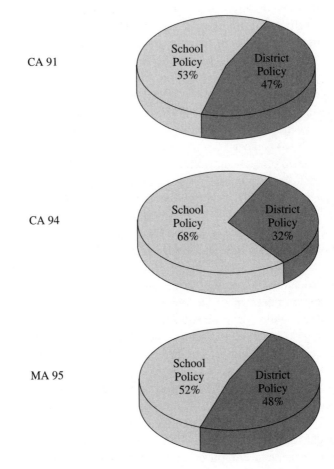

to experiment with untracking, the issue may appear on the agenda of faculty meetings for discussion, or a new principal may urge teachers to try a different system based on research in the latest journals. At the district level, central office administrators may review their curricular policies and recommend detracking, the school board may decide to implement a course of study leading to advanced placement courses, or a new superintendent may launch an initiative to diminish tracking and ability grouping.[10]

The study's survey asked principals whether district or school authorities decided their schools' tracking policies (see figure 5-1). To clarify the governance question, in other words, I forced the principals to pick one or

Table 5-4. Schools Deciding Own Tracking Policy, by Community
Percent

Community	CA 91	CA 94	MA 95
Urban	42.2	55.6	38.2
Suburban	51.5	73.8	63.6
Rural	62.9	75.0	83.3
Summary statistics			
Chi square	5.657	4.863	9.284
Degrees of freedom	2	2	2
p value	.06	.09	.01

the other as the dominant source.[11] Interestingly, California schools gained in controlling their own tracking policies from 1991 to 1994, and the percentage of autonomous schools rose from 52.5 percent to 68.0 percent. Massachusetts's policies, on the other hand, were developed almost equally by school and district decisionmakers in 1995. Authority over tracking is more centralized at the local level in Massachusetts than in California.

Recall the stability in the ratings reported in table 5-3 for CA 91 and CA 94. Changes in California's policy source from 1991 to 1994 apparently had no effect on the distribution of influence among various actors. California schools grew more responsible for tracking policies, but the relative power of district administrators, principals, and teachers remained unchanged. These data cast doubt on the notion that devolving authority to school sites, on this policy anyway, increases the influence of teachers and principals.

What leads to the district or the school possessing authority on tracking? In addition to the actors already discussed, environmental conditions affect the governance of tracking reform.

A school's institutional setting, especially the community in which it is located, makes a difference in its governance (see table 5-4). The 1991 California results show that 42.2 percent of urban schools exercised autonomy on tracking policy, 51.5 percent of suburban schools, and 62.9 percent of rural schools. In all three samples, urban schools were more likely to receive policy direction from central authorities, while rural schools were more likely to go their own way. The differences are statistically significant in Massachusetts, where rural schools were more than twice as likely as urban schools to formulate their own tracking policies (83.3 percent vs. 38.2 percent). What explains the urban systems' tendency to centralize tracking policy?

The Organizational Explanation

Cycles of centralization and decentralization have been described in several classic studies of big city school systems.[12] One explanation for urban centralization focuses on the relationship of bureaucracy to organizational size. Due to the heightened demand for educational services, urban school districts develop into highly complex organizations.[13] Like all large organizations, educational systems differentiate labor and create hierarchies that define executive, managerial, and operational roles. These positions are distinguished by their relative power over different operations of the organization.[14] Even in the most worker-empowered organization imaginable, executives and central office managers hold authority that lower-level employees do not possess. The central office coordinates far-flung activities. Serving a larger population, urban districts employ more administrators than suburban and rural districts.

Although this portrait of city school districts undoubtedly holds some truth, a considerable amount of organizational research rebuts the notion that growing size leads to centralization. Studies on the distribution of authority within organizations suggest that centralization and organizational size are often inversely related. As small firms expand, executives have neither the time nor the resources to make all necessary decisions. Internal differentiation takes place, and authority is delegated. Growth boosts the creation of administrative positions, but, strictly speaking, this is not synonymous with centralization.[15] Power can migrate upward only to be dispersed over a larger number of administrative offices. John W. Meyer and W. Richard Scott refer to this feature of educational bureaucracies as "fragmented centralization."[16] However, for the purpose at hand, determining whether districts or schools decide tracking policy, merely detecting if authority over tracking shifts upward will suffice. Moreover, research also shows that numerous areas of policy, including those dealing with public relations and the external environment, are often kept under top-echelon control in the large organization.[17]

To test whether district population drives centralization, I categorized districts as small, medium, or large (see table 5-5). To place these categories in a national context, small districts, those enrolling 5,000 or fewer students, are a whopping 85.6 percent of all districts in the country, but they serve only 35.8 percent of students; 10.4 percent of districts fall in the "medium" category, enrolling 34.3 percent of students; and a mere 1.4 percent of districts have enrollments of 25,000 or more, but these districts enroll 29.9 percent of students.[18]

Table 5-5. Schools Deciding Own Tracking Policy, by District Size
Percent

District size	CA 91	CA 94	MA 95
Small (5,000 or less)	69.3	76.2	63.8
Medium (5,001 to 25,000)	55.7	68.1	35.0
Large (25,001 or more)	28.6	59.5	25.0
Summary statistics			
Chi square	32.9	2.5	11.4
Degrees of freedom	2	2	2
p value	< .001	> .10	< .01

Bear in mind, despite the table's preoccupation with the characteristics of districts, that the unit of analysis remains the school. In CA 91, for example, 69.3 percent of schools in small districts reported that they decided their own tracking policies; this slipped to 55.7 percent of the schools in medium-size districts and all the way down to 28.6 percent in large districts. MA 95 shows a similar pattern, with power over policy exercised by 63.8 percent of schools in small districts, 35.0 percent in medium districts, and 25.0 percent in large districts (although with only eight schools in the cell, the figure for large districts in MA 95 should be taken with a grain of salt).

This helps clarify the trend toward decentralization in California that was noted earlier (figure 5.1). The movement to enhance school authority over policy has been most pronounced in large districts, with the percentage of autonomous schools doubling from 1991 to 1994 (from 28.6 percent to 59.5 percent). In the mid-1990s, bureaucratic constraints on California schools were apparently relaxed, allowing schools even in large districts to assert authority over their own curricular practices. But at the same time, central bureaucracies maintained their power over tracking policy in the large and midsize districts of Massachusetts.

The Political Explanation

A second explanation for why centralization occurs in urban districts involves politics. In comparison to suburban and rural officials, urban educational leaders must contend with heterogeneous and often fractious con-

Table 5-6. Schools Deciding Own Tracking Policy, with and without School Board Tracking Discussion
Percent

Board action	CA 91	CA 94	MA 95
Discussion	46.3	53.5	51.3
No discussion	62.1	77.8	54.2
Summary statistics			
Chi square	8.554	9.633	0.102
Degrees of freedom	1	1	1
p value	< .01	< .01	> .10

stituencies.[19] Elections for school board, or "school committee," as they are called in Massachusetts, attract powerful political interests. Teachers unions exert formidable influence and a vigilant press keeps the community informed of school controversies. Unstable political environments tend toward centralized policymaking, and to diminish conflict, urban districts may reduce the discretion of teachers and school principals on issues such as tracking.[20]

School boards are good barometers of local school politics.[21] In these three surveys of tracking policy, I asked principals if tracking policy had been discussed by their local boards. Where tracking looms as a political issue, quite likely it appears on the board's agenda. Note that the survey asked simply if tracking were discussed, not whether the discussion led to policy action.

When school boards discussed tracking, it was about an even bet, across all three samples, whether the source of the policy was the school or the district (see the first row of table 5-6). Differences emerged when there was no board discussion. Authority flowed to schools in CA 94, as 77.8 percent of schools in districts with no board discussion decided their own policies. In Massachusetts the percentage of autonomous schools remained basically unchanged, regardless of school committee discussion of the tracking issue. Perhaps the routines of policymaking are so deeply institutionalized within districts in Massachusetts that a calm political environment has no effect on policy devolution. The Massachusetts Education Reform Act of 1993, which had not been fully implemented at the time of the MA 95 survey, promises to alter this tendency. The act mandates the establishment of school councils to advise on policy matters. With parent, teacher, and community representatives serving on these councils, a new engine of policy development will be erected at school sites. Future surveys of policy-making in Massachusetts are likely to show schools stepping into any policy vacuum, developing their own policies when school committees are quiescent.

The patterns revealed here raise an interesting paradox. Local tracking policies in Massachusetts are more centralized at the district level than one would predict from its legacy of decentralized state governance. And in contrast to California's history of state control over numerous aspects of schooling, local districts there have increasingly allowed their schools to decide their own tracking policies. Determining the dispersion of authority within the educational system depends on the specific intergovernmental relationship that one examines, state-local or district-school. In addition to state political cultures, local political cultures may also take root that direct the flow of decisionmaking to schools or to districts.

Modeling the Source of Tracking Policy

I ran logistic regression models to untangle the various factors influencing whether districts or schools decide tracking policy. A few housekeeping items before proceeding: the variables are the same as those presented in chapter 4 except for a few changes. District population is included in equations instead of school population. And the influence variables for teachers, school principals, and district officials are dropped from the analysis since assessing their impact would be tautological (that is, the influence of school personnel strengthens when schools decide and the influence of district officials increases when districts decide).

The results of the analysis are displayed in table 5-7. Positive coefficients indicate a tilt toward school policies, negative coefficients toward district policies. To simplify the discussion, I will once again convert the best-fitting models' coefficients to odds ratios and apply them to a mythical sample of 100 schools, a sample that I have rigged so that the probability of school or district policy source is equal. Before anything else occurs, this imaginary sample is set so that fifty schools develop their own tracking policies and fifty schools receive policies from their districts. I now focus on the institutional, organizational, and political factors driving policy source—such as district size, school board discussion of tracking policy, state influence, a school's SES and percentage of nonwhite students—and show how the coin-flip samples change when each of these factors is altered.

Table 5-7. Logit Models of Source of Tracking Policy [a]

Clusters and factors	CA 91		CA 94		MA 95	
	Full model	Best fit	Full model	Best fit	Full model	Best fit
Institutional						
Urban	.929	...	1.136	...	−.609	...
	(.592)	...	(.870)	...	(1.143)	...
Suburban	.747	...	1.151	...	−.363	...
	(.458)	...	(.790)	...	(.929)	...
SES	−1.566***	−.361*	−1.361**	...	.530	...
	(.528)	(.192)	(.654)	...	(.640)	...
Percent nonwhite	−.013	...	−4.535***	−2.301***	.028	.034**
	(.010)	...	(1.576)	(.807)	(.019)	(.015)
Math score	.012	...	−.019	...	−.001	...
	(.008)	...	(.037)	...	(.075)	...
Technical						
Spread in achievement	.286	...	.003	...	−.001	...
	(.340)	...	(.002)	...	(.003)	...
Organizational						
District population	−.546***	−.441***	−.415**	...	−1.337***	−1.666***
	(.144)	(.094)	(.204)	...	(.494)	(.411)
Grade levels	.461	.436*	−1.006*	−.758*	.009	...
(6–8 in CA)	(.293)	(.248)	(.516)	(.418)	(.315)	...

Political

State	-.348**	-.329**	-.521**	-.574***	.212	⋮
	(.160)	(.132)	(.249)	(.219)	(.271)	⋮
Parents	-.066	⋮	-.088	⋮	.127	⋮
	(.204)	⋮	(.310)	⋮	(.301)	⋮
Community groups	-.349	⋮	.348	⋮	-.356	⋮
	(.230)	⋮	(.334)	⋮	(.336)	⋮
School board discussion	-1.097***	-.901***	-1.724***	-.975**	-.443	⋮
	(.308)	(.252)	(.541)	(.421)	(.516)	⋮
Constant	8.589	6.472	12.328	4.385	9.804	13.511
	(2.571)	(1.250)	(3.202)	(.880)	(5.222)	(3.242)
Summary statistics						
Chi square	62.87	53.44	37.82	28.34	23.58	27.22
Degrees of freedom	12	5	12	4	12	2
p value	<.001	<.001	<.001	<.001	<.001	<.001
Correctly predicted policies (percent)	68.8	66.0	78.8	73.9	72.3	69.5

*$p < .10$, **$p < .05$, ***$p < .01$.
a. Positive values favor school-based policy. Standard error indicated in parentheses.

Figure 5-2. Effect of District Population on "Coin-Flip" Sample, MA 95[a]

Increase of. . .

1,000 Students

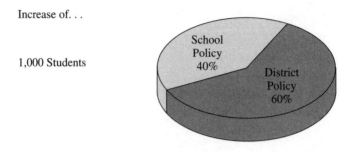

School
Policy
40%

District
Policy
60%

a. Computed from district with 3,681 students (mean of log of district population).

Organizational Factors

The tendency of urban districts to centralize tracking policy dissipates with district population and school board activity controlled in the regression equation.[22] District size exerts an especially powerful effect on who decides policy in Massachusetts (see figure 5-2). By increasing each district's enrollment by 1,000 students in MA 95's mythical 50-50 sample, the group tilts 60-40 toward district authority. This increase should be put in perspective, for it represents a huge gain, about a 26 percent increase for the median district in the state. The salient point is that Massachusetts's large districts are more likely to decide tracking policy for their schools—and schools in small districts to decide tracking policy for themselves. Schools in districts experiencing rapid population growth can expect some of their independence to erode.

Big districts may develop cultures that routinize centralized policymaking. Larger districts have more of everything to manage—more administrators, fatter budgets, more teachers, more school buildings, more curricular offerings. This complexity fosters the adoption of district-level rules and procedures in order to keep operations coordinated across organizational subunits. When change is proposed, from the reform of tracking systems to the redesign of basketball uniforms, district officials in large districts typically have something to say on the subject.

Small districts' cultures work to do the opposite. Small districts are better able to form decisionmaking protocols based on personal relationships and collegial interactions, allowing for the devolution of policymaking to schools. In districts with only one or two schools, the same person may hold school and district positions. Department chairs at the local high

Figure 5-3. Effect of Grade 6–8 Configuration on "Coin-Flip" Sample, CA 91 and CA 94

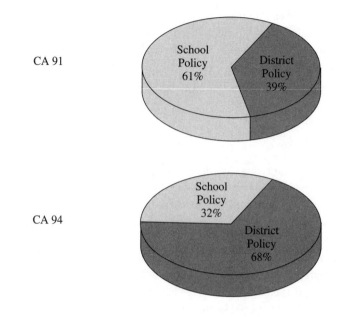

school or middle school, for example, may serve half-time as the district's curriculum coordinator in their disciplinary subject. The jurisdictional lines between school and district authority are blurred.

The second organizational factor, grade configuration, exhibits a curious effect in the two California samples. At schools serving grades 6–8, policies are solidly rooted in a school source in CA 91, but in CA 94, they tilt even more strongly toward a district source (see figure 5-3). How could this factor reverse direction in only three short years? The anomaly reinforces the point that districts can influence the school-level policy environment by controlling schools' organizational properties, in this case, by changing the grade levels that schools serve. From 1991 to 1994, there was a notable shift away from grade 7–8 and 7–9 configurations in California. Grade 6–8 schools grew from 45 percent to 55 percent of all middle schools. The state's untracking push was part of a general campaign for middle school reform. Districts decide the grade levels served by schools, not schools themselves. By reconfiguring schools, districts stamp them with a new identity, and in the case of grade 6–8 schools, it is an identity that shuns tracking. The classic grade 7–9 junior high dropped to 7.3 percent of the CA 94 sample.

Two cross-cutting trends are at work in the CA 94 numbers. The movement in favor of school-based management has persuaded districts, especially large districts, to grant more policymaking authority to educators at the site level. Districts have enhanced their control of tracking policies indirectly, however, by creating more grade 6–8 schools and then supervising these converted schools' adherence to the middle school philosophy on tracking reform. The net result is that grade 6–8 schools have lost autonomy on the tracking issue.

Political Factors

Districts routinely appoint advisory committees of educators, parents, and community members to tackle such controversial issues as sex education, multicultural curriculum, and tracking reform. These committees are charged with ironing out policy compromises. When advisory committee meetings turn bitter or divisive, an early warning system is triggered. Administrators prefer to solve controversies before they reach the board. Issues appearing on the school board agenda make existing policy vulnerable to alteration. If the conflict involves an organized group of parents, in extreme cases, district administrators may be forced to take the embarrassing step of overruling a school principal or lower-level district administrator. No wonder that parents' opposition to tracking reform has been taken so seriously by district officials.

School board discussion strongly influences the source of tracking policy in both California surveys. A 50-50 coin-flip sample with no discussion changes to only twenty-seven schools creating their own tracking policies once school board discussion takes place (see figure 5-4). This finding reaffirms the long-standing belief that political conflict exerts a centralizing effect on policy. School boards are the last stop for a district's political battles, the ultimate arbiter of political skirmishes.

Conflict may break out among people within the school system. Reform-minded teachers may strive to see tracking reduced in their schools and, after getting a negative response from their own principal or faculty, petition the district office to intervene. On the flip side of the issue, some districts that have reduced or eliminated tracking have seen resistant teachers band together to oppose the reform. Admittedly, such cases of open rebellion are rare. Open internecine conflict is infrequent because it exacts high costs in organizational morale and leaves the complainants at risk of reprisal. Nevertheless, such conflicts occasionally bubble up inside districts, gaining a spot on the school board's agenda.

Figure 5-4. Effect of School Board Discussion of Tracking Policy on "Coin-Flip" Sample, CA 94

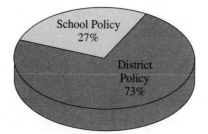

School board discussion of an issue can indicate administrative failure of two types—in managing the school system's external environment or in managing internal disagreements among personnel. What can boards do after discussing tracking? They can adopt district policy or leave tracking for schools to decide. But what if a school is involved in the conflict to be resolved, if parents have launched a petition drive against a particular school's policy or warring factions of a school's faculty have taken their dispute to the board? These deliberations almost certainly will result in district authority overruling school discretion.

Tracking reform often begins when district administrators initiate a re-evaluation of existing practices. This is an avenue for the influence of state policy to penetrate local districts. One of the responsibilities of a district's officer in charge of curriculum and instruction (typically an associate or assistant superintendent) is to monitor state policy on various curricular and instructional topics. These officials received copies of *Caught in the Middle* when it was distributed to California educators in 1987 and *Magic in the Middle* when it was released by Massachusetts state authorities in 1993. In some districts, the documents made no impression, but in others, administrators sympathized with the indictment of tracking and initiated steps to nudge districts toward reform.

A one-unit increase in state influence changes the mythical 50-50 sample for CA 91 to a 58-42 distribution favoring district policy creation (see figure 5-5). A two-unit increase creates a 66-34 breakdown. Generally speaking, state influence on tracking is weak. But when it becomes a factor in local decisions, it has a centralizing impact on the source of tracking policy. The finding is comparable to that of researchers in the 1970s who found that federal programs boosted the importance of state education departments. Researchers of state reforms in the 1980s and 1990s have also found that

Figure 5-5. Effect of State Influence on "Coin-Flip" Sample, CA 91[a]

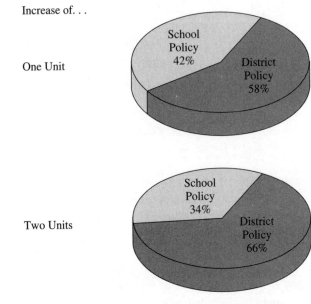

a. Categories of influence are no influence, moderate influence, considerable influence, and great influence.

regulation is not zero sum, that state activity may precipitate policy creation by local districts. In the schools I studied, state influence is felt through policies with district origins rather than policies formulated in schools.[23]

Local administrators can use state policy for political cover when issues draw political heat. This phenomenon occurred in both states. In districts where they were outnumbered and outgunned, tracking reformers cited state policy to bolster their cause. Administrators asked incredulously: How can resistant teachers, principals, and parents question the judgment of the state's experts? In a few extreme cases, officials declared that tracking had been "outlawed." Words like these are intended to shield local policymakers from public rebuke. They cannot be blamed for following the law.

Institutional Factors

Socioeconomic status (SES) is a significant factor in CA 91 and racial composition in CA 94. In CA 91, wealthier schools lack autonomy on tracking. The SES effect is the opposite of what I expected, having thought that Title I programs serving schools with low income populations would favor centralization at the district level. However, a wealthy school may face pressure to offer the same honors courses every other school in its district offers, thereby standardizing tracking policy. Local districts may grant schools serving poor students autonomy to experiment with detracking.

In CA 94, schools with a larger percentage of nonwhite students are more likely to receive tracking policy from their districts than formulate it themselves (the opposite occurs in MA 95). To check whether the CA 94 finding reflects administrative centralization of bilingual programs, I ran separate regressions using Hispanic, black, white, and Asian percentages as predictors. Neither Hispanic nor black enrollment has an effect on policy source but greater Asian enrollment does. It also predicts greater support of tracking (see chapter 4). Something related to the issue of tracking happened in predominantly Asian schools between 1991 and 1994, and possibly parents opposed to detracking went through district channels to influence policy. Further research is needed on the special experience of tracking reform in schools with large Asian populations. These data are ambiguous on this and the more general question of how racial composition affects the governance of tracking reform.

When Policies Collide: Creekside and Parkview Schools

This analysis of why policymaking flows to either districts or schools may leave the false impression that the exercise of authority in school systems is an orderly process, one that responds to patterns of inert forces. On the contrary, policymakers rarely relinquish decisions to others when the policies in question involve issues that they steadfastly believe are important. When the tracking wars pit schools against their own districts or state, the battle over policy jurisdiction can develop into a supreme test of wills. Let me illustrate with two California schools' experiences.

Creekside Middle School is located in a rural area that is rapidly becoming suburbanized. The school had untracked all academic subjects except mathematics until 1990. In that year, a parent group petitioned the district school board to reinstate advanced classes, pointing out the inconsistency of the district's policy that guaranteed gifted programs at elementary schools and advanced placement courses at high schools but made no provision for advanced courses at middle schools. The board directed the district administration to ensure that Creekside offered honors-level sequences in English, history, and science. Teachers were furious.

It was mainly because of a minority of vocal parents of advanced students who . . . said, "Well, elementary has gifted programs, and the high school has advanced placement, and we want something for our kids at your school." So that's where advanced came in, to appease a half a dozen loud parents.   —*Teacher, Social Studies*

He [the parent group's leader] ran for the board and was not elected. And I think he's looking for a constituency and has found that GATE [gifted and talented education] is a good topic—he rallied a group of parents, and they went to the board.   —*Principal*

He showed up at the school board with a petition with 300 or 400 names signed to it. Most of them were not names of parents of our students here. A number of people also addressed the board at that time, and we feel . . . that they had not investigated what's on our campus, what's available here, what sort of enrichment programs and options. They didn't take advantage of the school site council and, therefore, couldn't have made an informed decision as to what we needed to do here.   —*Teacher, English*

Now, my assistant superintendent . . . [is] very much in favor of heterogeneous grouping also. So she was my ally; she was a real support. And she had talked to the superintendent, and I thought we pretty well had the superintendent convinced. But . . . I don't know if it was easier to give in or it was the course of least resistance or it was a windmill he didn't feel at the time he wanted to tilt with—the board got it in their head, and that was something, for whatever reason, he was just not going to fight with them over.   —*Principal*

The teachers and principal at Creekside oppose tracking, believing it harms the school's large Latino population. They feel that by skimming off the best students, honors courses leave no role models in the regular classrooms and, in particular, leave no high achievers to facilitate cooperative learning, a favored instructional strategy at the school. Heterogeneous grouping also gives administrators the flexibility to move kids from class to class, whether to attain better racial and ethnic balance across classrooms or to separate an impressionable student from bad peer influences. Tracking also violates the staff members' egalitarian philosophy of education. Although most teachers did not attribute the parents' actions to racism, one teacher suspected it was at the heart of the protest.

You know, if we see a bright Hispanic—particularly a Hispanic kid who's hanging out with the home boys—we try real hard to get [him] out of that class and move him right away. Because the homeys, as they're called, tend to have a real negative effect on each other. But separately or with other groups, they're real positive, great kids.

—Principal

We have a couple of teachers that are real die-hards as far as "all kids are equal," you know, and "let's really make [classes] heterogeneous." And we say, "everybody takes it, everybody takes it."

—Teacher, Science

When we start ability grouping here, what we see is the upper-end kids, who are mostly white, going into the advanced classes, and the lower-end kids, who are mostly Hispanic or black, going into the other classes. And now we're even further accentuating any differences between white and black. And that, in itself, is a reason to say, "No. We don't want to do this." And that may be, in fact, the parental motivating factor for doing it in the first place. It wasn't to get their kids into advanced classes. It was to get their kids away from the minority students. *—Teacher, Science*

The campaign to overturn the district's tracking ultimatum was led by teachers in the English and social studies departments. Creekside's traditionally tracked math department did not participate in the protest. But science teachers joined in the defense of heterogeneous grouping because of the de facto effect tracking in one subject can have on all classes.

We put our protest through channels. . . . The principal heard from the department chairs and teachers who said, "You know, this is not good. This goes totally against our middle school philosophy." But, on the other hand, the parents must be appeased.

—Teacher, Social Studies

I think the only people who do not want heterogeneous grouping [are in] the math department, which, of course, I fully concur with as far as math is concerned. But that's the only class where I see they need to have ability grouping. *—Teacher, Social Studies*

The only thing is that when you group even one bunch of kids or offer something like algebra only one period, it tends to . . . track them a little bit anyway. . . . As a result of that, I have a class where I've got a whole bunch of really bright kids; and then some of the other ones are a little vacant on that.   —*Teacher, Science*

Their opposition was ignored. Several Creekside teachers engineered a creative way to comply with the district's order while simultaneously accomplishing their own objectives. The following year they would place all students in the same level classes for English, science, and history—and label all of these classes "advanced." The school would still have heterogeneous grouping, but the district would not know about it, and all the GATE parents would know is that their children were taking advanced classes. The plan was written into the recommendations of the state's Program Quality Review (PQR), which, coincidentally, took place only a few months after the board's decision. The state had been drawn into the Creekside faculty's effort to outfox its own school board. Teachers describe the plan:

Well, we have found a way now to get around it. It [was] decided— we just had our PQR last week or week before last week. And one of the things that is going into our plan is that all language arts and social studies classes beginning in July are advanced. So we won't have any generic classes. We will have all advanced language arts and social studies. So the parents have their advanced classes and we have our heterogeneous grouping. Funny how that works, isn't it? We can play the same game.   —*Teacher, Social Studies*

We wrote a letter to the board complaining that this decision was made without our input (well, the language arts [teachers] did), that the decision was made without involving us, and we didn't get a chance to present our program or answer to anything. And they just did it, which is typical. . . . The board did this to appease a group of parents. And so instead of having one advanced class, we have three. And the kids that are in there are not advanced, you know, and it isn't even in order to fill those classes. It's just . . . to sabotage the system, and we did.   —*Teacher, English*

For a year, they [the parent group demanding tracking] won't notice. When their little kids come home and it says "Advanced English" on their schedule, they'll be happy. . . . I think that the district office administration treads lightly around us anyway. They know that we can make as much noise as any parent group and, in fact, have. I think they're going to let this advanced issue slide next year.

—Teacher, English

The scheme did not work. The following year, district administrators discovered Creekside's subterfuge when district computers began printing students' schedules. Someone noticed that every Creekside student was taking honors courses, and thinking it was a computer glitch, investigated further. The district's assistant superintendent informed the principal, in the principal's words, that "the handwriting is on the wall." The principal sadly notified the staff that the plan had failed. The school would provide both honors and regular classes.

The passage of time and several changes in the community quelled the controversy. Honors classes were accepted begrudgingly at Creekside. Two years later, sixth graders were added as the school expanded to grades 6–8. Sixth graders were heterogeneously grouped. A new middle school opened nearby with an accelerated GATE cluster, and the district adopted an open enrollment policy, allowing parents, on a space available basis, to choose their children's school of attendance. Creekside lost parents who favored tracking but also picked up some favoring detracked classes. Perhaps the strongest signal that the conflict had calmed: One of the school's most energetic opponents kept her son at the school, changed her mind about tracking, and became an enthusiastic supporter of heterogeneous grouping. A cease-fire took hold in Creekside's tracking wars.

I turn to Parkview Intermediate School, the second school that differed with upper-level policy on the tracking issue. Parkview is located in a working class neighborhood of a major metropolitan area. Like Creekside Middle School, it serves an ethnically diverse population. And as at Creekside, the state's Program Quality Review played a part in the controversy. In 1991 the state review team sharply criticized Parkview's heavily leveled curricular structure and recommended reductions in tracking, especially in the four-track mathematics department.

The principal and teachers were outraged. They argued that detracking threatened popular and effective programs for remedial and advanced students, citing the numerous state and national awards Parkview had received.

[The state would] have an exemplary school program one year. And then the next year, the distinguished school. And so we got the first

two. We've done it on grouping. And we had an interesting experience. We knew it [detracking] was coming because [state superinten-
dent] Honig comes out with, "You've got to heterogeneously group."
We tried to resist it. But then this year, we got a state review. And, of
course, we didn't try to hide anything. So they knew we had [track-
ing]. Actually, we modified it somewhat this year because we knew
the state review was coming and we thought we'd do something toward it.   —*Principal*

The state review team criticized us severely for our homogeneous
grouping. And, in fact, they are telling us that the state is demanding
that we not ability group, except for algebra. They said this is a state
mandate.   —*Teacher, Math*

Yes, the math students are still tracked. But we just did a state review,
and that's one of the areas that we have to address. All of our classes
have to be heterogeneous to bring us in line with the state framework.
The math teachers—some of the math teachers were not very happy
about this. One of the review team members, though, comes from a
school where they have integrated all of the math classes heterogeneously, and he could not foresee any problems. But we do have some
math teachers that were quite upset about this.   —*Teacher, History*

The district urged Parkview to comply with the recommendations, but
the school resisted. Led by one of Parkview's veteran teachers, the math
department took its opposition to the school's parent council. The council
passed a unanimous resolution opposing any reductions in ability grouping
at the school. The math teachers argued that mathematics requires a hierarchical ordering of curriculum, that mastery of prerequisite concepts and
skills is necessary before students can advance through the math curriculum. They believed both high- and low-achieving students are ill-served in
heterogeneous classes and cited the experience of a local school to support
their position.

They have attempted some of this heterogeneous grouping [this year].
And they are finding that it is a disaster. As he [a teacher at the untracked school] has explained it to me, the fast students in the class
are the ones that are controlling the class, in that they have all the
answers. And the really slow students in the class are absolutely lost.
They have no idea what's going on. And they are causing mayhem in

the classrooms. . . . Teachers who have had good control in the classroom in the past are finding that they are ineffective in working with
these heterogeneous groupings.   —*Teacher, Math*

Our site council voted unanimously that we should keep our grouping. It didn't mean much, but at least it showed we had community
support.   —*Principal*

There is one math teacher who pushed it through, made sure it was
pushed through. He was very vocal. . . . And that's why it went
through the site council. And it was very obvious to the review team.
They saw it as, you know, you're resisting something that the state
says that you must do that is done in other school districts successfully.   —*Teacher, History*

The teachers and the principal of Parkview School saw the state's tracking reform as a recommendation based on politics, on elite "politically
correct" interests that dominate state policy. They viewed detracking as out
of touch with what happens in classrooms, in conflict with what was
wanted by parents, and oblivious to the classroom conditions required for
good teaching. The district's administrators typically took a hands-off approach on such issues. A veteran teacher was convinced that the state, too,
could be kept at bay.

I think it, frankly, is a school policy. The district doesn't have . . . any
policy on this. And . . . the [district] administration has no idea what
goes on in a junior high school anyway. They've never had any personal experience at the intermediate level. They are all elementary
school people, and so they have some awareness of it, but they've
never actually been involved with it. . . . Fortunately, the state is far
enough away, so we only see them once every three years. And I think
what's going to happen is they go, "Now, you're out of compliance.
When we come back in three years, you'd better be in compliance."
And if we're not, well then, "Well, we'll come back in three years;
you'd better be in compliance." And by that time, the compliance
idea will be gone, and we'll be going back to what we're doing.
                                                         —*Teacher, Math*

The two schools I have discussed in this section take strikingly different positions on tracking, but both schools see outside forces attempting

to impose a curricular policy upon them. A conflict existed between the school and district policy in the case of the first school and between the school and state policy in the case of the second. These conflicts can be viewed as bureaucratic struggles between different levels of the educational system for authority over school practices, and, in that sense, they flesh out the findings from the study's survey data.

They also contradict at least one finding. The state looms larger than the survey data would predict, even for California schools. This is reminiscent of chapter 4's finding on the effect of parent influence on policy. Parents were not rated as influential on tracking policy overall, but when they were a factor, their influence swung policy toward tracking. The state is usually weak in its influence, but when drawn into local deliberations, as happened with both Parkview and Creekside, it makes a difference.

The two schools reveal important information on how protracted struggles over school tracking policy get started, how they develop, and how they are finally resolved. When first threatened, both schools sought allies from outside the local system. The untracked school used the state PQR for support; the tracked school rallied parents to defend its policies. In neither case did the controversy divide the staff. Differences of opinion about the wisdom of tracking were evident, especially among teachers from different departments, but most of the teachers tolerated these different views. If anything, the controversies united the two schools' staffs. The freedom to decide school practices assumed greater importance than the particulars of tracking policy.

Both schools had strong principals, and they were pivotal in determining the final policy outcomes. Both were willing to fight for the policies their respective faculties wanted, but neither was willing to launch a jihad for the cause. When "the handwriting was on the wall," they gave in to the wishes of district officials. And that might be the most telling lesson of these two schools' experiences: they compromised. Creekside School's curriculum is more differentiated than its teachers would prefer. Honors courses are offered in academic subjects. And Parkview School's classes are less differentiated than its teachers would like, with three ability groups in math and two levels in the other academic subjects. Governance of tracking reform, like governance more generally, demands pragmatism and compromise to make policy that endures. When I visited these two schools in 1996, six years after the first shots were fired in their tracking wars, a few faculty members continued to grumble, but the policies were holding fast.

Summary and Conclusion

This chapter has examined the governance of tracking reform within the educational systems of California and Massachusetts. Tracking reform has transpired in accordance with the two school systems' contrasting histories. State policymakers wield powers in California that are unheard of in Massachusetts. State textbook adoptions, Program Quality Reviews, and curriculum frameworks clearly articulated a desire to detrack middle schools, and, in the crafting of school policy, principals in both California surveys judged the influence of state policymakers as about equal to that of parents in the local community. In Massachusetts, the state's position was significantly less influential.

In neither state do these patterns of power sharing carry over to the local level. California districts have been more willing to delegate authority to schools, while Massachusetts districts maintain authority over tracking policy. Since the site-based-management provisions of the Massachusetts Education Reform Act had not been fully implemented at the time of the MA 95 survey, schools may acquire more control over tracking in the future.

The degree of centralization of local tracking policy can be explained by several factors. District officials in urban areas were likely to decide policy, but in suburban and rural communities, schools decided policy for themselves. This discrepancy disappears, however, when organizational and political factors are statistically controlled. Centralization in urban districts, in other words, appears to be a product of their complex bureaucracies (related to the size of student population) and their contentious political environments (related to school board discussion of an issue). The power of bureaucracies and politics also hints at the existence of deeply entrenched political cultures at the local level, but this study's data, confined as they are to a single educational issue, are inadequate to trace the full dimensions of these cultures.

Other aspects of local organization and politics also influence the source of policy. In both California samples, who decides policy is related to the grade configuration of schools and the influence of state policymakers. These findings underscore effective strategies for pursuing tracking reform. District administrators invoke the legitimacy of state policy to persuade reluctant schools to detrack. Districts also couch detracking within a campaign for reforming middle schools, including changing the grade levels of schools from grades 7–9 or 7–8 to grades 5–8 or 6–8. Grade conversions are typically accompanied by changes in staffing—shifting faculty from teachers with secondary credentials to teachers with elementary licenses and training. Secondary teachers possess licenses for teaching single subjects and may not be skilled at teaching the interdisciplinary courses often found at middle schools. They may even transfer to the high school level when middle schools adopt reforms reflecting an elementary school orientation.

Schools can also fight to defend policies from pressure from above, as demonstrated by Creekside and Parkview schools. Creekside took on its own district and school board, and Parkview battled the state. Both schools were forced to compromise. In handling these conflicts, the two schools' principals exhibited indefatigable control of their institutions. Among the tough challenges they successfully managed were responding to teachers' anger and frustration, accommodating the demands of actively involved parents, and keeping administrators satisfied in the central office.

This chapter has helped to explain how states, districts, and schools interact to govern tracking reform. The next two chapters enter schools and investigate how their internal organization and operation affect tracking policy.

6

Tracking and the Subject Area

U P TO THIS POINT, I have depicted tracking and untracking as policies of schools. This chapter looks
inside schools to investigate how individual academic subjects affect tracking policy. Tracking exists as a subsystem of the school, with teachers,
students, and curriculum organized into tracks within schools. The school
subject area is another subsystem of the school, and the two affect each
other when they interact.[1]

The subject area influences student learning every bit as powerfully as
the curricular track. In fact, the knowledge and skills learned by students
can be more readily identified by disciplinary origins than by correspon-
dence to track. If you talk to a middle school student about what he or she
has recently learned in school, you will assume that identifying parts of
speech was covered in an English class and the value of pi in a math course
without ever knowing the student's track placement. These topics are found
in either high or low tracks, depending on the grade level in which they are
taught.

Subject Area Subsystems

The subject area subsystem operates along three dimensions. The first
concerns intellectual disciplines. From universities to kindergartens, disciplinary boundaries delineate the intellectual content of what is learned.
Middle school subjects only acquaint students with a tiny segment of the
larger corpus of disciplinary knowledge, but the basic parameters of subject areas remain in force across all educational settings. Middle and high
school teachers generally teach the same subject all day, unlike elementary
school teachers. Yet disciplinary jurisdictions are so well grasped that very

little coordination of curriculum across classes is required to avoid needless repetition of content or to ensure that all subjects are covered. English and history teachers may collaborate to present curricula around common themes, but neither has to worry about students studying, say, *A Tale of Two Cities* or the French Revolution in a science or gym class.

Disciplines not only define the substance of what is taught, but they also guide the teacher's choice of instructional methods. As Susan Stodolsky affirms in the title of her book, the subject matters. Even in the elementary classroom, where the same teacher teaches all subjects, the subject area affects the variety of instructional approaches, the amount of time students spend working in groups, and the pacing and organization of content.[2] Like their colleagues at universities, K–12 math teachers tend to organize curriculum hierarchically, while English teachers arrange literature units by genre or cultural origin (for example, poetry, the novel, British literature, Asian literature). English teachers also evidence more variety in their instruction than math teachers.[3]

The second dimension of this subsystem refers to the subject area as part of a larger curricular order spanning grade levels and schools, a planned course of study that progresses from basic to advanced material. The predictability of this arrangement is essential. Middle school teachers expect students to arrive with an adequate preparation for middle school coursework. In turn, they are expected to prepare students for high school. These expectations are reinforced by parental demands, achievement tests, district administrative regulations, state curricular frameworks, and high school graduation requirements. Teachers of the same subjects from elementary, middle, and high schools occasionally (but all too rarely) meet or correspond to exchange concerns. The purpose is to coordinate the flow of curriculum from one level of schooling to the next.

Subject area subsystems, then, function on at least two levels that transcend the school—as instruction in a recognized field of knowledge and as part of a K–12 course of study. The subject area subsystem also operates on a third level—as an organizational unit within the school, the subject department. Whether made up of English or math teachers, the department brings together instructors teaching the same subject and sharing the vocabulary, values, and interests inculcated by training in a common discipline. In many schools, departments are important units of decisionmaking. They schedule classes, determine course prerequisites, select and order textbooks, write and administer exams, and establish and enforce grading policies. The department also functions as a political actor. When school faculties are split on school policy, factions often develop along departmental lines.

Subject Areas and Tracking

Researchers have discovered that subject departments react differently to the tracking issue. Leslie Santee Siskin found English departments generally opposed to tracking and math departments generally in favor "because of the understandings of teaching and curriculum within each subject." [4] Stephen J. Ball discovered the clash of "subject subcultures" in his study of a British high school's attempt to "destream" its curriculum. Again, the main combatants were math teachers on the side of tracking and teachers of English and social science on the side of reform. [5]

Other studies indicate that departments formulate tracking policies independently of one another. A study of the educational paths of California high school students concluded that tracking affects students' experiences, but that the "approaches vary within schools by department, that is, each subject reflects differences in beliefs and traditions about content and sequence and differences in institutional requirements." [6] Such differences even appear in subjects that one would intuitively expect to behave similarly. An analysis of almost 2,000 student transcripts in five Maryland high schools discovered that only 35 percent of students' movement up or down in math tracks correlated with movement in science tracks. [7]

The studies cited above examine the role of high school departments. The few studies involving middle schools have also uncovered subject differences. [8] In Maureen Hallinan's study of middle school tracking, math classes in the eleven schools contained more tracks than English classes. [9] In a study from the early 1990s, Elizabeth Useem discovered marked variation in track assignment in mathematics. Focusing on differences among twenty-six Massachusetts school districts, she concluded that students of equal ability living in different districts do not have the same opportunity to enroll in advanced mathematics. Assignment policies differed by the surrounding community's socioeconomic level and the attitude of administrators toward acceleration in mathematics. Useem notes that departmental chairpersons were powerful: "These chairs, who remain in their jobs for many years, are in a position to put their own stamp on course offerings, ability grouping configurations, placement criteria, and rules about parental intervention." [10] She also shows that taking algebra in the eighth grade was related to enrollment in calculus at the high school four years later

Table 6-1. Number of Levels in English and Math
Percent of schools, unless otherwise noted

Subject	Number of levels	CA 91	CA 94	MA 95
English	1	47.6	56.1	55.1
	2	36.3	39.6	15.0
	3+	16.1	4.3	29.9
Math	1	11.2	17.1	15.2
	2	34.3	46.3	30.3
	3+	54.5	36.6	54.5

($r = .68$), suggesting that grouping in middle and high school math departments may be connected.

Tracking in English and Math

In this study's three surveys, sharp differences are exhibited in mathematics and English (see table 6-1). English is significantly less tracked than math. More than half of all schools in CA 94 and MA 95 report that they heterogeneously group students in English classes (that is, offer only one level), while less than 20 percent of schools heterogeneously group math students. The most stratified systems in MA 95—those with three ability levels or more—are almost twice as common in mathematics as in English (54.5 percent vs. 29.9 percent). In CA 94, the same comparison is extremely lopsided (36.6 percent vs. 4.3 percent).

The most popular system in CA 94 has two ability levels in math, and in MA 95, three levels. What do these systems look like? Two-level math systems typically offer an algebra class for the school's highest-achieving eighth graders. For all other students, they offer a class usually called "eighth grade math" or "math 8." Students at grade level and below are assigned to this course. Three-level systems, the most popular in MA 95, either break out low-achieving students into a separate third track, with a curriculum centering on basic skills, or break out students who are almost ready for algebra into a separate pre-algebra class. Three-track systems might consist of "algebra," "pre-algebra," and "eighth grade math," or "algebra," "eighth grade math," and "remedial math." Course titles vary because schools frequently invent their own labels. Labels can be misleading, therefore, when comparing courses from school to school. Algebra classes are not all the same. More often than not, however, labels accurately outline the hierarchy of courses within a single school.

What explains the stark differences between tracking in math and English? The three dimensions of subject area subsystems shed light on this question.

Middle School Subjects as Part of a Discipline

Educational issues such as tracking are viewed differently by those who toil in separate educational fields. This became obvious to me as I visited schools and talked to teachers about tracking. They were not just teachers but teachers of English and mathematics and other subjects. They scrutinized innovations for their contribution to the task of teaching a particular discipline's skills and knowledge. An effective approach in one subject may be worthless in another.

I was surprised at the respect paid to disciplinary differences when educators discussed tracking policy, especially the near unanimous agreement among teachers that such differences should be factored into policy decisions. Even at schools where tracking had been hotly debated, teachers recognized differences in the essential nature of mathematics and English. This recognition led true believers on both sides of the issue to think twice before imposing a single policy on their adversaries. Substantive characteristics of math and English foster such mutual tolerance.

Mathematics

Math teachers and their colleagues tend to view mathematics as a hierarchical sequence of concepts requiring mastery. This view is explicitly rejected by the math standards enunciated by the National Council of Teachers of Mathematics in 1989 and by the 1992 California and 1996 Massachusetts math frameworks.[11] These documents, which seek to reform traditional practice, portray mathematics as knowledge constructed by learners. Most of the math teachers I interviewed from 1991 to 1997 did not subscribe to this belief. Instead, learning mathematics was seen as mastering a series of skills and concepts, with prerequisite knowledge essential to further progress along the continuum. As with the math teachers encountered in other studies, skepticism was expressed about reforms initiated by state and district curricular leaders, specifically about reforms challenging the sequential character of mathematical learning.[12] Policymakers who favor detracking were often described as out of touch with the realities of classrooms.

It's all about the framework and the latest drafted framework. . . . I
don't know; I find it hard to believe that it's coming from math teachers themselves, you know, the ones that are strong in the classroom.
—*Teacher, Math*

I'm sure [the district math coordinator] has some real good arguments. And things have always looked good on paper. But my personal opinion is I think he's lost his perspective . . . from being out of
the classroom so long.   —*Teacher, Math*

Deemphasizing content knowledge as the primary criterion for assigning students to courses directly challenged these math teachers' beliefs
about what is valuable in the curriculum. The math teachers regarded content, rather than process or affect, as the lodestar of their teaching. With
content coverage seen as a critical dimension of good teaching, heterogeneously grouped classes were viewed as unmanageable. A math teacher
anticipates the frustrations he will encounter while teaching classes of students grouped heterogeneously, a situation he has experienced before.

There are . . . some concepts you must cover. Otherwise, you're not
going to go on, and you're going to have problems later on. So that's
what bothers me. Are you going to be playing around here? Are you
going to make sure you cover everything you're supposed to cover?
—*Teacher, Math*

These sentiments support a mathematics that is hierarchical, content
driven, and conducive to ability grouping. Two school principals who are
against tracking lament the persistence of ability grouping in math, but
beneath the regret, a note of understanding can also be detected:

It's a different kind of subject, but they all want to teach the top end.
Nobody wants to teach the bottom. Nobody is breaking down my
door and saying, "Oh, I'll be glad; I'll be happy; I'm thrilled." I
don't know. . . . Maybe it's more quantifiable, more cut-and-dry, more
linear.   —*Principal*

That's only because it's vertical. And almost every other learning is
horizontal. So because math is vertical, there are certain kids at certain levels. But, theoretically and philosophically, I think as a school,
we would not have algebra.   —*Principal*

Principals must deal with cleavages inside the school that are institutionalized around subject areas. Whether mathematics is truly more vertical, more quantifiable, or more linear, educators on both sides of the tracking issue agreed that something is different about math.[13]

English

English is a subject conducive to heterogeneous grouping. At the middle school level, the content of English is decidedly nonhierarchical. In both states at the time of this study, seventh grade typically featured literature from various world cultures and eighth grade studied American authors. Learning objectives were cast in broad language—for example, read, analyze, and discuss literature, express oneself clearly in written and spoken language.[14] State and district advisories may recommend certain literary works for use in the English classroom, but discretion is granted to teachers as to compliance. Unlike mathematics students, whose demonstration of mastery in pre-algebra is often required to proceed into algebra, English students may advance by simply avoiding retention in grade level (though many districts require summer school to make up failed classes). An accelerated seventh grade student who fails pre-algebra repeats the same course the following year. A student who fails seventh grade English, on the other hand, might be placed in a lower track, but moves on to eighth grade English nevertheless.

Student promotion is not the only practice on which math and English tracks differ. Familiar course titles—honors, regular, and remedial—describe the levels of curriculum in English, but course titles in mathematics name both level and content—algebra, geometry, advanced algebra, and so forth. The extent to which math courses represent stratified curriculum is clear, but English tracks have no comparable authoritative form. State mechanisms for regulating curriculum leave this situation undisturbed. Curriculum frameworks are silent on what each English track will cover, although a list of recommended literature is frequently provided for each grade level. The same English textbook might be used in three different tracks at the same school, with teachers acquiring supplementary materials that correspond to students' reading levels. Completing coursework in any track usually fulfills graduation requirements in English.

English teachers wield power over curriculum that math teachers do not enjoy. English tracks with the same name may diverge as teachers adjust the curriculum to respond to different populations of students. Some teachers of low tracks argue that they modify the curriculum to better meet the needs of students, while, paradoxically, other low-track teachers claim that, in the name of equality, they give students a curriculum identical to that of higher tracks. In her book about lower-track English classes, Reba Page notes that since the spread of tracking early in this century, American educators have embraced a pair of contradictory aims—the same education for all and an education that suits individual differences. Tracking attempts to harmonize this contradiction, and, as Page observes, "Teachers assuage their doubts by differentiating lower-track lessons but asserting that the differentiation is imperceptible." [15]

Teacher discretion in English is enhanced by the subject's nonlinear, flexible structure. A nonlinear structure makes ability grouping less necessary, a phenomenon evident to this English teacher when comparing the subject to math.

> You have to teach to mastery in math; you don't have to in English. You don't have to master all of the aspects, so it's not the same building block thing. It should be, in my estimation—it's just not.
>
> —*Teacher, English*

In English classes, process can compete equally with content as valued learning. The theory behind process-oriented approaches to the teaching of writing, for instance, is that students who might struggle with spelling, subject-verb agreement, and the proper use of subordinate clauses can learn how to write well by experiencing the writing process. Students go through the stages of brainstorming ideas, engaging in peer editing, and composing final drafts. The belief is that learning accrues from each writing project, without following a predetermined sequence or direction. The rhythm of a student's own development, not a subject's intrinsic structure, calls the tune on curricular content. Believers in this type of teaching give credence to the old saw, that English teachers are free to teach the student, but math teachers must teach the subject.

Middle School Subjects as Part of a K–12 Curricular System

Middle schools, intermediate schools, and junior high schools find themselves situated between elementary schools and high schools in the educational system, depending on elementary schools for the learning provided to students before their arrival, and preparing students, before they depart, for the learning expected by high schools. Educators who work in middle schools are keenly aware of their place in the K–12 continuum. Grade 7–8 schools are the most dramatically affected. Every student is in either the first or last year at the school. Preparation for entrance and exit permeates the life of these schools.

The ebb and flow of middle school reform has affected tracking policies. A veteran counselor described how, over the last twenty-five years, the counselor's school had gone from tracking to untracking and back to tracking. The counselor attributed the impetus for the school's return to tracking to the influence of high schools.

> We eventually went back into an honors situation because the high school was that way and parents were demanding that we do it. So we did. It started in the math department. We included algebra in the eighth grade for those top math students who were able to do it, so they could move into geometry and get into higher math in high school.   —*Counselor*

In its latest incarnation, the middle school movement recommends detracking as part of a broad package of reforms. The reforms impute an independent and organic purpose to the middle school, especially in terms of its organization, curriculum, and instruction. The middle school movement advances a basic organizational objective, the quest for institutional autonomy—in this case, middle school autonomy from high schools. A common thread running through these educators' reflections is the need to divorce middle schools from secondary school conventions.

> Going to middle school is going to change the nature of teaching because we're moving away from being like a mini–high school, and we're going to more student-oriented learning, more hands-on activities, more cooperative groupings, and problem solving. —*Counselor*

> It was clear from the quality review that we had to do some things to make our school better and teaming answered the majority of questions. So the philosophy is heterogeneous grouping—but I think it's almost impossible to be totally heterogeneous. Our philosophy— and I think every middle school's philosophy—needs to be student-oriented rather than subject-oriented. When you look at subject-oriented places, they're homogeneously grouped. I don't ever want to get into the mini–high-school mode.   —*Principal*

Linkages to High Schools

Mathematics may hinder the middle school's emergence from the high school's shadow. Middle schools earn legitimacy by supplying able students for the high schools' advanced math courses. Mathematics at the high school level is organized into carefully defined tracks, and the rules for placement are clearly stated. Middle schools provide algebra to about one-fourth of all eighth graders, who then go on to a four-year sequence of high school math that typically consists of geometry, advanced algebra, trigonometry-precalculus, and calculus.[16] College admission requirements heighten the concern of parents that their children receive the preparation necessary to achieve in the high school setting. Moreover, central office administrators monitor students' matriculation from middle school to high school. A math teacher who is also a detracking advocate describes the barriers preventing schools from eliminating tracking in math.

> If you go with the heterogeneous grouping, you wouldn't have eighth grade algebra—but the state demands that eighth graders have access to algebra. Our department wouldn't have it philosophically—we believe in heterogeneous. I have many students who don't have the background for algebra—they're not ready—so you can't give it to everyone, but we're told we must provide it here. In order to get fifth-year math as a senior and the AP classes, you have to have algebra in eighth and pre-algebra in seventh.   *—Teacher, Math*

The middle school's relationship with the high school involves conflicting objectives when it comes to tracking. Educators in the middle school movement strive to differentiate their practices from high school conventions. They push to detrack their schools. Cutting the middle school's ties to the high school curriculum poses risks for math departments, however, especially in preparing advanced students for high school work and in reaping the status that math departments acquire when they do this successfully. An algebra imperative exists for almost all middle school math departments. They feel compelled to offer algebra in eighth grade, and unless they are willing to offer it to everyone, then tracking in some form inevitably occurs.

Middle School Departments as Bureaucratic Actors

State policies governing achievement testing, textbook selection, and course requirements attract the interest of professional groups representing different subject areas. At the local level, teachers from various academic fields sit on district and school curriculum committees. Tensions may arise among various disciplines. There are different views, from subject to subject, about the structure of curriculum, appropriate teaching methods, and the relative importance of content and process. Departments act to sway school curricular policies toward their own institutionalized interests, beliefs, conceptions, and values.

One way of dissipating such tensions is to grant departments the authority to formulate their own policies. Although most tracking policies were implemented schoolwide, a substantial number of schools granted exceptions to departments: 36.4 percent of schools in CA 94 and 23.6 percent in MA 95 (this question was not asked in CA 91). Some departments were allowed to track in otherwise untracked schools, and vice versa. What kinds of policies did this departmental autonomy produce? Math departments within untracked schools frequently continued tracking, usually by offering two levels of mathematics. A small number of schools offered algebra to all eighth graders, but ability grouped within the subject. The more able students took a standard one-year algebra course, while students with less preparation in mathematics took the first of a two-year algebra sequence, with the second year taken in ninth grade at the high school. In contrast to math departments, English or history departments, when allowed to part from their school's overall system, experimented with heterogeneous grouping while the rest of the school continued tracking.

Teachers' affinity for departmentalization has deep historical roots. In the late nineteenth century, high school teachers envied departmentalization in colleges. Departments gave teachers a point of reference for anchoring their work. Teachers in nondepartmentalized high schools complained about the difficulty of preparing lessons in several subjects each day, and departments grew in popularity. They brought collegiality, shared specialization, and common intellectual interests to a profession noted for its isolation. They also imposed a disciplinary order on the unruly secondary curriculum.[17]

Departments are important players in local districts' informal traditions of power sharing. In many districts, implicit treaties are negotiated whereby teachers are granted authority over instructional decisions in exchange for school and district authority over other decisions. Susan Moore Johnson describes teachers' special affiliation with their departments:

These subunits command teachers' respect and receive their involvement because decisions at these levels are close to the classroom and concern substantive issues that matter to them, such as elective offerings, course sequence, student discipline, scheduling, and student assignment. Teachers feel confident that decisions they make with their peers will be implemented, though in other parts of the school, decisions about policy may never find their way into practice. . . . Teachers may view their responsibilities to departments, teams, and clusters more seriously because these subunits are rarely distant bosses with managerial concerns, but rather peers familiar with teaching and their colleagues' concerns, sharing the burden of transforming policy into practice.[18]

In terms of school politics, schools track differently in the subjects of mathematics and English because math and English departments think about the tracking issue very differently. The following vignette illustrates that when one of these departments also thinks differently than a reform-minded principal, problems can arise that threaten harmony at the school.

A Math Department Rebellion: Hillcrest Middle School

Ted Winters was excited that his first principalship was at Hillcrest Middle School. He had long believed that schools would not improve without a profound change in the conduct of teaching. In his own high school science classroom, he had worked hard to become more student-centered and less beholden to textbooks, to get students working in groups, and to engage students in real experiments so that they could learn the "how" of science as well as the "what." Ted believed these practices had been successful in twenty-seven years of teaching, and he looked forward to implementing them as principal of his town's only middle school.

When I came in and I was reading the literature, *Caught in the Middle* and all those kinds of things, it seems as though the emphasis is changing somewhat from our function of gaining academic skills to maybe learning how to live together a little better. I see lots of movement and work in cooperative learning. You also read the research that says that the tracks have a negative impact on kids, and kids in the lower tracks . . . conceive of themselves as being slow; therefore, they don't have to do much. And then the expectations of the teachers are reduced.

Over the summer, Ted learned that much of his own educational philosophy was reflected in the middle school movement. He met frequently with the district's curriculum specialists and the assistant superintendent in charge of curriculum, all supporters of middle school reform. He appointed a task force of activist teachers from the school to study the latest literature on reform, and plotted a strategy for changing Hillcrest. Ted wanted to hit the ground running by presenting an aggressive agenda in the fall.

So what we're working toward is—at least what I'm working toward is—establishing some teams. I see this as a big school. One of our major problems is the fact that there's not a lot of . . . contact on a . . . close, personal level. And so we're going to establish some teams; and when we're establishing those teams, we're going to do heterogeneous groups.

In his first faculty meeting, Ted laid out a plan for restructuring the school consisting of three reforms: (1) heterogeneous grouping, (2) interdisciplinary teams, and (3) advisory periods, in which students would be able to connect with adults taking a personal interest in their success.

The conversion from tracking to heterogeneous grouping was to proceed incrementally. In the first year, four or five volunteer teachers at each grade level would form an interdisciplinary team and instruct students in mixed-ability classrooms. Language arts, science, and social studies teachers who were not part of teaming would heterogeneously group their classes later. Math teachers were to reduce their groupings from three to two levels, eliminating the remedial class and placing those students in grade-level math. This was intended as a conciliatory gesture toward the math teachers. They wanted no reductions in tracking at all, and two levels seemed like a reasonable, middle-ground proposal.

The year began and the math teachers immediately encountered difficulties. The range of abilities within classes was so large that the teachers felt they were losing kids, especially low-ability students. At the end of the semester, the math teachers took action as a department. They sat down and traded kids, period by period, to restore homogeneity to their classrooms.

It didn't work. . . . I exchanged twelve students. I picked out my very best, gave them to another teacher, and I took her lowest. . . . It's better for the kids to have them homogeneously grouped. So we did that. Other people in other departments agree that math should not be part of this. They feel, too, that math is one of those things that . . . [is]

structured, the concepts and the things that you have to learn to do. They agree that it should not be [part of detracking].

—*Teacher, Math*

We moved them back in January, which was after our first testing, and we found we were going nowhere with the lower kids. It was not done based on teachers just saying, "Hey, it's not working." It was based on standardized tests in textbooks, comparing them to previous years as to how our lower-level kids achieved and our average kids; and then it was compared on the CTBS [Comprehensive Test of Basic Skills] scoring. We found our lower-level kids were not obtaining as good a developmental increase as . . . in the past. Now, we also compared that to how these same kids did in the sixth and fifth grades. So we do not just look at this year and say, "Well, you know, they're low," because we might have a low class coming in. Not all years are equal. So we went back and looked at the sixth grade and found, well, they were pretty normal; went back to fifth grade and found they're fairly normal.   —*Teacher, Math*

Ted Winters was notified of the change in groupings, which he approved reluctantly. The reality was that the decision had already been made. The counselor at Hillcrest sympathized with the teachers' actions, having heard from students that they were not learning very much.

Heterogeneous grouping and math—that didn't really work out real well. We had kids going to the math teachers and coming to me and saying, "This is the work I did in the third and fourth grade. It's too easy." And other kids in the math class saying, "It's so hard I can't do it." So math really wanted to go completely homogeneous again this year.   —*Counselor*

Ted expressed his disappointment to the math department. The math teachers bluntly told him that he was wrong on the tracking issue—and on a lot of his other reforms as well. A new agreement was hammered out in which two levels would be tried again the following year. However, this time, the two top groups would be joined in a single class, allowing for a separate remedial class. This addressed the math teachers' belief that low-ability students were not learning in heterogeneous classes because they lacked the basic skills to handle grade-level math. A seventh grade teacher comments:

I think what happened is everybody was attempting to teach the same way that they had taught before and were running into copious quantities of students who just flat couldn't add and subtract. Because we do get students in here that can't add and subtract. I had a student in class the other day, and I asked her what 1 more than 56 is and stumped her.   —*Teacher, Math*

I originally visited the school in May 1991. When I returned in March 1996, Ted Winters was still principal. He was a chastened reformer, however. Only traces remained of the reforms that he had so enthusiastically pursued five years earlier. Two teams were operating, but they were interdisciplinary in name only, with little coordination of curriculum across subject areas. Heterogeneous grouping had never taken hold. In most subjects, students were ability grouped into two tracks. In math, the three-track system remained.

What led to tracking reform's failure at Hillcrest? The math department's initial resistance provided a rallying point for other dissidents at the school. Allowing the math department to operate as an exception to the school's tracking reforms tacitly acknowledged that modifications in detracking might be warranted. Every department at the school had teachers who were against detracking. They frequently shared their frustrations, swapped stories about the problems that interdisciplinary teams were encountering, and took solace in the math department's successful avoidance of the reform.

Teacher support for detracking was also affected by tying it so closely to interdisciplinary teaming and the advisory period. Frustrations from implementing one reform infected the others. Teachers who were spending enormous amounts of time and energy on the practical aspects of instructing mixed-ability classes suddenly had to plan lessons with colleagues and find time to counsel students on their personal problems. Each innovation had opponents. Some who were neutral on detracking became strong opponents because they disliked the other reforms. The advisory class was deeply resented, mainly because it essentially added a new period to the school day. Several teachers filed grievances. The teachers union supported their case, and Ted Winters suddenly found himself in arbitration hearings.

Ted Winters's support completely collapsed both inside and outside the school. Events seemed to conspire against the reforms. Just as former allies on the teaching staff were turning against heterogeneous grouping, a new school board was elected. The new members promised a return to basic skills instruction. The district opened a new middle school, reducing Hillcrest's population from 1,350 to 850. Eighteen teachers transferred to the new school, and many of them confided that they were fleeing a bad situation. The district superintendent, perhaps the most important supporter of Ted Winters's reforms, decided to retire. The new superintendent surveyed the turmoil at Hillcrest and, in Ted's words, directed him to "do something about it or you're gone." Tracking reform was finished.

The Hillcrest experience says something about the difficulty of implementing tracking reform. It also casts doubt on a popular theory of school change. The belief that adopting detracking incrementally would win over nonbelievers turned out to be wrong. At the beginning of his tenure in 1991, Ted Winters expressed the faith of all reformers that the innovations he held dear would ultimately catch fire and spread. Speaking of ambivalent staff members, Winters said:

> If we're successful, they'll see that. If these people on these teams say, "Hey this is better for kids, this is what you want to do," then I'll have some of the fence-sitters come over.

A similar hope was held out for community resistance.

> If these teams are successful, and it gets around the community that this is a good idea and our kids are going to learn a great deal in those—I think a lot of people will want to get into this school because they'll feel that academically their kids will get more in this school.

This theory of diffusion, that reform's successes are noticed and duplicated, may be true for some reforms. But failure travels the same pathway. Frustration, doubt, and full-scale political opposition can rise up, spread out of control, and overwhelm well-intentioned efforts at reform. In the case of Hillcrest Middle School, the seed of failure was sewn in the math department's initial opposition to tracking reform.

Summary and Conclusion

Subjects exert policy influence through a subject area subsystem that operates on three levels. First, as the embodiment of widely recognized intellectual fields, subject areas mold curricular content and pedagogical practices to correspond to disciplinary characteristics. Higher education's hierarchical organization of mathematics and horizontal organization of

English curriculum has carried over to high schools and middle schools. Second, middle schools offer the introductory courses of secondary education. This position is particularly significant for math, as it meshes with the hierarchical sequencing of high school courses. Subject area differences coalesce formally within organizational subunits of the schools, providing the third dimension of the subject area subsystem, the department. Functioning as bureaucratic actors, subject departments bargain with each other, and with administrative authorities, to defend their interests in school policymaking.

Thus despite the habit of researchers, including myself, to depict schools simply as either tracked or untracked, in many schools, policy emerges as a collage of independent policies governing semi-autonomous departments. What are the implications of this arrangement?

Schools serving small student populations may look untracked even though de facto tracking takes place. Because of scheduling constraints, untracked English classes in small schools are still relatively homogeneous in student ability when mathematics classes continue to group students by ability. Small schools may offer only a single section of a particular subject in a single period of the day. The assignment of high-ability eighth graders to an algebra course, for example, means these students receive similar schedules for the entire day, and the same is true for students placed in remedial math courses. Elective courses (where students may pick, for instance, between shop and foreign language) also heighten de facto stratification.

At one of the case study schools, this situation led to resentment on the part of English teachers, who took a strong stand against tracking in their department. Mathematics continued with three ability levels. The English teachers felt that the de facto tracking of their heterogeneously grouped classes undermined the curricular and instructional changes they had implemented, causing a few tense confrontations with the math department. These kinds of structural constraints on tracking policy make bargaining and compromise among departmental units more difficult to achieve in smaller schools. And, as demonstrated in the case of Hillcrest Middle School, departmental objections can strongly influence the fate of reform in an entire school.

Tracking policies that are differentiated by subject area could also affect the middle school's relationship with its elementary and high school counterparts, especially in terms of the status accorded different subjects. If mathematics remains the only tracked subject in the middle school curriculum, high school educators may come to regard math as the only "real" subject in middle schools. Math's status might grow to overshadow all other subjects. The fact that most districts grant high school credit to students who take algebra in eighth grade is already one sign of math's differential status.

The findings of the book's previous chapters may need qualification because of the subject area differences discussed here. Take chapter 4's conclusions about influences on policy. Parents might get up in arms over detracking math, but not English. And chapter 5's finding that large districts tend to centralize policy may be more applicable to mathematics than other subjects. The way that I have defined policies attempts to model a school's tracking system as a whole while at the same time recognizing math's uniqueness by allowing two levels of math for the "untracked" designation. Departmental independence is still not so prevalent as to negate the validity of this approach. But future studies may need more finely grained measures of influence and policy to analyze different subjects properly.

Researchers should also pay attention to variations in curriculum arising in untracked situations. Reducing the stratification of content relaxes a potent course constraint. Algebra teachers receive strong signals as to the content that must be covered in their class. These signals would vanish if students of all abilities took a course that included algebraic concepts but was simply called "eighth grade math." Teachers of heterogeneous English classes are permitted to choose from a number of topics, each with a different degree of difficulty. What one learns is a function of what is taught. Future achievement in English could become completely dependent on the teachers that students encounter; achievement in math, on the courses that students take.

This carries the discussion to the classroom and to teachers' work, the subject of the next chapter.

7

The Classroom, the Teacher, and Tracking Reform

W HAT IS THE IMPACT of tracking reform on teachers and classrooms? This chapter describes the ways teachers cope when several school reforms are taking place at once, the changes in instruction and curriculum materials that often accompany detracking, the use of alternative grouping strategies in tracked and untracked schools, the role of professional development in encouraging change, and the unresolved questions surfacing from classrooms engaged in tracking reform.

Tracking's critics frequently assert that detracking must be accompanied by a transformation in teachers' deeply held beliefs, among these, beliefs about how learning occurs and assumptions about what constitutes valuable knowledge.[1] Robert Slavin argues that schools should not expect untracking to have a significant impact on student achievement "unless they also undertake changes in curriculum or instruction likely to improve actual teaching."[2] This is a tall order. As two researchers familiar with classrooms have observed, "Changing one's teaching is not like changing one's socks."[3] Each teacher's opinions on educational issues, including tracking, interlock to create a personal philosophy of schooling. To achieve widespread detracking, skeptical teachers must be persuaded to reject personal educational beliefs in favor of a radically different system of values.

Sifting Reform

Critics and defenders of tracking agree that detracking is a formidable undertaking for teachers. Exacerbating the difficulty, the reform frequently takes place in a school simultaneously implementing several additional innovations, such as transforming a school from a junior high to a middle school (which entails moving a sixth grade into a school and a ninth grade out), reorganizing teachers from departmental units into grade-level teams, teaching a new interdisciplinary curriculum, adopting block scheduling or a year-round calendar, and employing child-centered instructional strategies for the very first time. Some teachers discover that these reforms complement each other. Others are overwhelmed by the scope of change.

Frequently, schools that launch major reform projects decide details on the run. Listen to a counselor whose school was encouraging interdisciplinary instruction:

> I think we've blurred the curriculum and kind of crossed boundaries already, starting last year and certainly this year, where we're doing writing in math now and we're doing math problems in other subjects. There's a real blur, and so we don't have the departmental delineation that we had in the past. I think the concern is just how are we going to figure it all out—who does what?   —*Counselor*

Faced with countless reforms to implement, teachers cope the same way administrators cope in similar situations. They pick and choose reforms, separating the ones deserving their energy and enthusiasm from those they will ignore or deemphasize. This sifting of reform is an integral part of mutual adaptation, the notion that policy may succeed in changing existing practice, but, as practitioners harmonize policy with existing ways of doing business, practice also changes policy.

One of the ways practitioners adapt policy is by breaking down big reform proposals into manageable parts, addressing the agreeable components and ignoring the rest. The following case study participants describe this process at different levels of the school system. The first speaker, a teacher representative on a district curriculum committee, talks of selectively interpreting state curriculum frameworks. The second, a school principal, discusses how she acquainted her school's faculty with the recommendations in *Caught in the Middle*. And the third, a science teacher, teaches in an untracked school.

> We [the district curriculum committee members] look at the frameworks and say, "what can we use, what can we set aside, what can we just offer in a broad sense so that the teacher can use his or her knowledge and input?"   —*Teacher, English–Social Studies Core*

Most of the reports I read—I ask if it's coming from a practitioner or is it coming from a theory base. I can't always implement "a program," but there's usually something good I can draw on—find things that meet our program—and we've approached *Caught in the Middle* the same way. We spent a year going through *Caught in the Middle,* with the staff assigned chapters—and we discussed concepts. We decided which of those areas meet our needs. Effective schools set up the best systems that fit their students' needs, so I think you're going to see tracking in some places and nontracking in other places.

—Principal

None of us [teachers] ever gets [the district-adopted curriculum] all done. So it's kind of pick and choose and decide what you're going to emphasize.

—Teacher, Science

Mutual adaptation is not confined to a single step in the implementation process. At every level of the educational system, policy from above is digested and recast in terms agreeable to educators' own objectives and the demands of the local environment.

What Is Different about Untracked Classes?

Teachers in untracked classrooms emphasize practices that they believe are effective with heterogeneous groups of students. Students who have fallen behind academically are a key concern. Teachers favor instructional formats that draw struggling students into class activities. Instead of assigning large chunks of textbooks to be read at home, for example, teachers in heterogeneous English and history classes often have the whole class read passages orally in class. Teachers also attempt to shelter low-ability students from public failure. Poor readers are given shorter, easier passages to read out loud so they will not be embarrassed. Though no substitute for literacy, reading text aloud in class at least permits low-ability students to hear readings, to ask about particular concepts, to witness what classmates have to say about the material, and to participate in class discussion.

The pace of this approach is slower than assigning readings for completion at home and reserving class time for discussing and extending concepts. Indeed, more oral reading reduces the amount of time for discussion, a scarcity that is compounded if the teacher provides one-on-one help to a large number of students who do not understand the lesson. Teachers are divided on the value of these changes.

You do it orally. Certainly, there will be kids that can't read stuff. But that doesn't mean they can't learn the material. If you felt they couldn't do it, then you're assuming that you only learn through reading, which is not . . . in [terms of] learning modalities, that isn't necessarily true.   —*Teacher, English–Social Studies Core*

You've got that mixture. You've got kids that can't read the text. In the same room, we've got children who can read the text. . . . For instance, I'll give a specific assignment. I'll go through the board exercise, showing them exactly what has to be done. And you look around the room, and you can just see the difference. Some kids are picking up on it, and they're already doing their work. . . . But others, there go the hands. So you go one on one; and these kids have no idea what's happening, how to do it. And you can sit there with them, one on one, and spend a lot of time.   —*Teacher, Math*

Right now, I still plan to read orally. And the other teacher on the other team plans not to. So we will see which one of us—you know, it's a trade-off. Mine won't be able to cover quantities. She's going to lose the low ones because . . . they can't read independently. It will be interesting to see how we find the common ground in between there.
                    —*Teacher, English*

We have kids down to about the third grade reading level. We do an awful lot of reading in class. I read to them, the good readers read also, so the kids are hearing it and seeing it. If you do about two-thirds of whatever it is in class, they get some grasp of what's going on—what they don't get is the depth of understanding.
                    —*Teacher, English*

This testimony underscores that middle school instruction is challenged more by student heterogeneity in the ability to comprehend text than by heterogeneity in any other student characteristic, save perhaps behavior. In many cases, students who are unable to read on their own can gain exposure to new knowledge only by having someone else read to them. Students must read to gain access to a vast store of critical information in school, from simple directions in a history text, to problem solving activities in mathematics, to background information on a science experiment. Basic literacy is essential in all subjects.

Tracking's critics frequently recommend that teachers divide heterogeneous classes into small groups for cooperative learning activities. Cooperative groups are composed of students with varying abilities and interests. Each group works on a common problem or completes a common assignment. Studies indicate that well-structured cooperative learning approaches may boost academic achievement.[4] However, it is not simply a matter of placing students in small groups. Approaches vary by reward structure (whether incentives such as grades are rewarded individually or to a group as a whole), the amount of teacher-led direct instruction preceding group work, and how tasks are divided and assigned to group members.[5] There is nothing inherently contradictory about tracking and cooperative learning. Cooperative groups can be formed within tracked classes. But the technique seems to fit hand in glove with detracking.

[Detracking] is not as bad as I thought it would be, particularly if I use cooperative learning in some areas.   *—Teacher, English*

Cooperative learning is frequently tied in with the issue of advanced and remedial tracks and all that sort of thing. I think that cooperative learning works better with heterogeneous classes. There's more to draw from. But, more importantly, we have not just that technique but a number of other techniques and things that we should have been doing for years but kind of gave up when we gave up one-room schoolhouses—peer tutoring, different grouping practices, flexible grouping practices, kids working in pairs.   *—Teacher, English*

Teachers in untracked classes find that they must alter curriculum and modify course materials to accommodate various ability levels. They also report using differentiated grading criteria so that low-achieving students do not get discouraging report card grades. These changes are not taken lightly. Teachers hone their skills through an iterative process. Lessons, materials, and grading practices that work well are kept for future use. Those that fall flat are discarded. From year to year, this culling process saves teachers precious time and labor. Nothing is as valuable as tried and true techniques, and nothing as disquieting as finding out, because of a sudden change in assignment or tracking policy, that reliable practices have been rendered obsolete, that one must start from square one.

Heterogeneous grouping demands a greater variety of materials, especially materials amenable to hands-on learning and group work.

I can't see heterogeneous working in the old lecture-worksheet thing. There's going to have to be a whole lot more hands-on materials and things for them to play with.   *—Teacher, Math*

Heterogeneous teachers have to be more diversified in their methodology. I mean they have to look at the visual learner, the auditory learner, the kinesthetic learner. They have to have materials that are at a more complex level and some that are at a simpler level. They have to create ways for kids to work together so that the more able students can support the less able students.   *—Assistant Principal*

Alternative Instructional Strategies

The teachers and principals cited up to this point have testified to heterogeneous classes' distinct instructional milieu, that detracking demands a shift toward more oral reading in class, more cooperative learning, and more hands-on materials. Less time is spent on lecture and discussion, less reading is assigned as homework, and there is less dependence on textbooks.

The study's survey data, however, suggest that the changes in instructional strategies may not be as great as teachers think. The survey asked principals to report the frequency of use for within-class ability grouping and four alternative grouping strategies: cooperative learning; temporary grouping by task, in which students are regrouped for each assignment and receive small-group instruction from the teacher; peer tutoring, in which students work in dyads consisting of a student who understands the material instructing one who does not; and cross-age tutoring, like peer tutoring except for the difference in students' ages. The four alternative schemes are embraced by tracking reformers as preferable to ability grouping.

First, a caution. These data should be viewed skeptically. It is unclear how knowledgeable principals are of teachers' instructional strategies. Past research shows that most principals spend little time directly observing teachers, so the estimates in the surveys are probably based on their conversations with teachers. Nevertheless, in representing principals' impressions of the most common practices at their schools, the figures are interesting and important.

Cooperative learning is used most frequently in classrooms, followed by temporary grouping by task and peer tutoring (see table 7-1). Cross-age tutoring remains rare. Within-class ability grouping comes in at the bottom of the list in California, but near the middle in Massachusetts. All four

Table 7-1. Use of Grouping Strategies
Ratings based on (4) commonly used, (3) considerably used,
(2) moderately used, (1) never used.

Strategy	CA 91	CA 94	MA 95
Cooperative learning	3.26	3.41	3.04
Temporary grouping by task	2.63	2.82	2.58
Peer tutoring	2.42	2.60	2.25
Cross-age tutoring	1.97	2.01	1.76
Ability grouping	2.00	1.88	2.29

alternatives grew in use from the CA 91 survey to CA 94, but ability grouping declined. And all four alternatives were used more frequently in California than in Massachusetts schools. Considering that these strategies are advertised as signature elements of untracked classrooms, this finding is consistent with data examined in earlier chapters showing Massachusetts schools more likely to continue tracking than California schools.

The disparity between the states in embracing these innovations becomes clearer by comparing tracked and untracked schools. Alternative grouping methods were more common in California's traditionally tracked schools in 1991 (see table 7-2, the first column) than in Massachusetts's reformed, untracked schools in 1995 (the final column). Detracking does not seem to transfer ability grouping from the schoolwide level to that of the classroom. In fact, within-class ability grouping is more likely to occur in tracked than untracked schools. Once a school buys into or rejects ability grouping, teachers apparently follow the general principle underlying school policy. Tracked schools clear the way for teachers to consider ability as a criterion for grouping students within classes. Untracked schools do not.

Table 7-2. Grouping Strategies in Tracked and Untracked Schools
Ratings based on (4) commonly used, (3) considerably used, (2) moderately used, (1) never used.

Strategy	CA 91		CA 94		MA 95	
	Tracked	Untracked	Tracked	Untracked	Tracked	Untracked
Cooperative learning	3.25	3.33	3.34	3.51	2.91	3.24*
Temporary grouping by task	2.65	2.59	2.84	2.79	2.57	2.60
Peer tutoring	2.39	2.49	2.55	2.65	2.22	2.27
Cross-age tutoring	1.98	1.98	2.01	1.99	1.77	1.72
Ability grouping	2.07	1.78**	1.92	1.85	2.55	1.88**

$*p < .05$, $**p < .01$.

Table 7-3. Schools Receiving Professional Development
by Strategy
Percent

Strategy	CA 94	MA 95
Cooperative learning	98.1	91.0
Temporary grouping by task	49.1	37.3
Peer tutoring	47.8	29.9
Cross-age tutoring	20.4	7.5
Ability grouping	21.7	32.8

Surprisingly, when it comes to practices other than ability grouping, only the use of cooperative learning in Massachusetts looks different in tracked and untracked schools. In both California surveys, the prevalence of cooperative learning and peer tutoring lean in the expected direction— toward untracked schools—but in neither case can it be stated confidently that the difference is not occurring by chance. This seems to contradict the impression that detracking requires new instructional approaches.

To dig a little deeper into other potential influences on instruction, I asked whether teachers had received professional development on these strategies (the question was not asked in 1991). Studies of "school restructuring" depict professional development, or "inservice," as a catalyst for change.[6] More than 90 percent of schools in both states reported that their staffs had received training on cooperative learning (see table 7-3). On the other techniques, professional development was spotty. In California, roughly one-half of the schools had been inserviced on temporary grouping by task and peer tutoring, but only about 20 percent on within-class ability grouping and cross-age tutoring. Special training was less evident in Massachusetts. Of the remaining strategies, inservice on within-class ability grouping was used in nearly a third of the schools and frequencies of the rest of the strategies ranged from 37.3 percent on temporary grouping by task to fewer than one in ten on cross-age tutoring.

Professional development does not appear to have been provided as part of a strategic plan for implementing tracking reform (see table 7-4). Tracked and untracked schools exhibit similar rates of training on alternative instructional strategies. Only one difference between tracked and untracked schools is statistically significant, training in cross-age tutoring for CA 94 schools. About twice as many untracked schools (27.5 percent) in the CA 94 survey received training on cross-age tutoring as tracked schools (14.4 percent).

Table 7-4. Professional Development in Tracked and Untracked Schools by Strategy
Percent

Strategy	CA 94		MA 95	
	Tracked	Untracked	Tracked	Untracked
Cooperative learning	97.8	98.6	88.6	95.7
Temporary grouping by task	47.5	39.2	35.4	40.4
Peer tutoring	48.9	46.4	26.6	34.0
Cross-age tutoring	14.4	27.5*	7.6	6.4
Ability grouping	24.4	17.4	34.2	25.5

*p < .05.

Is inservice training effective? Professional development seems to stimulate the use of targeted practices (see table 7-5). Schools that report having received training on particular strategies also report using them. Of the ten relationships examined in table 7-5, all ten point in the direction of training leading to increased use, and six are statistically significant (the p-value for CA 94's cooperative learning is a near miss at .059). Does this mean that professional development works in changing instruction? Not necessarily. The correlation should be regarded as merely suggestive. School principals are the source of data on both training and use. They are no doubt inclined to believe that inservice training, which they probably have a hand in selecting and providing, leads to teachers using new skills. More research must be conducted to identify the limitations and potential of professional development in promoting reform.

In sum, except for within-class ability grouping, grouping practices inside classrooms appear to be adopted independently of a school's tracking policy, perhaps as components of a middle school reform strategy. Coop-

Table 7-5. Use of Grouping Strategies by Professional Training
Ratings based on (4) commonly used, (3) considerably used, (2) moderately used, (1) never used.

Strategy	CA 94		MA 95	
	Trained	Untrained	Trained	Untrained
Cooperative learning	3.43	2.67	3.09	2.14**
Temporary grouping by task	3.17	2.46**	2.90	2.37**
Peer tutoring	2.69	2.52	2.58	2.10**
Cross-age tutoring	2.67	1.83**	2.00	1.74
Ability grouping	2.33	1.76**	2.40	2.23

**p < .01.

erative learning is now routine in middle schools, both tracked and untracked. Although this innovation has gained a foothold in the classroom, the complete overhaul of instruction envisioned by Robert Slavin and other tracking reformers does not appear imminent. Peer tutoring and temporary grouping by task experience only moderate use. Cross-age tutoring seldom occurs. These practices may be linked with detracking in the popular literature, but, except for cooperative learning in MA 95, they are no more evident in untracked schools than tracked schools. Professional development supports the use of alternative instructional strategies, but this type of training is provided equally in tracked and untracked schools.

The surveys portray tracked and untracked schools as similar in instructional practices. How can these data be reconciled with the case study evidence and teachers' statements that they are changing instruction to accommodate detracking?

The principals' answers in the survey and the teachers' answers in the interviews may be addressing different aspects of instruction. Three of the strategies listed in the survey—cooperative learning, peer tutoring, and cross-age tutoring—shift the source of instruction from teacher to pupil. They reflect the belief that classrooms should become student-centered rather than teacher-centered, a long-standing tenet of progressive education. Students instruct students, and the teacher's role is to create and manage these student interactions. Detracking seems to have no effect, either positive or negative, on the use of these student-centered practices.

The changes that teachers reported in the case study interviews, on the other hand, were changes that affected *their teaching,* not the locus of instruction in the classroom. Their concerns were teacher-centered. They did not describe a revolution in the teacher and student roles, but the practical adjustments that teachers must make to be effective in heterogeneous classrooms. Assigning less reading as homework, conducting more oral reading in class, and using manipulatives (hands-on materials) as teaching devices are instructional choices. Teachers are saying they make different choices in tracked and untracked classrooms. Tracking reform apparently has no effect on the traditional distribution of power between teacher and student, but it is impossible to tell whether this is an artifact of the study's questioning protocols or of the reform being in the early stages of implementation.

Unanswered Questions from the Classroom

The surveys were conducted during the first half of the 1990s, too early to determine the full effect of the widespread tracking reform that had taken place in California and Massachusetts. A few trailblazing schools had embarked on the slow, incremental process of detracking five or six years earlier. But most of the teachers in detracked schools had no more than one or two years' experience to judge how it changed their classrooms. What do they believe are the most important unresolved questions about detracking? The first question is what happens when students on the extreme ends of the achievement continuum—exceptionally high- and low-achieving students—are placed in untracked classrooms. This issue is at the heart of the tracking debate and is invariably raised when schools and districts consider tracking reform. Teachers worry about their ability to meet children's needs.

I think they [teachers in an experimental heterogeneous class] have found some real problems to some degree. They're trying to teach to the middle. The lower students are struggling to keep up; and then, of course, the higher students are bored and unchallenged.

—Chapter I Teacher

I have children in my classroom saying, "How come we have to do this?" or "How come we're moving so slow?"   *—Teacher, Math*

These people come up with these great ideas of heterogeneously grouping these children and thinking that the more astute ones are going to help the other ones. And it doesn't work that way. They get very impatient. And you hear kids making comments, "Oh, he's stupid." You know, they do that to each other. They know who they are.

—Teacher, Math

Their main book will probably, for the most part, be our grade-level textbook. But we will use sixth grade as a reinforcement. We don't have anything specific planned for the higher-achieving kids. I mean we will just have extra things that they will do. . . . By having them help, having them teach in a cooperative learning sort of atmosphere, they are going to learn more than they would just by listening to teachers—a peer teaching type of thing.   *—Teacher, Science*

The teacher offering the last quotation was planning instruction for an untracked class the following year. As the other speakers point out, high achievers may become bored with cooperative learning and the slower pace of heterogeneous classrooms. Nonreaders are unlikely to learn how to read through peer tutoring or by having text read aloud to them. To a degree, assignments can be individualized within classrooms, but tailoring work to each student's unique profile leaves the teacher little opportunity for direct instruction or detailed feedback to students. Unless class sizes are radically reduced in conjunction with a detracking program, heterogeneity in student ability runs the risk of hampering effective teaching.

In fairness to tracking reformers, extreme achievement heterogeneity also exists in many tracked classes. The challenge of adequately serving students with diverse needs is never fully addressed by tracking or any other ability grouping system.[7] But detracked classes cannot help but exacerbate the difficulties posed by widely varying achievement in classrooms. The slightest hint of this problem only confirms the suspicion and fear of wary teachers and parents. This does not mean that detracked classes are inherently incapable of handling diverse student abilities, but it does mean that the issue must still be addressed by tracking reformers.

The second unanswered question about detracking involves student behavior. Teachers at detracked schools observed that the behavior of low-ability students improved once they were dispersed over several classes.

> You have more behavior problems [in tracked classes] because you've grouped a bunch of unmotivated kids together. And so there's no peer pressure. You can't use that where you can . . . if they're heterogeneously grouped. They just stick all the home boys in one class. It makes it more difficult to control. You have to do more real structured things.   —*Teacher, English*

> I see [the effect of scheduling] especially at the lower end because that group of kids gets grouped together and frequently they also have behavior problems and all of those attendant things. Scheduling affects that, whereas if it were just heterogeneous, it wouldn't make such a difference.   —*Teacher, English*

These observations offer a strong argument for detracking. Low tracks frequently cluster together students exhibiting behavior problems. Whether poor behavior is the cause of, result of, or just coincidental to students' learning deficiencies, low track classrooms are frequently regarded as anarchic environments. Poor behavior feeds on itself. Dispersing poorly behaved students among separate, heterogeneous classrooms may tap peer influences that steer these students toward better behavior.

The third question involves teachers' workloads. Preparing new materials and learning new methods of instruction take time, and dealing with a wider range of student achievement is taxing. Also, recall that 31.9 percent of schools in CA 94 and 20.8 percent in MA 95 reported abolishing the remedial track. These classes were often capped in size so that teachers could give extra attention to below-grade-level students. The heterogeneous classes replacing them are probably larger, therefore increasing the demands on teachers.

On the other side of the ledger, detracking may save time and simplify teachers' work in one important respect. Eliminating different course levels decreases the number of preparations, or "preps," teachers must complete for classes. In a tracked school, for example, an eighth grade English teacher may prepare three separate lessons daily—for remedial, regular, and honors classes. In an untracked setting, the same teacher would only prepare one lesson, assuming that heterogeneous classes were all covering an identical curriculum. Detracking may ultimately require less work by drastically reducing preparation time.

Whether detracking makes teachers' work easier or more difficult, whether student behavior improves, and whether teachers can serve students with vastly different needs in the same classroom are important issues for schools debating tracking policy. All of these topics require additional research, and new issues will emerge as the number of detracked schools grows.[8]

Schools that have been able to untrack without rancor or internal turmoil have been willing to take the leap of faith that heterogeneous grouping is beneficial. How were they able to avoid the pitfalls that other schools experienced when embarking on reform?

Different Philosophies, Different Policies: Meadowview Middle School

Meadowview Middle School opened as a grade 7–8 school in the fall of 1992. Planning for the new school had taken three years. A middle school task force, including parents, teachers, and administrators, mapped out an educational program that reflected the latest thinking on exemplary middle schools. The plan was presented to the local school board in 1991. Meadowview would have interdisciplinary teams, the inclusion of non-English-speaking and special needs students in regular classrooms, technology as an integral part of instruction, community-school partnerships, common planning periods for teaching teams, and untracked, heterogeneously grouped classes.

The board was hesitant on the tracking issue. Only two years earlier, tracking had become a divisive issue in the community. A district administrator's report recommended phasing out tracking in junior and senior high schools. The town's local newspaper greeted the recommendation with a cartoon showing a for-sale sign indignantly planted on the front lawn of a home. Facing certain defeat at the time, the detracking recommendation was pulled from the school committee agenda without coming up for a vote.

The task force designing Meadowview Middle School understood, as a consequence of the earlier controversy, that radical tracking reform would not fly politically in the district. The new principal of Meadowview presented a more moderate proposal to the school board in what he called "a big song and dance."[9] Since the new school would feature teaming, he proposed that the school offer heterogeneous grouping on one team only, as "an experiment, a pilot program." No one would be forced into detracking. Teachers would volunteer to teach on the experimental team, and parents would voluntarily sign up their children to participate. The plan narrowly passed on a 4-3 vote, with the school committee adding a provision to collect data and review the program at the end of the first year.

The first year went smoothly. Strong teachers volunteered for the heterogeneous team. They fanned out to the elementary schools and explained the program to parents of the sixth graders attending the school the following year. Approximately 100 students signed up for the heterogeneous option in seventh grade. The local college provided consultants to assist teachers in revamping instruction. Meadowview also offered tracked teams (an honors team for academically advanced students, three teams at grade level, and a team for students below grade level).

The first-year evaluation judged the experiment a success. The attendance rate of students on the heterogenous team was 3 percent higher than that of comparable students on other teams. Test scores were comparable to the school's as a whole. Surveys showed that parents and teachers were happy with the program, and only a handful of students transferred out to one of the ability-grouped teams during the year.

When I visited the school in the spring of 1997, it was apparent that teaming, and the availability of a mixed-ability team, had been institutionalized at Meadowview Middle School. The founding principal still led the school. He described the parents of the heterogeneous team students as "active parents who are concerned." Surprisingly, despite this support and the favorable first-year review, the ranks of volunteers had not grown. The heterogeneous team had about eighty students. The appeal of heterogeneous grouping had never extended beyond this (about 20 percent of the students at each grade level) in the school's five-year history. Most students at the school sought placement on the tracked teams and continued to attend above-grade-level, grade-level, and below-grade-level classes.

Why was Meadowview School's experiment with heterogeneous grouping able to succeed, albeit without expanding, when reform at a school like Hillcrest, described in chapter 6, had failed so painfully? How had the school avoided fighting with other levels of governance, like Creekside and Parkview schools, described in chapter 5?

Detracking enjoyed a supportive context at Meadowview. This was not by accident. From the start, the school's policymakers addressed district concerns regarding heterogeneous grouping. Opponents were placated by offering tracking reform as a limited experiment with a review at the end of the first year. Teaming supported heterogeneous grouping at Meadowview while undermining the innovation at Hillcrest. At Meadowview, teaming meant that heterogeneous grouping could be tried with a willing segment of the school population without forcing it on the whole school. At Hillcrest, teaming was one of three reforms imposed upon a wary faculty and parent population. In other words, how teaming was used in conjunction with tracking reform determined whether it helped or hindered detracking.

The fact that Meadowview was a new school, opening with a new principal and faculty, certainly helped too. Faculty and students were explicitly recruited for the heterogeneous team; they were not members of an established school community only reluctantly persuaded to participate. Hillcrest was an old school with a new principal, an eager innovator who suggested, before first forging strong personal ties or bonds of trust, that people radically change their ways.

The heterogeneous team at Meadowview used its autonomy to develop a clear pedagogical identity. The team's classrooms sported the pronounced markings of progressive education: lots of cooperative and hands-on learning activities, student-centered instruction, projects involving inquiry and exploration, and a multicultural curriculum. This ideology contrasted with that of the tracked teams, which emphasized content mastery, a relatively traditional curriculum, and rigorous preparation for high school. Meadowview parents, therefore, were offered a choice between two different types of education, with clear differences on what students should learn and how teachers should teach. Teachers were also afforded a choice, the opportunity to teach in a setting compatible with their pedagogical style, to work with colleagues who shared their educational philosophy, and to serve parents who believed as they did.

Meadowview functioned as an ideological marketplace. Teachers and parents sorted themselves into teams compatible with their core educational beliefs. This contrasted with the reforms at Hillcrest, which were presented as the one best way of teaching and learning.[10] At Meadowview, opposing ideologies coalesced around different teaching teams. At other schools in this study, differences in educational approach coalesced around subject area departments. The result was the same result, schools with hybrid policies. Schools like Meadowview have found a way to resolve the tracking wars while recognizing diverse views on what constitutes a good education.

Summary and Conclusion

When schools abolish tracking, change occurs in classrooms. Teachers' lessons include more oral reading and more hands-on materials. Instruction is conducted at a slower pace, less time is spent on lecture and discussion, homework with extensive readings is assigned less frequently, textbooks are used less, and grading is individualized. But not everything changes. How students are organized for work within classrooms is largely unaffected by tracking policy. Tracked and untracked classrooms both use cooperative learning. Other alternative instructional strategies—peer tutoring and cross-age tutoring—are used infrequently in either setting.

These findings bolster a tentative conclusion from chapter 4, that school achievement heterogeneity may not affect tracking policy, but heterogeneity in the classroom can still affect teaching. They are also consistent with what is known about how mutual adaptation alters policies promoting reform. Teachers sift through reform programs, keep what they think is feasible, and ignore the rest. This limits how profoundly detracking changes the core of schooling. The adjustments noted above, such as giving fewer overnight reading assignments and conducting more oral reading in class, while important, do not trigger a revolutionary change in educational philosophy. Detracking has altered the planning and management of instruction in several ways, but these changes have been pragmatic rather than ideological. And the questions that remain are primarily about coping with heterogeneous classrooms, not the profound, self-critical evaluations of teaching that many tracking advocates had hoped for and predicted.

I met dozens of believers in progressive pedagogy during the course of this study, and they fervently supported tracking reform. I also met dozens of teachers with a more traditional approach to teaching. They opposed detracking with equal devotion. Most of the teachers in the study, however, fell somewhere in between, either appearing unaware of any pedagogical dimension to the tracking issue or seeing their own teaching as nonideological. Sometimes researchers focus too much on the philosophical implications of educational controversies and overlook the practical demands of teachers' work. In reality, the philosophical and the practical are often muddled in schooling. Cross-age tutoring continues to be a rarity. Undoubtedly this has as much to do with the difficulty of scheduling a time and place for students of different grades to work together as with any deep-seated objections to student-centered practices.

In schools where educational philosophies do matter, compromises must be struck. Meadowview Middle School offers an example of how opposing ideologies can be accommodated at the same school. A heterogeneous team allowed parents and teachers who oppose tracking and support progressive educational techniques to enjoy untracked classes. Parents and teachers who believed in tracking and traditional teaching practices could join tracked teams. This provided a durable solution to the tracking controversy at the school and solved the problem that I raised at the beginning of the chapter. Teachers can alter elements of their teaching, but changing one's overall teaching style is not an easy matter. Reforms that compel teachers to change every aspect of their work face a dubious fate after reaching the classroom door.

8

The Fate of Reform

HAVE THE TRACKING WARS changed the way schools group students? Can states persuade schools to alter traditional practices? In reviewing this study's most significant lessons, let me first step back and examine a simple, perhaps even naïve, model of state education reform, what I call a "right-angle" explanation of how state reforms influence schools (see figure 8-1). The horizontal dimension represents policymaking at the state level. Issues are framed, governmental agendas are set, options are debated, evidence is gathered, advocacy is marshaled, committees are formed, hearings are held, letters are written, op-ed articles are published, and the desires of special interest groups are heard. State policy is the product of these activities.

But a policy decision is just the starting point for implementation, shown in the vertical dimension. State reforms are handed down from state to district to school. They may be changed significantly along the way. They may even be rejected. The goal of reform is for policies to materialize at the level of the system targeted for change. In the case of tracking reform, state policy targets schools, but in some cases the power to track or not to track is vested in other levels of the system (for example, districts above the school level or departments below).

The two dimensions mark off distinct, commonly recognized periods in the life span of reform. Press coverage of controversial state reforms typically marks off and illuminates these phases. Policy is made. Policy is implemented. Policymaking is dominated by politics, policy implementation by management. Articles on policymaking tell us how a reform is born, the debates that rage, and why the state chooses one approach over another. Articles on implementation tell us how the different levels of the system work together to put a policy's objectives into force.[1]

The right-angle model is unequivocally top-down in orientation, focus-

Figure 8-1. Right-Angle Model of State Education Reform

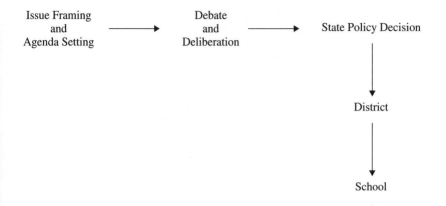

ing on reform initiated by upper-level governments. It omits change initiated at the grassroots, reforms that teachers, parents, and administrators develop on their own and agree to implement. The omission is significant. Even with state-initiated reforms, as this study has demonstrated, schools exercise tremendous discretion and ultimate control over implementation.

Implementing Tracking Reform

Detracking was originally framed as an equity issue with clear winners and losers. Advocates argued that students of color, students in urban schools, students from economically disadvantaged backgrounds, and low-achieving students would benefit from tracking's abolition. Opponents argued that high-achieving students would be ill-served in heterogeneously grouped classrooms, and, in California especially, groups supporting gifted education lobbied strenuously against the reform.

This "choosing up sides" during policymaking resonated in implementation. Although principals rated state influence on their schools' policies as inconsequential, responses to the state recommendation matched the demographic profiles that had been defined in the debate. The empirical support for either tracking or detracking is weak. The symbolic politics are strong. Schools were signaled how to respond to detracking. Urban schools and low-SES schools embraced the reform; suburban schools and high-SES schools shunned it.

This suggests that a modification in the right-angle model (figure 8-1) is warranted. Policymaking and implementation intersect on occasions other

Figure 8-2. Modified Model of State Education Reform

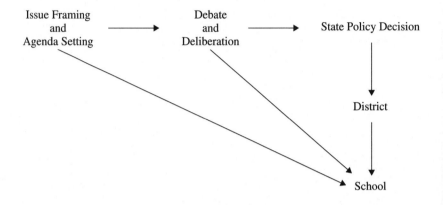

than when policy is decided (as depicted in figure 8-2). Local decisionmakers do not work in a vacuum. In California and Massachusetts, local educators were aware of how the tracking issue had been framed. Though it appears detracked schools followed the states' recommendations, educators at these schools can honestly claim that state policy had very little to do with their decisions. Instead, detracking had been dictated by their schools' institutional characteristics, more precisely, by local educators' understanding of the best policy for the kind of institutions they work in and govern.

Basing reform on symbolic politics unleashes a series of consequences. In essence, state officials in California and Massachusetts signed off on the causal theory pushed by antitracking advocates, that tracking contributes to the low academic achievement of low-income and minority children. Deborah Stone points out that a policy's causal theory is key to its politics, primarily because theories assign both blame and responsibility for action. As Jeannie Oakes stated in *Keeping Track*'s opening pages, earlier researchers and policymakers looked everywhere for the cause of inequality in achievement "except in the content and processes of schooling itself." Now state policy proclaimed tracking at fault for the achievement gap and assigned schools the responsibility for fixing it.[2]

Reforms steeped in symbolism also tend to shut off consideration of alternative solutions. Joseph Gusfield shows how drinking and driving has been framed as an issue of personal responsibility, with laws first levying penalties on drunk drivers alone, then expanding to include bartenders, tavern owners, party hosts, and others with tangential culpability. Gusfield asks us to imagine the policies that might have been considered if the problem had been defined as a deficiency in transportation systems. Proposed solutions would have concentrated on providing inebriated drivers other means of getting home, a radically different focus than that of current laws.[3] As this book has documented, detracking consumes vast amounts of time, energy, political capital, and expertise. It places extraordinary demands on schools' organizational structures, leadership, faculty morale, and parental support. What if California and Massachusetts officials had singled out low tracks as the problem? A program for boosting their productivity might have been launched. What if low standards and a general lack of intellectual rigor in schooling had been identified as depressing the achievement of poor and minority students? Tough new academic standards, expected equally of all students, might have been the proposed solution. Imagine if the problem had been framed as the lack of technical expertise to tackle students' difficulties with basic reading and math. An aggressive intervention might have been launched, with full funding for remedial classes of five or six students taught by specially trained experts. These options were foreclosed when tracking was identified as the problem and detracking as the solution.

The state's position on tracking, however, is not the last word. Schools are free-standing policymaking bodies. They consider decisions in their own right, not simply implement the decisions of others.

School leaders responded to the arguments framed in the tracking debate and formulated policies to match their school's institutional characteristics, including urbanicity and socioeconomic level. They crafted policies compatible with their school's grade configuration and student population. Parents were also influential. Schools where parents were actively involved with policymaking tended to hold onto tracking in academic subjects. Within schools, mathematics departments were likely to continue tracking and English departments to support heterogeneous grouping. In schools with interdisciplinary teaming, teams more oriented toward the beliefs of progressive education grouped students heterogeneously. Teams with more traditional teachers stuck to tracking.

Casting Doubt on the Prevailing Explanation of Tracking

A mix of institutional, organizational, technical, and political factors shaped tracking in California and Massachusetts middle schools. How does this square with the dominant explanation of why schools track? In a nutshell, the experience of schools in California and Massachusetts casts doubt upon it. The prevailing explanation depicts tracking as a tool for reproducing social inequality, a condition rooted in the maldistribution of wealth, bolstered by racist and classist conceptions of intelligence and achievement, and maintained by society's powerful so that they may continue their domination of the powerless.

This is a dramatic indictment, politically potent enough to sweep aside the neutral and inconclusive findings of research and to convince policymakers in California and Massachusetts to condemn tracking. But, ironically, the antitracking movement's impressive political success and the subsequent implementation of state admonitions have undermined the reformers' original rationale.

Three contradictions are glaring. First, the distribution of political power has been completely backwards. Tracking's defenders were hopelessly outmatched in policy deliberations in California and Massachusetts. Tracking's opponents held all the cards and emerged victorious. Notably, these political triumphs were accomplished without a revolution in the American economic and social structures that allegedly support tracking.

Second, detracking is taking place in low-achieving schools, in poor schools, and in urban areas. Schools serving inner city children and society's poorest children are not rejecting reform. They are embracing it. Suburban schools, schools in wealthy communities, and high-achieving schools are staying with curriculum differentiation. This runs counter to the notion of elites imposing a counterproductive policy on society's downtrodden. If tracking is bad policy, society's elites are irrationally reserving it for their own children.

Third, the major influences on tracking reform are primarily local, not societal. Local officials are responding to a multitude of forces, but they vary considerably from school to school. This is not to deny that societies erect structures, both explicit and hidden, that steer social interactions and institutional choices. But the power of these structures is not absolute, and their influence may be attenuated within local environments. The hundreds of schools that have turned away from tracking exist in the same society as those that continue tracking. In some cases, tracked math departments exist in the same school as detracked English departments.

The Future of Tracking Policy and Research

The future will almost certainly include both tracked and untracked schools. We do not know very much about untracked schools. They have not existed in sufficient numbers to find out, as tracking reformers claim, that low-achieving, poor, or urban students benefit from heterogeneous grouping. Detracking is a gamble. This study is the first to discover that the risks of the gamble are being assumed disproportionately by urban schools, low-SES schools, and schools with low achievement. This should cause great concern. Some of society's most disadvantaged children are now part of an educational experiment, with the outcome completely unknown.

What are the risks associated with detracking? One study of NELS data suggests that high-achieving students and students at grade level achieve less in heterogeneous math classes than in tracked classes. Low-ability students benefit. Another study found that students of all abilities learn more in tracked algebra classes than in untracked algebra classes. Where detracking has taken hold, educators should keep a close eye on math achievement in general and on algebra classes in particular. High-achieving minority students in low-income, urban schools are most at risk of suffering from the abolition of tracking. Their academic achievement should be carefully monitored and steps taken to ensure that they are academically challenged in detracked settings.[4]

Educators should also assess the political costs of detracking. Parents are hesitant to detrack, and the parents of high-achieving children are especially opposed to it. Researchers have described schools where parents threaten to transfer their children if tracking is abolished. In chapter 5, I described a school where students did indeed transfer out, but educators there claimed that other students transferred in to take advantage of the untracked environment. Schools that adopt heterogeneous grouping should carefully monitor the outflow and inflow of students. Schools that drive away their highest-achieving students must weigh that loss against any gains that they believe accrue from tracking reform.

Tracked schools, on the other hand, should carefully monitor their low tracks. Linda Valli has reported on an urban Catholic school with low tracks focused on achievement. The school pushes low-ability students to excel, emphasizing "a curriculum of effort." Margaret Camarena and Adam Gamoran have also described the characteristics of low-track classrooms where achievement is the norm. Tracked schools should adopt aggressive interventions targeting the academic deficiencies of struggling students.[5]

My study raises significant issues for future research, especially efforts to evaluate tracking and detracking's relative merits. Transfers of high achievers will make untracked schools appear lower in achievement. A fall in test scores resulting from changes in school population cannot be blamed directly on detracking. Researchers should also note that low-achieving schools were more likely to detrack in both California and Massachusetts. Comparing mean scores of tracked and detracked schools is an unfair way to judge detracking if the gap is merely an artifact of preexisting achievement differences. Research must be careful to account for initial differences between tracked and untracked schools, to control for other factors that may affect achievement, and to measure achievement effects over time.

Schools with hybrid tracking policies will no doubt grow in number. Tracking sparks heated debate, and compromise policies have been able to dissipate conflict. More mixed systems can be expected, with tracked and untracked classes at the same school. This presents serious challenges for researchers. For the sake of clarity, studies of tracking's effects have almost always modeled tracking policy as a dichotomy in statistical analyses (the present study is no exception). Schools are tracked or untracked. The reality is that several shades of gray exist between the two extremes. Moreover, studies of track effects typically describe schools as offering three tracks—academic, regular, and vocational (or remedial). This is hopelessly out of date when applied to contemporary high schools, and it is questionable whether it was ever appropriate for middle schools. Contemporary high schools usually group students on a subject-by-subject basis. Middle schools not only group by subjects, but some subjects are also tracked at the same time that other subjects are untracked. Researchers must be alert to whether schools' tracking practices are accurately portrayed in the data they are analyzing.[6]

A final point applies to both policymakers and researchers. This study has identified several influences on school tracking policy. Those thinking about tracking policy in the future, whether policymakers deliberating the issue or researchers attempting to measure effects, should consider whether these influences are also important to tracking's impact on achievement. What if big schools track and small schools untrack because that is the appropriate thing for big and small schools to do? What if schools follow the preferences of parents because to oppose parents on policies about which they feel so deeply is educationally unsound? What if low-achieving schools detrack because heterogeneous grouping truly benefits low-achieving students?

In other words, what if principals, teachers, and parents know what they are doing, know what is best for their particular schools when they decide policy? The debate over tracking has carried on for so long and at such a shrill pitch that this question has never been asked. It should be asked now.

Appendix A

The Study's Methods and Data

THE FIRST CALIFORNIA SURVEY was mailed to the 894 schools serving grades 6–8, 7–8, and 7–9. Usable surveys were returned by principals at 373 schools, a return rate of about 42 percent. The 1994 California survey ("CA 94") was mailed to a random sample of 343 schools, with 166 usable surveys returned, a response rate of approximately 48 percent. The Massachusetts survey ("MA 95") was conducted in 1995 and, like the first survey in California, was mailed to all middle schools in the state, 230 schools. But unlike the California surveys, schools serving grades 5–8 were also included since the grade 5–8 school is a relatively common grade configuration in Massachusetts. The Massachusetts survey was returned by 134 schools, a 58 percent response.

In both states the first survey was mailed to all middle schools for a simple reason. I had no idea how many schools were engaged in tracking reform. When I prepared the CA 91 survey, as part of my doctoral dissertation research, state education department officials in Sacramento told me that they knew that some schools were detracking, but they would not hazard a guess as to how many. These same officials also warned that because California school principals are inundated with research surveys, a healthy portion of them from well-intentioned doctoral students, I could expect only a 10 percent to 20 percent response rate to the mailing. Contemplating the disastrous consequences for my own well-intentioned efforts if only 10 percent of schools responded to the survey—and if only 10 percent of these schools were detracking—I abandoned the idea of random sampling and instead administered the survey to all 894 middle schools in the state (see table A-1).

The worry was unnecessary. The 42 percent return rate yielded a substantial number of schools wrestling with the tracking issue. A little more

Table A-1. Surveys[a]
Number of surveys, unless otherwise noted

Survey	Sample	Mailed	Returned	Response rate (percent)
CA 91	CA middle schools	894	373	41.7
CA 94	Random	343	166	48.4
MA 95	MA middle schools	230	134	58.3

[a] Eighty-four schools in CA 91 are also in CA 94. The three surveys were returned by a total of 589 different schools (373 + 82 + 134).

than half of the 373 responding schools had reduced tracking in at least one subject. The schools also varied widely on the factors that I thought might be influential in deciding tracking policies.

It is useful to know how respondents to the surveys compare with non-respondents or how respondents match up on statistics reported for all eighth grades in the respective states. These comparisons are reported in tables A-2 and A-3. For CA 94 and MA 95, I am only able to compare the samples to state means. On these measures, the schools in CA 94 and MA 95 look almost identical to state averages. For CA 91, the sample with the lowest response rate, I am able to compare responding to nonresponding schools on several variables: eighth grade enrollment, socioeconomic status (SES), reading achievement, and racial composition. Nonresponding schools had more eighth graders (299 vs. 286, standard deviation of 150), lower SES ratings (2.81 vs. 2.93, sd of 0.66), lower reading achievement (252 vs. 263, sd of 47), and more nonwhite students (61 percent vs. 54 percent, sd of 24 percent).

Table A-2. Comparison of CA 91 Respondents and Nonrespondents on Selected Characteristics
Mean score[a]

Characteristic	Respondents (n = 373)	Nonrespondents (n = 515)
Reading score	263.1	252.4
	(45.64)	(47.7)
Percent nonwhite	53.7	60.6
	(23.5)	(24.8)
Socioeconomic status	2.93	2.81
	(0.66)	(0.66)
Eighth grade population	285.5	298.7
	(143.7)	(154.7)

a. Standard deviation indicated in parentheses.

Table A-3. Comparison of CA 94 and MA 95 with State Test Data
Percent of students scoring at performance level

CLAS Test, 1994	All CA schools	CA 94 survey sample	MEAP Test, 1996	All MA schools	MA 95 survey sample
Level 6	3	3	Level 4	5	5
Level 5	8	8	Level 3	15	15
Level 4	13	13	Level 2	40	39
Level 3	20	20	Level 1	33	34
Level 2	24	25	< Level 1	7	7
Level 1	33	31			

How these differences bias the CA 91 results is unknown, but three things suggest the skewing is small. First, most of the findings for CA 91 were confirmed in CA 94. Second, as noted below, I augmented the CA 91 survey data with extensive case studies. The case study sample was designed to be representative of the state's middle schools on demographic, achievement, and school-size variables. Third, it would be misleading if the survey's respondents and nonrespondents differed significantly on how tracking policy, the dependent variable in most analyses, is related to independent variables. Although CA 91's response rate for schools is 42 percent, these schools are located in approximately 61 percent of California's districts having at least one middle school (249 out of 507). Schools in the same district are likely to share characteristics, including similar tracking policies. This does not eliminate the self-selection problem, but chances are diminished that the unsampled schools have the radically different policy environments that would reverse the results reported here.

Any selection bias on the measurement of tracking itself probably leans toward inflating the estimate of reformed schools. School principals are undoubtedly more willing to tout their schools' exciting new innovations than well-established routines. They are also sensitive to the claim that tracking is a racially discriminatory practice and that it contradicts a school's democratic mission. Indeed, the mere fact that tracking is openly condemned by the state probably discourages principals of tracked schools from responding to a survey on the topic. In my case visits, however, I found only three schools with policy misreported in the survey. All three underreported tracking in math. I model detracking in a way that, by allowing two ability levels, gives some leeway to reductions in math grouping. This should reduce the chance of misreported policies. Nevertheless, it seems prudent to regard the untracking reported here as a high estimate of the actual amount of reform transpiring in schools.

Case Studies: Wave I, 1991

The first wave of case studies were conducted in California in the spring of 1991. The sample was selected to be representative of California's middle schools and to maximize a variety of tracking policies and local decisionmakers (district or school). Volunteer sites for fieldwork were solicited on the CA 91 survey. The ninety-three schools expressing an interest were sorted into six cells created by a 2 × 3 matrix. One axis on the matrix was defined by two values modeling tracking policy, whether schools averaged 2.0 or more levels of tracked classes in academic subjects or fewer than two levels. The other axis was defined by three values modeling policy source, whether tracking was decided at the district level or school level, or by a combination of both. I then selected four schools from each of the six cells, seeking balance on achievement, SES, racial composition, school population, and geography. This produced a sample of twenty-four schools.

Backup sites were selected for the schools. One school canceled at the last minute, and the backup was unable to schedule a visit, leading to a final sample of twenty-three schools that I visited. Sample medians on characteristics such as eighth grade population, SES, reading achievement, and percent minority enrollment were close to state means (see table A-4). On each of these dimensions, in other words, eleven or twelve schools fell above the state mean and eleven or twelve fell below.

I asked the principals at each site to solicit volunteers for interviews and to make sure that, in addition to themselves, at least one math, English, social studies, and science teacher took part. While at the school, I also sought out educators, including counselors, who were mentioned as important to their school's policymaking on tracking. Interviews ranged from fifteen to ninety minutes long. All but a handful of interviews were tape-recorded and extensive field notes were kept at each site. Interviews were semistructured (see protocol below), but I did not ask all subjects the same questions. Once information on a school, such as the number of tracks and the ability levels they served, had been collected and verified, I dropped these questions. Documents describing the school, course offerings, tracking policies, and test scores were also collected. In all, 175 educators were interviewed.

Based on interview notes, I selected four schools that I thought captured the most important issues of all twenty-three sites. Verbatim transcripts

Table A-4. CA 91 Case Study Sample Statistics [a]

School	Mean subject levels	Eighth Grade Population	Nonwhite students (percent)	Socio-economic status	CAP reading score
A	1.000	low	high	low	low
B	1.000	high	high	low	low
C	1.125	low	low	high	high
D	1.250	high	low	high	high
E	1.250	low	low	high	high
F	1.250	high	high	low	low
G	1.250	low	low	high	high
H	1.250	low	high	high	high
I	1.625	low	high	low	high
J	1.750	high	high	low	low
K	1.875	high	high	low	low
L	2.000	low	low	low	low
M	2.000	high	high	low	low
N	2.000	low	low	high	high
O	2.000	high	high	low	low
P	2.125	low	low	high	low
Q	2.250	high	high	low	low
R	2.375	high	low	high	high
S	2.375	low	low	high	high
T	2.500	high	low	high	high
U	2.625	low	low	high	high
V	2.750	low	high	low	low
W	2.750	high	high	low	low
Case study sample median	301	56		2.78	252
State mean ($n = 888$)	293	58		2.86	257
State SD	150	24		0.66	47

a. Values dichotomized to shield identity. HIGH represents value above state median, LOW below state median.

were prepared from the interviews at these four schools—695 pages of text. The transcripts were analyzed, and coding categories were developed. Using this coding scheme, I coded each interview using field notes from the interviews and 144 hours of audio tape recordings. Major trends and recurring themes in the data were then identified.

Case Studies: Wave II, 1996–97

I used a less structured strategy to select case studies in Wave II. I wanted to study schools that had faced and overcome significant opposition to detracking and schools that had either failed in detracking or continued to struggle to implement it. The purpose was to learn about challenges to implementing tracking reform that had arisen since the earlier study. I was also interested in schools that reported a significant district role in their detracking plans, a facet of tracking that I had not learned much about in Wave I. And I wanted to follow up on some of the more interesting cases from the earlier interviews. Based on these criteria, I selected six California schools from the original sample of twenty-three and six new schools in Massachusetts.

Interviews were conducted with teaching teams and individuals. Interviews followed the Wave I protocol, except that I tape-recorded interviews at only six of the twelve sites. A total of 89 interviews were conducted.

Use of Quotations and Cases in the Book

Quotations presented in the book were not selected to be representative of all interviews but to illustrate various facets of tracking policy. Quotes were lightly edited for clarity. Ellipses denote deleted utterances, and brackets denote editorial insertions. Cases were randomly assigned pseudonyms (Hillcrest, Creekside, Meadowview, Parkview). I also randomly used gender pronouns (he, she, his, her) in the sentences introducing quotations and altered superficial characteristics to shield the speaker's identity.

Appendix B

Statistical Issues in Chapter 4

Computing the Index of Achievement Heterogeneity

FOR CA 94 AND MA 95, I computed the index of hetero-geneity by multiplying the percent of students scoring at the very lowest and highest levels of proficiency on state tests. Computed this way, higher indices are assigned to schools with lots of students at both ends of the achievement distribution and lower indices to schools with more students bunched up at the middle.

Computing an index for CA 91 schools was more complicated. Data on the number of students tested, the mean scaled score in reading, and the standard error (SE) were gathered for each school. Pseudo-standard deviations (SD) were first computed from standard errors (multiplying SE by the square root of n). Since the distance of a particular score from the test mean strongly influences the pseudo-SD, this was corrected by dividing the SD by $|Z|$ (adding 1 to avoid a 0 denominator). This quotient exhibited a skewed frequency distribution. A log transformation gained a near normal distribution. I call this statistic the index of achievement heterogeneity, or index of spread, for short.

To test the validity of the index, I sought an alternative measure of achievement heterogeneity in the CAP data. Fortunately, for every school the database reports the percentage of students scoring in each quartile of the state's distribution of scores. Assuming that a 25-25-25-25 quartile breakdown would represent the most heterogeneous schools in the state, I summed each school's deviation from this pattern by adding the absolute values of the quartile deviations from 25. Schools with a high value on this index, which I call the summation index, represent the most homogeneous schools in the state. A school with all of its students scoring in the top quartile, for instance, would have a 0-0-0-100 quartile breakdown, and a summation index of 150 (the sum of the four deviations from 25). A school with all of its students scoring in the bottom quartile, or in any of the four quartiles, would yield the same summation index, 150, indicating homogeneity of achievement. This measure also exhibited a skewed frequency, so I standardized the scores (mean of 0, standard deviation of 1). The two indexes should be inversely related. The zero-order correlation coefficient for the standardized summation index and the index of spread is −.902, a good confirmation.

Computing the Coin-Flip Sample Effects

Coefficients in logistic regression express the effect that one unit of an independent variable has on a dependent variable, with all of the other variables in the equation controlled at their sample means. The change is measured in log odds. In chapter 4, I illustrate each variable's effect on tracking policy by using an imaginary sample of 100 schools that start evenly divided, with a 50-50 distribution of tracked and untracked schools, and then report how a change in the independent variable alters this distribution.

The purpose in statistical modeling is to find the simplest, most accurate way to explain an event. My purpose in chapter 4 is to explain what factors influence tracking policy. In table 4-7, the full and best-fitting models are presented for the three samples—CA 91, CA 94, and MA 95. The full model represents an equation that includes the variables that I theorized might affect tracking policy. Many of these influences overlap, measuring essentially the same force on policy. Some have no effect on policy whatever. Deleting weak and extraneous variables leaves the best-fitting model. The best fit is the model that gives the simplest, most powerful explanation of tracking policy.

I will use the influence of parents in CA 91 to show how the coin-flip sample's change in distribution is computed. The coefficient, −.444, represents the change in log odds for schools detracking when parent influence increases by one unit on the survey's four-level rating scale. Positive values favor detracking, negative values are opposed. The negative coefficient means that parent influence decreases the odds of detracking. An odds ratio is the probability of an event occurring (p) divided by the probability of an event not occurring (1 − p). Therefore, the coin-flip odds are p/1 − p, or .50/.50, or 1.00.

The coefficient for parent influence means that the odds of detracking decrease by a factor of $e^{-.444}$, or .641. This is the new odds ratio after a one-unit increase in parent influence. The task now is to solve for p, the new probability of detracking, using the equation, $.641 = p/(1 - p)$. The result is $p = .39$, which, when applied to a sample of 100 schools, yields 39 detracked schools. Raising parent influence by one unit changes the 50-50 sample to 39 detracked schools and 61 tracked, as displayed in Figure 4.4. Parents affect tracking policy.

Variables Receiving Special Treatment

Community. Respondents filled out a sheet separate from the survey in which they identified the school community as rural, urban, or suburban. Mixed responses were coded as the dominant type. Nonresponses to this item were significant: 14 percent in CA 91, 11 percent in CA 94, and 23 percent in MA 95. Some simply overlooked the item, but I think the main problem was the difficulty of categorizing communities using the three descriptors, especially in Massachusetts's small towns. The nonrespondents appeared to be random on key independent variables—population, achievement, SES—and on the dependent variables, tracking policy and policy source.

As an additional check on the effect of nonresponses, I coded the communities of the nonrespondents based on my own knowledge and the wisdom of acquaintances who know the two states well. I then ran new regressions, with no significant differences noted. In chapter 4 and 5's analyses, I decided to use the original codes, even though this reduces the sample size by 23 percent in MA 95. This choice has little effect on the analyses and possesses the advantage of accurately reflecting respondents' perceptions of the community in which their school is located. My argument concerning urbanicity is that city schools have embraced detracking because they consider it a reform especially appropriate for urban schools.

School Board Discussion. In CA 91, the survey asked whether school boards had discussed policy and gave a "yes" and "no" to be circled. A series of potential forums were asked about in this manner (media, school meeting with parents, staff meeting, district meeting). A significant number of respondents, eighty-eight, circled neither yes nor no to the school board question. These were defaulted to no discussion if the survey had at least one response in the cluster of questions. I assumed that the item had been left blank to indicate no school board discussion. Subsequent surveys asked respondents to circle all forums where the policy was discussed, making it clear that nonresponses would be considered negative responses.

Actors' Influence. Ratings were solicited on several actors' influence on

tracking policy. If one actor was rated in the set, all other blanks were defaulted to 1, no influence. Again, respondents appeared to interpret the directions as saying "circle all that apply," or in this case, "rate all who
mattered." Teachers' influence was left blank on twelve surveys, for example, but the influence of community groups was omitted on forty-one
surveys.

Notes

Chapter One

1. Teachers' opinions on tracking are reported in *The Carnegie Foundation for the Advancement of Teaching, 1987 National Survey of Public School Teachers* (Princeton, N.J.: Carnegie Foundation), p. 77. In the survey, 63 percent agreed with the statement, "Tracking students by ability is a useful way for schools to deal with diversity." The Public Agenda Foundation polls indicate that only 34 percent of the public and 40 percent of teachers believe heterogeneous grouping will improve education, as reported in Steve Farkas and Jean Johnson, *Given the Circumstances: Teachers Talk about Public Education Today* (New York: Public Agenda Foundation, 1996), p. 41.

2. Steve Bates, "Academic Mixing Stirs Pot in Alexandria," *Washington Post,* January 31, 1993, p. B5; Christine Dempsey, "Students of All Abilities Mixed as Parents Fume," *Hartford Courant,* July 25, 1994, p. A1; Peter Maass, "Study of Howard Middle Schools Criticizes Focus on Self-Esteem," *Washington Post,* October 11, 1996, p. B1; Lori Olszewski, "Teacher Union Sues Livermore District: Suit Says Principal Stifled Discussion over Curriculum," *San Francisco Chronicle,* June 3, 1997, p. A13; Tanya Schevitz, "Livermore Teachers, School District Settle Suit," *San Francisco Chronicle,* September 11, 1998, p. A17.

3. The Rand Change Agent Study spearheaded the research of federal programs (Paul Berman and Milbrey W. McLaughlin, *Federal Programs Supporting Educational Change,* vols. 1–8, [Santa Monica, Calif.: Rand Corporation, 1974–1978]).

4. Diane Ravitch succinctly states the lesson of these efforts: "the curriculum reform movement exemplified the pitfalls of trying to impose sweeping change on an institution as multidimensional as the American school. Regardless of what the state superintendent or the school superintendent or the principal may recommend, classroom teachers have a considerable degree of control over what and how they teach; even when a new curriculum is put in their hands, the way they use it may alter it beyond recognition." Diane Ravitch, *The Troubled Crusade* (Basic Books, 1983), p. 265. On the troubled fate of the 1960s science reforms, see Robert E. Stake and Jack A. Easley, *Case Studies in Science Education,* vols. 1 and 2 (Urbana: Center for Instructional Research and Curriculum Evaluation, University of Illinois, 1978).

5. Reflecting on the innovative programs of the early 1970s, the implementation researcher Milbrey W. McLaughlin comments, "for many teachers these policy goals

and activities were simply part of a broader environment that pressed in on their classrooms. Thus, to ask about the role or consequences of a program or strategy for practice risked misspecification because it gave policy a focus or significance it did not have in the daily matter of classroom life" (p. 151). Milbrey W. McLaughlin, "The Rand Change Agent Study: Ten Years Later," in Allan R. Odden, ed., *Education Policy Implementation* (SUNY Press, 1991), pp. 143–55.

6. Linda Darling-Hammond, "Instructional Policy into Practice: 'The Power of the Bottom Over the Top,'" *Educational Evaluation and Policy Analysis,* vol. 12, no. 3 (1990), 233–41.

7. William A. Firestone, S. Rosenblum, B. D. Bader, and Diane Massell, "Recent Trends in State Education Reform: Assessment and Prospects," *Teachers College Record,* vol. 94, no. 2 (Winter 1992), 254–77; Diane Massell and Susan Fuhrman, *Ten Years of Education Reform, 1983–1993* (New Brunswick, N.J.: Consortium for Policy Research in Education, 1994); Richard F. Elmore and Susan Fuhrman, eds., *The Governance of Curriculum* (Alexandria, Va.: Association for Supervision and Curriculum Development, 1994). See also several articles on CPRE research in *Educational Researcher,* vol. 24, no. 9 (1995).

8. David K. Cohen and Deborah Ball, "Relations between Policy and Practice: A Commentary," *Educational Evaluation and Policy Analysis,* vol. 12, no. 3 (Fall 1990), 331–38; James P. Spillane, "How Districts Mediate between State Policy and Teachers' Practice," in Richard F. Elmore and Susan Fuhrman, eds., *The Governance of Curriculum* (Alexandria, Va.: Association for Supervision and Curriculum Development, 1994).

9. Susan Fuhrman, William H. Clune, and Richard F. Elmore, "Research on Education Reform," *Teachers College Record,* vol. 90, no. 2 (Winter 1988), 237–57; Susan Lusi, *The Role of State Departments of Education in Complex School Reform* (Teachers College Press, 1997).

10. Thomas Corcoran and Margaret Goertz, "Instructional Capacity and High Performance Schools," *Educational Researcher,* vol. 24, no. 9 (1995), 27–31.

Chapter Two

1. California State Department of Education, *Caught in the Middle* (Sacramento: CSDE, 1987); Massachusetts Department of Education, *Structuring Schools for Student Success: A Focus on Ability Grouping* (Quincy, Mass.: MDOE, 1990); Massachusetts Department of Education, *Magic in the Middle* (Malden, Mass.: MDOE, 1993). Maryland and Nevada are two other states that condemned tracking as part of their middle school reform initiatives.

2. The course enrollment figures are 1996 NAEP data reported in Catherine A. Shaughnessy, Jennifer E. Nelson, and Norma A. Norris, *NAEP 1996 Mathematics: Cross-State Data Compendium for the Grade 4 and Grade 8 Assessment* (Washington: U.S. Department of Education, 1998), table 6.26, pp. 167–68. For a critique of the "spiral curriculum" that leads to repetition of mathematical content, see Curtis C. McKnight and others, *The Underachieving Curriculum: Assessing U.S. School Mathematics from an International Perspective* (Champaign, Ill.: Stipe Publishing Company, 1987).

3. Dominick Esposito, "Homogeneous and Heterogeneous Ability Grouping: Prin-

cipal Findings and Implications for Designing More Effective Educational Environments," *Review of Educational Research,* vol. 43, no. 2 (1973), pp. 163–79. See also Claude S. Fischer and others, *Inequality by Design: Cracking the Bell Curve Myth* (Princeton University Press, 1996), pp. 163–67.

4. James E. Rosenbaum, *Making Inequality* (Wiley, 1976); Samuel Bowles and Herbert Gintis, *Schooling in Capitalist America* (Basic Books, 1976).

5. To appreciate the stability and persistence over time of the social and functional orientations on tracking, see Guy Montrose Whipple, ed., *The Grouping of Pupils, Thirty-fifth Yearbook of the National Society for the Study of Education,* part 1 (Bloomington, Ill.: Public School Publishing Company, 1936); and Alfred Yates, ed., *Grouping in Education* (Wiley, 1966). Then contrast the indictment of tracking in Jeannie Oakes's *Keeping Track: How Schools Structure Inequality* (Yale University Press, 1985) with Charles Nevi, "In Defense of Tracking," *Educational Leadership,* vol. 89, no. 3 (1987), pp. 283–304.

6. Frederick Mosteller, Richard J. Light, and Jason A. Sachs, "Sustained Inquiry in Education: Lessons from Skill Grouping and Class Size," *Harvard Educational Review,* vol. 66, no. 4 (1996), p. 812.

7. Adam Gamoran and Mark Berends, "The Effects of Stratification in Secondary Schools: Synthesis of Survey and Ethnographic Research," *Review of Educational Research,* vol. 57, no. 4 (1988), pp. 415–35.

8. Robert E. Slavin, "Ability Grouping and Student Achievement in Elementary Schools: A Best Evidence Synthesis," *Review of Educational Research,* vol. 57, no. 3 (1987), pp. 293–336; Chen-Lin C. Kulik and James A. Kulik, "Effects of Ability Grouping on Elementary School Pupils: A Meta-analysis," paper presented at the annual meeting of the American Psychological Association, Toronto, 1984; James A. Kulik and Chen-Lin C. Kulik, "Meta-Analytic Findings on Grouping Programs," *Gifted Child Quarterly,* vol. 36, no. 2 (1992), pp. 73–77.

9. Robert E. Slavin, "Achievement Effects of Ability Grouping in Secondary Schools: A Best Evidence Synthesis," *Review of Educational Research,* vol. 60, no. 3 (1990), pp. 471–99.

10. Chen-Lin C. Kulik and James A. Kulik, "Effects of Ability Grouping on Secondary School Students: A Meta-Analysis of Evaluation Findings," *American Educational Research Journal,* vol. 19, no. 3 (1982), pp. 415–28. Slavin does not include gifted classes in his review (see note 9) because of the possibility of selection effects, the skewing of the comparison from educators screening and identifying good students for placement in gifted classes. It is difficult to see why Slavin tolerates this problem with evidence from the other tracks, however. Educators also screen and identify students with achievement problems for placement in remedial tracks, and sometimes these problems are more serious than indicated by test scores.

11. I discuss the Slavin and Kulik reviews in depth in Tom Loveless, "The Tracking and Ability Grouping Debate," *Fordham Report,* vol. 2, no. 8 (1998), 1–27.

12. William E. Shafer and Carol Olexa, *Tracking and Opportunity* (Scranton, Penn.: Chandler, 1971); Barbara Heyns, "Selection and Stratification within Schools," *American Journal of Sociology,* vol. 79, no. 6 (1974), pp. 1434–51.

13. Adam Gamoran, "The Stratification of High School Learning Opportunities," *Sociology of Education,* vol. 60 (July 1987), pp. 135–55. Quote on p. 152. For middle school students, Hoffer found a high-track benefit exceeding heterogeneous and low-

track deficits in science and math; Thomas B. Hoffer, "Middle School Ability Grouping and Student Achievement in Science and Mathematics," *Educational Evaluation and Policy Analysis,* vol. 14, no. 3 (1992), pp. 205–27. For an interesting discussion of intertrack differences, and an example where researchers modified their position (from claiming large track differences to questioning whether differences exist) after obtaining and evaluating additional data, see Karl L. Alexander, Martha A. Cook, and Edward L. McDill, "Curriculum Tracking and Educational Stratification," *American Sociological Review,* vol. 43 (February 1978), pp. 47–66; and Karl L. Alexander and Martha A. Cook, "Curricula and Coursework: A Surprise Ending to a Familiar Story," *American Sociological Review,* vol. 47, no. 5 (1982), pp. 626–40.

14. The charge that ability grouping promotes race and class discrimination has a long history. See Ray C. Rist, "Student Social Class and Teacher Expectations: The Self-fulfilling Prophecy in Ghetto Education," *Harvard Educational Review,* vol. 40, no. 3 (1970), pp. 411–51; Jeannie Oakes, "More Than Meets the Eye: Links between Tracking and the Culture of Schools," in Harbeson Pool and Jane A. Page, eds., *Beyond Tracking: Finding Success in Inclusive Schools* (Bloomington, Ind.: Phi Delta Kappa Educational Foundation, 1995). Quantitative studies employing appropriate controls for prior achievement rebut the assertion, however, and no discriminatory effect in group placement is detected, at the elementary level, in Emil J. Haller and Susan Davis, "Does Socioeconomic Status Bias the Assignment of Students to Reading Groups?" *American Education Research Journal,* vol. 17, no. 4 (1980), pp. 409–18; Emil J. Haller, "Pupil Race and Elementary School Ability Grouping: Are Teachers Biased against Black Children?" *American Educational Research Journal,* vol. 22, no. 4 (1985), pp. 465–83. At the secondary level, Gamoran and Mare actually uncover a 10 percent advantage, with background variables held constant, for black students to be assigned to high tracks; Adam Gamoran and Robert D. Mare, "Secondary School Tracking and Educational Inequality: Compensation, Reinforcement, or Neutrality?" *American Journal of Sociology,* vol. 94, no. 5 (1989), pp. 1146–83. In a reevaluation of the data using transcript records, however, Lucas and Gamoran found that the advantage evaporates when the racial composition of schools is controlled, suggesting that predominantly minority, inner city schools bias the estimate; they are more likely to place students with low test scores into the academic track than are predominantly white, suburban schools; Samuel R. Lucas and Adam Gamoran, "Race and Track Assignment: A Reconsideration with Course-Based Indicators," Working Paper (University of Wisconsin–Madison, 1993).

15. A few studies have modeled elements of instruction. Adam Gamoran, Martin Nystrand, Mark Berends, and Paul C. LePore, "An Organizational Analysis of the Effects of Ability Grouping," *American Educational Research Journal,* vol. 32, no. 4 (1995), pp. 687–715. Differential effects of instructional strategies are uncovered, with authentic questioning by teachers and class discussion positively associated with achievement in high-ability classes but negatively associated in low-ability classes. Epstein and MacIver found that an emphasis on problem solving activities promoted higher math achievement, and they also found that homogeneously grouped algebra classes were more productive than heterogeneously grouped classes, Joyce L. Epstein and Douglas J. MacIver, *Opportunities to Learn: Effects on Eighth Graders of Curriculum Offerings and Instructional Approaches,* Report 34 (Baltimore: Center for Research on Effective Schooling for Disadvantaged Students, The Johns Hopkins University,

1992). In their study of first-grade reading groups, Barr and Dreeben document differential curricular coverage of high- and low-ability groups but expressly warn against using these instructional differences as justification for moving struggling readers to higher groups; Rebecca Barr and Robert Dreeben, *How Schools Work* (University of Chicago Press, 1983). I discuss ways of improving low tracks in Loveless, "The Tracking and Ability Grouping Debate."

16. Valerie E. Lee and Anthony S. Bryk, "A Multilevel Model of the Social Distribution of High School Achievement," *Sociology of Education,* vol. 62, no. 3 (July 1989), pp. 172–92.

17. Laura M. Argys, Daniel I. Rees, and Dominic J. Brewer, "Detracking America's Schools: Equity at Zero Cost?" *Journal of Policy Analysis and Management,* vol. 15, no. 4 (1996), pp. 623–45.

18. National Center for Educational Statistics, *Reading and Mathematics Achievement: Growth in High School* (Washington: National Center for Educational Statistics, 1997).

19. For more on problem definition, see David A. Rochefort and Roger W. Cobb, eds., *The Politics of Problem Definition: Shaping the Policy Agenda* (University Press of Kansas, 1994). For two different perspectives on agenda setting, see the institutional-environmental equilibrium analysis of Frank R. Baumgartner and Bryan D. Jones, *Agendas and Instability in American Politics* (University of Chicago Press, 1993); and the communications and media analysis of James W. Dearing and Everett M. Rogers, *Agenda-Setting* (Thousand Oaks, Calif.: Sage Publications, 1996).

20. Nancy C. Roberts and Paula J. King, *Transforming Public Policy: Dynamics of Policy Entrepreneurship and Innovation* (San Francisco: Jossey-Bass, 1995). For descriptions of the impact of *Sputnik* see Diane Ravitch, *The Troubled Crusade* (Basic Books, 1983); and for discussion of *A Nation at Risk,* see Rick Ginsberg and David N. Plank, eds., *Commissions Reports, Reforms, and Educational Policy* (Westport, Conn.: Praeger, 1995).

21. John W. Kingdon, *Agendas, Alternatives, and Public Policies* (Harper Collins, 1984), p. 187.

22. John I. Goodlad, *A Place Called School* (McGraw-Hill, 1984); Kenneth A. Tye, *The Junior High* (University Press of America, 1985).

23. The *Social Science Citation Index* is available on Hollis Plus, Harvard University's online library reference service.

24. Oakes, *Keeping Track,* pp. xiii–xv.

25. Although varying from year to year, the standard deviation of NAEP scores is approximately 38. In standard deviation units, then, the black-white gap in reading shrank from about one full standard deviation to one-half from the early 1970s to the mid-1980s and then added about one-fourth of a standard deviation from the mid-1980s to the mid-1990s. For a full discussion, see Larry V. Hedges and Amy Nowell, "Black-White Test Score Convergence Since 1965," in Christopher Jencks and Meredith Phillips (eds.), *The Black-White Test Score Gap* (Brookings, 1998).

26. Status dropout rates lump together GED recipients and high school graduates. Since minority students disproportionately receive GED certificates, the race gap is wider than shown in table 2-4. However, event dropout rates, measuring dropouts in grades 10–12, show essentially the same trend—steady improvement among African

Americans that stalled in the middle to late 1980s. See U.S. Department of Education, National Center for Educational Statistics, *Dropout Rates in the United States, 1996* (U.S. Department of Education, 1997).

27. Paul Peterson, *The Politics of School Reform, 1870–1940* (University of Chicago Press, 1985); Diane Ravitch, *The Revisionists Revised* (Basic Books, 1978).

28. Oakes, *Keeping Track,* pp. 16, 17.

29. Ibid., p. 21.

30. William J. Reese, *The Origins of the American High School* (Yale University Press, 1995), p. 14.

31. David L. Angus, Jeffrey W. Mirel, and Maris A. Vinovskis, "Historical Development of Age-Stratification in Schooling," *Teachers College Record,* vol. 90, no. 2 (1988), pp. 211–36.

32. David B. Tyack, *The One Best System: A History of American Urban Education* (Harvard University Press, 1974), p. 44–45.

33. Reese, *American High School,* pp. 153–54.

34. Michael B. Katz, *The Irony of Early School Reform: Educational Innovation in Mid-Nineteenth Century Massachusetts* (Harvard University Press, 1968). Katz's emphasis on class conflict as the deciding element in the referendum is questioned in Maris Vinovskis, *The Origins of Public High Schools: A Reexamination of the Beverly High School Controversy* (University of Wisconsin Press, 1985). Both Vinovskis's and Katz's views are presented in Maris A. Vinovskis, *Education, Society, and Economic Opportunity* (Yale University Press, 1995). See also David L. Angus, "Conflict, Class, and the Nineteenth-Century Public High School in the Cities of the Midwest, 1845–1900," *Curriculum Inquiry,* vol. 18, no. 1 (1988), pp. 7–25.

35. Harold Rugg, "Three Decades of Mental Discipline: Curriculum-Making Via National Committees," in *The Foundations and Technique of Curriculum-Construction,* Guy Montrose Whipple, ed., *The Twenty-sixth Yearbook of the National Society for the Study of Education,* part 1 (Bloomington, Ill.: Public School Publishing Company, 1926), p. 40.

36. David L. Angus, "A Note on the Occupational Background of Public High School Students prior to 1940," *Journal of the Midwest History of Education Society,* vol. 9 (1981), pp. 158–83. Maris Vinovskis's study of 1875 school attendance in Massachusetts shows that 16.7 percent of children attended at least some high school. See chapter 9 in Vinovskis, *Education, Society and Economic Opportunity.* Jeffrey Mirel, book review of *The Once and Future School* by Jurgen Herbst, *American Journal of Education,* vol. 106, no. 2 (1998), pp. 334–40.

37. Rugg, "Three Decades." See also Herbert M. Kliebard, *The Struggle for the American Curriculum 1893–1958* (Routledge, 1987).

38. David F. Labaree, *The Making of an American High School* (Yale University Press, 1988). Labaree explicitly rejects both the functionalist and reproductionist explanations for Central High's introduction of tracking in 1889. No rapid growth in enrollment preceded the differentiation of curriculum, and though the tracking system obviously played to middle class interests, to ignore them would have been unthinkable; middle class parents were the school's primary constituents. But contrary to the reproductionist idea of class dominance, the school was altering its curricular structures as a defensive response to environmental changes. In Labaree's telling, Central High's decision is an institution's pragmatic response to changes in the value of its diploma,

the demands of its clients, and the professional outlook of its faculty. See also David F. Labaree, "Curriculum, Credentials, and the Middle Class: A Case Study of a Nineteenth-Century High School," *Sociology of Education*, vol. 59 (January 1986), pp. 42–57.

39. Oakes, *Keeping Track*, pp. 27 and 35. Oakes's account of G. Stanley Hall is incomplete. Although his bigotry was real, far from being representative of fellow educators' thinking on social issues, Hall was thought to be a bit of a crackpot. His biographer, Dorothy Ross, reports, "There was some feeling in the profession that Hall had so tainted child study with popular pseudoscience that no 'respectable' scientists wanted anything to do with it." In Dorothy Ross, *G. Stanley Hall: The Psychologist as Prophet* (University of Chicago Press, 1972), p. 286. Hall's child study movement, a subgroup of the movement generally known as progressive education, supported curricular differentiation as an outgrowth of his theories on human development, in particular, the notion that cognitive capacities develop sequentially along a course dictated by nature. In the 1990s, the influence of Hall's theories is reflected in such practices as developmentally appropriate instruction, the use of manipulatives in instruction, exhortations to teach "the whole child," constructivism, the concern that schooling may be too centered on academic learning, and viewing the education of adolescents as a specialized field. Curiously, detracking advocates have not asserted, as they have with curriculum differentiation, that Hall's social Darwinism contaminates these practices and beliefs, and, in fact, notable tracking critics have even embraced some of them. See Jeannie Oakes, Amy Stuart Wells, Makeba Jones, and Amand Datnow, "Detracking: The Social Construction of Ability, Cultural Politics, and Resistance to Reform," *Teachers College Record*, vol. 98, no. 3 (1997), pp. 482–510.

40. Selwyn K. Troen, *The Public and the Schools: Shaping the St. Louis System, 1838–1920* (University of Missouri Press, 1975), p. 175. See footnote 26 on p. 175 for an extensive list of studies culled from *American Apprenticeship* by Paul Douglas. The term "retardation" evolved into "overageness" by the 1920s, when studies documented that it was still a problem. (See Fred Engelhardt, "Pupil Classification As Affected by Organization and Administrative Practice," in Guy Montrose Whipple, ed., *The Grouping of Pupils, Thirty-fifth Yearbook of the National Society for the Study of Education*, part 1 [Bloomington, Ill.: Public School Publishing Company, 1936], p. 21.)

41. UCLA's antitracking researchers have urged a redefinition of "what it means to be smart," supported dividing high school history and English curricula into ethnic and gender concentrations, and criticized advanced placement (AP) courses as an affront to "more creative, multidisciplinary ways of thinking about learning and instruction." See Jeannie Oakes, Amy Stuart Wells, and Associates, *Beyond the Technicalities of School Reform* (Los Angeles: UCLA Graduate School of Education and Information Studies, 1996).

42. Rugg, *The Foundations and Technique of Curriculum-Construction*, pp. 44–45. Two examples of turn-of-the-century urban superintendents who struggled with the question of curriculum differentiation before deciding that it helped to democratize education, especially for poor immigrant students, are William Henry Maxwell of New York City (see Diane Ravitch, *The Great School Wars: A History of the New York City Public Schools* [Basic Books, 1988], pp. 167–83); and Frank Cody of Detroit (see Jeffrey Mirel, *The Rise and Fall of an Urban School System: Detroit, 1907–81* (Ann Arbor: University of Michigan Press), pp. 66–72.

43. Mirel, *Rise and Fall of an Urban School System*, p. 71; Peterson, *The Politics of School Reform*, p. 59.

44. Lawrence Cremin, *The Transformation of the School* (Random House, 1961), p. 42; Peterson, *The Politics of School Reform*.

45. David Tyack and Larry Cuban, *Tinkering toward Utopia* (Harvard University Press, 1995) pp. 69–70.

46. In the interest of fairness, when analysts attribute evil motives to the establishment of past policies, they should document policymakers' intentions with hard evidence. A simple illustration: in the 1960s, reformers promoting greater social equality developed a Title I program to which participating students were assigned by their families' economic status. In the 1970s, reformers developed a bilingual program which gathered students into special classes on the basis of their ethnicity. Although both programs led to a degree of class and ethnic segregation, these policies' supporters were certainly not social Darwinists.

47. Anne Wheelock, *Crossing the Tracks: How Untracking Can Save America's Schools* (New York: New Press, 1992), p. x.

48. For a collection of articles written in the wake of *A Nation at Risk*, see Beatrice and Ronald Gross, eds., *The Great School Debate: Which Way for American Education?* (New York: Touchstone, 1985). The book also includes the complete text of *A Nation at Risk*. American public opinion on schooling is summarized in Stanley Elam, *How America Views Its Schools: The PDK/Gallup Polls, 1969–1994* (Bloomington, Ind.: Phi Delta Kappa Educational Foundation, 1995). The role of the press in shaping views on education is critically reviewed in George R. Kaplan, *Images of Education: The Mass Media's Version of America's Schools* (Washington, D.C.: Institute for Educational Leadership, 1992). I give my own interpretation of the ambiguous public opinion data, arguing that public confidence in education consists of both attitudes and behaviors, in Tom Loveless, "The Structure of Public Confidence in Education," *American Journal of Education*, vol. 105 (February 1997), pp. 127–59.

49. "The Educational Reform Movement of the 1980s: A Comprehensive Analysis," in Joseph Murphy, ed., *The Educational Reform Movement of the 1890s* (Berkeley, Calif.: McCutchan Publishing, 1990, p. 25.

50. Louis G. Romano, Nicholas P. Gerogiaddy, and James E. Heald, eds., *The Middle School* (Chicago: Nelson-Hall, 1973); Mauritz Johnson, ed., *Toward Adolescence: The Middle School Years, Seventy-ninth Yearbook of the National Society for the Study of Education* (University of Chicago Press, 1980).

51. Jerry Valentine, Donald C. Clark, Neal C. Nickerson, Jr., and James W. Keefe, *The Middle Level Principalship: A Survey of Middle Level Principals and Programs* (Reston, Va.: National Association of Secondary School Principals, 1981); Gordon Cawelti, "Middle Schools a Better Match with Early Adolescent Needs, ASCD Survey Finds," *Curriculum Update*, November 1988, pp. 1–12 (quotation from p. 8); Joyce L. Epstein and Douglas J. MacIver, *Education in the Middle Grades: Overview of National Practices and Trends, Report No. 45* (Baltimore: Center for Research on Elementary and Middle Schools, The Johns Hopkins University, 1990).

52. Jomills H. Braddock II, "Tracking the Middle Grades: National Patterns of Grouping for Instruction," *Phi Delta Kappan*, vol. 71, no. 6 (1990), pp. 445–49 (quotation on p. 449). See also Paul S. George, "Tracking and Ability Grouping: Which Way for the Middle School?" *Middle School Journal*, vol. 20, no. 1 (1988), pp. 21–

28; Jeannie Oakes and others, "Creating Middle Schools: Technical, Normative, and Political Considerations," *The Elementary School Journal*, vol. 93, no. 5 (1993), pp. 461–80.

53. Anne Wheelock, *Crossing the Tracks.* The popular press accounts are from Susan D. Allan, "Ability Grouping Research Reviews: What Do They Say about Grouping and the Gifted?" *Educational Leadership*, vol. 48, no. 6 (March 1991), pp. 60–67.

54. Carnegie Council on Adolescent Development, *Turning Points: Preparing American Youth for the Twenty-first Century* (New York: Carnegie Corporation, 1989), p. 49.

55. Kingdon, *Agendas,* p. 187.

56. Jane J. Mansbridge, *Why We Lost the ERA* (University of Chicago Press, 1986).

57. Sarah Lake, *Equal Access to Education: Alternatives to Tracking and Ability Grouping,* Practitioner Monograph #2 (Sacramento: California League of Middle Schools, 1988).

58. Wheelock, *Crossing the Tracks.*

59. CSDE, *Caught in the Middle,* p. 56.

60. Ibid., p. vii.

61. California State Department of Education, *Mathematics Framework for California Public Schools* (Sacramento: CSDE, 1992).

62. California State Department of Education, *Quality Criteria for Middle Grades* (Sacramento: CSDE, 1988), p. 38; California State Department of Education, *English–Language Arts Framework* (Sacramento: CSDE, 1987); CSDE, *Mathematics Framework. Mathematics Framework,* p. 60.

63. MDOE, *Magic in the Middle,* pp. 5–6. See also MDOE, *Structuring Schools for Student Success.*

64. *Magic in the Middle,* p. 20.

65. *Intercom,* "CAG Meets with Superintendent Honig" (Canoga Park: California Association for the Gifted), May 1989, p. 2, and December 1989, p. 1.

Chapter Three

1. See Jeannie Oakes, Amy Stuart Wells, and Associates, *Beyond the Technicalities of School Reform* (Los Angeles: UCLA Graduate School of Education and Information Studies, September 1996). Also see Oakes's "Can Tracking Research Inform Practice? Technical, Normative, and Political Considerations," *Educational Researcher,* vol. 21, no. 4 (May 1992), pp. 12–21.

2. Jeannie Oakes, Amy Stuart Wells, Makeba Jones, and Amand Datnow "Detracking: The Social Construction of Ability, Cultural Politics, and Resistance to Reform," *Teachers College Record,* vol. 98, no. 3 (1997), pp. 482–510.

3. Amy Stuart Wells and Jeannie Oakes, "Potential Pitfalls of Systemic Reform: Early Lessons from Detracking Research," *Sociology of Education,* extra issue (1996), pp. 135–43. Quotation from page 140.

4. Oakes, Wells, and Associates, *Beyond the Technicalities,* p. 21.

5. Ibid., p. 17.

6. Ibid., p. 24.

7. L. Bernstein, *Policy Changes and School Climate: An Analysis of the NAEP School Questionnaire, 1987–1988* (Princeton, N.J.: Educational Testing Service, 1990);

A. M. Huberman and M. B. Miles, *Innovation Up Close* (New York: Plenum Press, 1984).

8. David Tyack, "Public School Reform: Policy Talk and Institutional Practice," *American Journal of Education,* vol. 100, no. 1 (November 1991), pp. 1–19. Paul Berman and Milbrey McLaughlin (*Federal Programs Supporting Educational Change,* vols. 1–8, [Santa Monica, Calif.: Rand Corporation, 1974–1978]) provided some of the earliest documentation that failing schools tend to embrace reform. Also see John W. Meyer and Brian Rowan, "The Structure of Educational Organizations," in M. Meyer ed., *Environments and Organizations* (San Francisco: Jossey-Bass, 1978), pp. 78–109. Balridge and Deal portray educational reform as a symbolic alternative to substantive change, a conclusion reached again over a decade later in Hess's study of urban school reform; V. J. Balridge and T. Deal, eds., *The Dynamics of Organizational Change in Education* (Berkeley, Calif.: McCutchan, 1983); and Frederick M. Hess, *Spinning Wheels: The Politics of Urban School Reform* (Brookings, 1999).

9. Paul Berman, "Educational Change: An Implementation Paradigm," in Rolf Lehming and Michael Kane, eds., *Improving Schools: Using What We Know* (Beverly Hills, Calif.: Sage Publications, 1981), p. 269.

10. The idea that voters respond to cues when deciding their vote is a classic theory of political science. Bernard R. Berelson, Paul F. Lazerfeld, and William N. McPhee, *Voting: A Study of Opinion Formation in a Presidential Campaign* (University of Chicago Press, 1954); Angus Campbell, Philip E. Converse, Warren E. Miller, and Donald E. Stokes, *The American Voter* (University of Chicago Press, 1960).

11. Rebecca Barr and Robert Dreeben, *How Schools Work* (University of Chicago Press, 1983). See also Rebecca Barr and Robert Dreeben, "The Formation and Instruction of Ability Groups," *American Journal of Education,* vol. 97, no. 1 (1988), pp. 34–64.

12. Maureen T. Hallinan, "The Organization of Students for Instruction in Middle School," *Sociology of Education,* vol. 95, no. 2 (1992), pp. 114–27; Brain DeLany, "Allocation, Choice, and Stratification: How the Sorting Machine Copes," *American Journal of Education,* vol. 99, no. 2 (1991), pp. 181–207.

13. Carolyn M. Evertson, Julie P. Sanford, and Edmund T. Emmer, "Effects of Class Heterogeneity in Junior High School," *American Educational Research Journal,* vol. 18, no. 2 (Summer 1981), pp. 219–32; Susan Moore Johnson, *Teachers at Work* (Basic Books, 1990).

14. Everston, Sanford, and Emmer, "Effects of Class Heterogeneity in Junior High School." In contrast, Jeffrey Leiter found no significant effect of class heterogeneity on third grade math or reading achievement in Jeffrey Leiter, "Classroom Composition and Achievement Gains," *Sociology of Education,* vol. 56 (July 1983), pp. 126–32. The argument that tracking makes teaching more efficient is presented by C. Nevi, "In Defense of Tracking," *Educational Leadership,* vol. 89, no. 3 (1987), pp. 283–304.

15. A. Michael Huberman and Michael B. Miles, *Innovation Up Close* (New York: Plenum Press, 1984), p. 176; Lawrence Bernstein, *Policy Changes and School Climate: An Analysis of the NAEP School Questionnaire, 1987–1988* (Princeton, N.J.: Educational Testing Service, 1990).

16. John H. Lounsberry, *Perspectives: Middle School Education, 1964–1984* (Columbus, Ohio: National Middle School Association, 1984). For an early book on junior highs, see Aubrey Augustus Douglass, *The Junior High,* The 15th Yearbook of the Na-

tional Society for the Study of Education (Bloomingon, Ill.: Public School Publishing Company, 1916).

17. David H. Monk and Emil J. Haller, "Predictors of High School Academic Course Offerings: The Role of School Size," *American Education Research Journal,* vol. 30, no. 1 (Spring 1993), pp. 3–21. On the vertical relationship of organizational size in districts, schools, and classrooms, see Charles E. Bidwell and John D. Kasarda, "School District Organization and Student Achievement," *American Sociological Review,* vol. 40 (February 1975), pp. 55–70; and Robert W. Jewell, "School and School District Size Relationships: Costs, Results, Minorities, and Private School Enrollments," *Education and Urban Society,* vol. 21, no. 2 (1989), pp. 140–53.

18. J. B. Conant, *The American High School Today* (McGraw-Hill, 1959).

19. United States Department of Education, *120 Years of American Education* (Washington: U.S. Department of Education, 1993), table 20.

20. James Q. Wilson, *Bureaucracy* (Basic Books, 1989). Academic and practitioner perspectives are presented as a clash of cultures in J. Ruddick, "Dissemination as Encounter of Cultures," *Research Intelligence,* vol. 3 (1977), pp. 3–5. Teacher conservatism in the face of instability is documented in Dan C. Lortie, *Schoolteacher: A Sociological Study* (University of Chicago Press, 1975). The "creative insubordination" of urban school principals is described in Van Cleve Morris, Robert L. Crowson, Emanuel Hurwitz, Jr., and Cynthia Porter-Gehrie, "The Urban Principal: Middle Manager in the Educational Bureaucracy," *Urban Review,* vol. 63, no. 10 (1982), pp. 689–92.

21. Wallace S. Sayre and Herbert Kaufman, *Governing New York City* (New York: Russell Sage Foundation, 1960).

22. Amy Stuart Wells and Irene Serna, "The Politics of Culture: Understanding Local Political Resistance to Detracking in Racially Mixed Schools," *Harvard Educational Review,* vol. 66, no. 1 (1996), pp. 93–118.

23. Jean Johnson and John Immerwhar, *First Things First: What Americans Expect from the Public Schools* (New York: Public Agenda, 1994), pp. 18–19.

24. Sam D. Sieber, "Knowledge Utilization in Public Education: Incentives and Disincentives," in Rolf Lehming and Michael Kane, eds., *Improving Schools: Using What We Know* (Beverly Hills, Calif.: Sage Publications, 1981), 115–16, 142. Paul Berman and E. W. Pauly, *Federal Programs Supporting Educational Change,* vol. 1 (Santa Monica, Calif.: Rand Corp., 1975). For more on the ground-level politics of implementation, see Michael Lipsky, *Street-Level Bureaucracy* (New York: Russell Sage Foundation, 1980). Two seminal texts on politics and education policy are Ernest R. House, *The Politics of Educational Innovation* (Berkeley, Calif.: McCutchan, 1974); and Frederick M. Wirt and Michael W. Kirst, *Schools in Conflict* (Berkeley, Calif.: McCutchan, 1976).

Chapter Four

1. Jomills Henry Braddock II, "Tracking the Middle Grades: National Patterns of Grouping for Instruction," *Phi Delta Kappan,* vol. 71 no. 6 (February 1990), p. 449.

2. Quote referring to the Massachusetts State Department of Education as a leader is from Diego Ribadeneira, "State Seen as Leader in Urban School Reform," *Boston Globe,* July 23, 1990, p. 17. Also see Diego Ribadeneira, "Schools Panel Calls for End to 'Tracking,' " *Boston Globe,* June 26, 1991, p. 1; Margaret Combs, "Aiming for

Equity in Springfield," *Boston Globe,* February 28, 1993, p. 37; Jay Caldwell, "In Amherst, Minds Meet on the Tracks," *Boston Globe,* September 21, 1993, p. 17; Jennifer Kingson Bloom, "Panel Recommends Cambridge Schools End Tracking," *Boston Globe,* November 1, 1993, p. 17.

3. Consistent with the findings of this study, Chubb and Moe found Asian students more likely enrolled in tracked classes in the NELS sample. And black students were slightly more likely enrolled in heterogeneously grouped classes. John E. Chubb and Terry M. Moe, "Politics, Markets, and Equality in Schools," paper delivered at the Annual Meeting of the American Political Science Association, September 3–6, 1992.

4. Paul Berman and Milbrey Wallin McLaughlin, *Federal Programs Supporting Educational Change,* vol. 7: *Factors Affecting Implementation and Continuation* (Santa Monica.: Rand, 1977), p. 165. Also see V. J. Balridge and T. Deal, eds., *The Dynamics of Organizational Change in Education* (Berkeley, Calif.: McCutchan, 1983); and Frederick M. Hess, *Spinning Wheels: The Politics of Urban School Reform* (Brookings 1999).

5. As an alternative strategy, I modeled achievement and heterogeneity in a single variable, sorting schools into three categories—high-homogeneous, middle-heterogeneous, and low-homogeneous—and ran the analyses again. The findings were the same. High-homogeneous schools tended to be tracked; low-homogeneous schools tended to be untracked; and the middle-heterogeneous schools fell somewhere in between. I concluded that heterogeneity does not drive policy. Schools with equally narrow bands of performance adopted different policies, tracking at the high end of achievement and detracking at the low end.

This noneffect is interesting, but I may have misspecified heterogeneity, measuring the right factor at the wrong level of analysis. As the case study interviews show, the spread of achievement within classes, rather than schoolwide, probably has a greater effect on teachers' positions on tracking. School officials can dampen achievement heterogeneity before it reaches the classroom by taking such measures as scheduling, during the same period, electives that differentially attract high- and low-achieving students (for example, foreign language and shop, orchestra and teen world). Students sort themselves into these electives, and because of the vagaries of scheduling, share academic classes with the same classmates during the rest of the day.

6. Robert Jewell, "School and District Size Relationships: Costs, Results, Minorities, and Private School Enrollments," *Education and Urban Society,* vol. 21, no. 2 (February 1989), pp. 140–53.

7. Unks (pp. 182–84) points out that small schools often exhibit innovations that are adopted out of necessity. Gerald Unks, "Differences in Curriculum within a School Setting," *Education and Urban Society,* vol. 21, no. 2 (Febraury 1989), pp. 175–91. The difficulties encountered by small rural districts are detailed in Richard A. Schmuck and Patricia A. Schmuck, *Small Districts, Big Problems* (Newbury Park, Calif.: Corwin Press, 1992).

8. Peter M. Blau, "A Formal Theory of Differentiation in Organizations," *American Sociological Review,* vol. 35, no. 2 (April 1970), pp. 201–18.

9. T. B. Gregory and G. R. Smith, *High Schools as Communities: The Small School Reconsidered* (Bloomington, Ind: Phi Delta Kappan Educational Foundation, 1987).

10. The survey showed 167 schools reporting schoolwide teaming out of 625 respondents. California Department of Education, *Implementation of Middle Grade Re-*

forms in California Public Schools: 1988–89 through 1992–93 (Sacramento: California State Department of Education, 1993), p. 7.

11. See James M. McPartland, J. Robert Coldiron, and Jomills H. Braddock II, *School Structures and Classroom Practices in Elementary, Middle, and Secondary Schools,* Report No. 14 (Baltimore: Center for Research on Elementary and Middle Schools, Johns Hopkins University, June 1987). Note that 90 percent of Massachusetts schools serve either grades 5–8 or grades 6–8. Grade 6–8 schools are the most popular graded form in both states, and grade 7–9, the traditional junior high grade levels, and the most popular configuration as recently as the 1970s, is fading into oblivion.

12. A 1981 survey reported the following percentages of middle school principals held secondary administration credentials: 77 percent in grade 7–9 schools, 61 percent in grade 7–8 schools, and 51 percent in grade 6–8 schools. Jerry Valentine, Donald C. Clark, Neal C. Nickelson, Jr., and James W. Keefe, *The Middle Level Principalship: A Survey of Middle Level Principals and Programs* (Reston, Va.: National Association of Secondary School Principals, 1981). Grade 7–9 schools are about three times more likely than grade 6–8 schools to have three-quarters of faculty holding secondary certification. The breakdown: grade 6–8, 22.1 percent; grade 7–8, 42.4 percent; grade 7–9, 70.8 percent. James M. McPartland, "Staffing Decisions in the Middle Grades," *Phi Delta Kappan,* vol. 71, no. 6 (February 1990), pp. 465–69.

13. McPartland, Coldiron, and Braddock, *School Structures and Classroom Practices,* p. 20.

14. Jean Johnson and John Immerwahr, *First Things First: What Americans Expect from the Public Schools* (New York: Public Agenda Foundation, 1994), pp. 18–19.

15. I first presented this argument in "Parents, Professionals, and the Politics of Tracking." Tom Loveless, "Parents, Professionals, and the Politics of Tracking Policy," in Kenneth K. Wong, ed., *Advances in Educational Policy,* vol. 1 (New York: JAI Press, 1995), pp. 187–212.

16. Talcott Parsons, *The Social System* (New York: Free Press, 1951).

17. Dan C. Lortie, *Schoolteacher: A Sociological Study* (University of Chicago Press, 1975); Susan Moore Johnson, *Teachers at Work: Achieving Success in Our Schools* (Basic Books, 1990).

Chapter Five

1. David Tyack, Thomas James, and Aaron Benavot, *Law and the Shaping of Public Education, 1785–1954* (University of Wisconsin Press, 1987).

2. Lawrence A. Cremin, *American Education: The National Experience, 1783–1876* (Harper & Row, 1980), p. 182.

3. Ibid., data from table 2, pp. 182–85. On the early years of California's educational system, see Nicholas C. Polos, *John Swett: California's Frontier Schoolmaster* (University Press of America, 1978); Leighton Henry Johnson, *Development of the Central State Agency for Public Education in California, 1849–1949* (University of New Mexico Press, 1952).

4. Samuel Eliot Morison, *The Intellectual Life of Colonial New England* (Cornell University Press, 1956).

5. Cremin, *American Education.* I discuss historical tensions created by the state's role in education in Tom Loveless, "Uneasy Allies: The Evolving Relationship of

School and State," *Educational Evaluation and Policy Analysis,* vol. 20, no. 1 (Spring 1998), pp. 1–8.

6. Wirt bases his state centralization scale on Daniel Elazar's theory of state political cultures. Wirt uses the scale to test whether centralization is correlated with traditional, moral, or individualistic traditions. See Frederick M. Wirt, "School Policy Culture and State Decentralization," in Jay D. Scribner, ed., *The Politics of Education,* The Seventy-Sixth Yearbook of the National Society for the Study of Education, part 2 (University of Chicago Press, 1977), pp. 164–87; Daniel J. Elazar, *American Federalism* (Thomas Y. Crowell Co., 1972).

7. Wirt, "School Policy Culture and State Decentralization," p. 184.

8. At the time of the study California districts had to spend 85 percent of their allotted textbook monies on state-approved texts or seek a waiver for the purchase of nonapproved texts. Kenneth K. Wong and Tom Loveless, "The Politics of Textbook Policy in the United States: Proposing a Framework," in Philip G. Altbach, ed., *Textbooks in American Education: Politics, Policy, and Pedagogy* (SUNY Press, 1991), pp. 27–41.

9. California State Department of Education, *Quality Criteria for Middle Grades* (Sacramento: California State Department of Education, 1988); California State Department of Education, *Guide and Criteria for Program Quality Review—Middle Grades* (Sacramento: California State Department of Education, 1990).

10. For case studies of one superintendent's detracking initiative and another superintendent's response to public outcry when it was announced that an advanced placement class would be abolished, see Susan Moore Johnson, *Leading to Change: The Challenge of the New Superintendency* (San Francisco: Jossey-Bass Publishers, 1996).

11. Responses indicating "both" sources were coded as district policy so that "school" policy in this analysis reflects maximal autonomy in school decision-making.

12. Jeffrey Mirel, *The Rise and Fall of an Urban Public School System* (University of Michigan Press, 1993); Paul Peterson, *School Politics Chicago Style* (University of Chicago Press, 1976); Diane Ravitch, *The Great School Wars: A History of the New York City Public Schools* (Basic Books, 1974); David Tyack, *The One Best System: A History of American Urban Education* (Harvard University Press, 1974).

13. John Chubb and Terry Moe, *Politics, Markets, and America's Schools* (Brookings, 1990).

14. For a comprehensive, fascinating discussion of governmental organizations, see James Q. Wilson, *Bureaucracy* (Basic Books, 1985). Must-reads analyzing school districts' organizational characteristics include Charles E. Bidwell, "The School as a Formal Organization," in James G. March, ed., *Handbook of Organizations* (Chicago: Rand McNally, 1965), pp. 972–1022; and Roald F. Campbell and others, *The Organization and Control of American Schools,* 4th ed. (Columbus, Oh.: Merrill, 1980).

15. Peter M. Blau, "A Formal Theory of Differentiation in Organizations," *American Sociological Review,* vol. 35, no. 2 (1970), pp. 201–18.

16. John W. Meyer and W. Richard Scott, *Organizational Environments: Ritual and Rationality* (Beverly Hills, Calif.: Sage, 1983).

17. See L. Peter Jennergen, "Decentralization in Organizations," in Paul C. Nystrom and William H. Starbuck, eds., *Handbook of Organizational Design* (Oxford University Press, 1980), pp. 39–59.

18. National Center for Educational Statistics, *Digest of Educational Statistics* (Washington: Department of Education, 1995), table 89. Districts do not add up to 100 percent because of 2.5 percent not reporting size.

19. Peterson, *School Politics Chicago Style;* James G. Cibulka, Rodney Reed, and Kenneth K. Wong, eds., *The Politics of Urban Education in the United States,* The 1991 Yearbook of the Politics of Education Association (Washington, D.C.: Falmer Press, 1992).

20. Jane Hannaway, "Political Pressure and Decentralization in Institutional Organizations: The Case of School Districts," *Sociology of Education,* vol. 66, no. 3 (1993), pp. 147–63.

21. George S. Counts, *The Social Composition of Boards of Education* (University of Chicago Press, 1927); Laurence Ianaccone, *Politics in Education* (New York: Center for Applied Research in Education, Inc., 1967); Frederick M. Wirt and Michael W. Kirst, *Schools in Conflict,* 2d ed. (Berkeley, Calif.: McCutchan Publishing Corporation, 1989). On reforming school boards, see Jacqueline P. Danzberger, Michael W. Kirst, and Michael D. Usdan, *Governing Public Schools: New Times, New Requirements* (Washington, D.C.: Institute for Educational Leadership, 1992).

22. A residual centralizing effect remains for urban schools in Massachusetts.

23. James P. Spillane, "How Districts Mediate between State Policy and Teachers' Practice," in Richard F. Elmore and Susan H. Fuhrman, eds., *The Governance of Curriculum,* 1994 Yearbook of the Association for Supervision and Curriculum Development (Alexandria, Va.: ASCD, 1994), pp. 167–85. For an analysis of recent trends in educational governance, see Michael W. Kirst, "Who's in Charge? Federal, State, and Local Control," in Diane Ravitch and Maris A. Vinovskis, eds., *Learning from the Past* (Johns Hopkins University Press, 1995).

Chapter Six

1. An earlier version of this chapter is presented in Tom Loveless, "The Influence of Subject Areas on Middle School Tracking Policies," in Aaron Pallas, ed., *Research in Sociology of Education and Socialization* (New York: JAI Press, 1994), pp. 147–75.

2. Susan S. Stodolsky, *The Subject Matters: Classroom Activity in Math and Social Studies* (University of Chicago Press, 1988).

3. William. H. Schmidt and M. M. Kennedy, *Teachers' and Teacher Candidates' Beliefs about Subject Matter and Teaching Responsibilities,* Research Report 90-4 (East Lansing, Mich.: National Center for Research on Teacher Learning, 1990); Stephen W. Raudenbush, Brian Rowan, and Y. F. Cheong, "Higher Order Instructional Goals in Secondary Schools: Class, Teacher, and School Influences," *American Education Research Journal,* vol. 30 (1993), pp. 523–53.

4. Leslie Santee Siskin, "Departments as Different Worlds: Subject Subcultures in Secondary Schools," *Educational Administration Quarterly,* vol. 27, no. 2 (1991), pp. 134–60; quote from p. 147. Also see Leslie Santee Siskin, *Realms of Knowledge: Academic Departments in Secondary Schools* (Bristol, Penn.: Falmer Press, 1994); Leslie Santee Siskin and Judith Warren Little, eds., *The Subjects in Question: Departmental Organization and the High School* (New York: Teachers College Press, 1995).

5. Stephen J. Ball, *The Micro-Politics of the School* (London: Methuen, 1987).

6. Nancy M. Sanders, "Organizational Meanings of Curriculum Differentiation

Practices," in Reba Page and Linda Valli, eds., *Curriculum Differentiation* (SUNY Press, 1990), pp. 207–29; quote from p. 229.

7. Bruce L. Wilson and Gretchen B. Rossman, *Mandating Academic Excellence: High School Responses to State Curriculum Reform* (New York: Teachers College Press, 1993).

8. Gordon Cawelti, "Middle School a Better Match with Early Adolescent Needs, ASCD Survey Finds," *Curriculum Update*, November 1988, pp. 1–12; Joyce L. Epstein and Douglas J. MacIver, *Education in the Middle Grades: Overview of National Practices and Trends*, Report 45 (Baltimore: Center for Research on Elementary and Middle Schools, 1990).

9. Maureen T. Hallinan, "The Organization of Students for Instruction in Middle Schools," *Sociology of Education*, vol. 65, no. 2 (April 1992), pp. 114–27.

10. Elizabeth L. Useem, "Middle Schools and Math Groups: Parents' Involvement in Children's Placement," *Sociology of Education*, vol. 65, no. 4 (October 1992), pp. 263–79; Elizabeth L. Useem, "Getting on the Fast Track in Mathematics: School Organizational Influences on Math Track Assignment," *American Journal of Education*, vol. 100, no. 3 (May 1992), pp. 325–53, quote from p. 341.

11. California State Department of Education, *Mathematics Framework for California Schools* (Sacramento: California State Department of Education, 1992); Massachusetts Department of Education, *Mathematics Curriculum Framework* (Malden, Mass.: Massachusetts Department of Education, 1995). The 1992 California math framework was extensively revised and released, along with separate K–12 math standards, in 1998, after this study's conclusion. The latter documents present a mathematics curriculum markedly different from the NCTM recommendations. The California documents are available online at http://www.cde.ca.gov. The Massachusetts framework is available at http://www.msde.ma.gov.

12. J. A. Schwille, J. A. Porter, G. Belli, R. Floden, D. Freeman, L. Knappen, T. Kuhs, and W. Schmidt, "Teachers as Policy Brokers in the Content of Elementary Mathematics," in Lee S. Shulman and Gary Sykes, eds., *Handbook of Teaching and Policy* (New York: Longman, 1983); David K. Cohen and Deborah L. Ball, "Relations between Policy and Practice: A Commentary," *Educational Evaluation and Policy Analysis*, vol. 12, no. 3 (Fall 1990), pp. 331–38.

13. Romberg provides an extensive review of the research supporting the reform of mathematics along the lines of the NCTM proposals in Thomas A. Romberg, "Problematic Features of the School Mathematics Curriculum," in Phillip W. Jackson, ed., *Handbook of Research on Curriculum* (MacMillan, 1992).

14. The English curriculum changed in both states after 1996, moving toward greater specificity in learning objectives. Despite these changes, the differences between English and math still hold. See California State Department of Education, *English–Language Arts Framework* (Sacramento: California State Department of Education, 1987). The 1998 standards document may be retrieved online at http://www.cde.ca.gov. The 1997 Massachusetts framework was the state's first in English, Massachusetts State Department of Education, *English–Language Arts Curriculum Framework* (Malden, Mass.: Massachusetts State Department of Education, 1997).

15. Reba Page, *Lower Track Classrooms: A Curricular and Cultural Perspective* (New York: Teachers College Press, 1991), p. 182.

16. The 1996 NAEP data indicate 24 percent of eighth graders were in algebra

classes, 27 percent in pre-algebra, 44 percent in eighth grade math, and 5 percent in other placements. Catherine A. Shaughnessy, Jennifer E. Nelson, and Norma A. Norris, *NAEP 1996 Mathematics: Cross-State Data Compendium for the Grade 4 and Grade 8 Assessment* (Washington: U.S. Department of Education, 1998), table 6.26, pp. 167–68.

17. Siskin, *Realms of Knowledge;* David F. Labaree, *The Making of an American High School: The Credentials Market and the Central High School of Philadelphia, 1838–1939* (Yale University Press, 1988).

18. Susan Moore Johnson, *Teachers at Work* (Basic Books, 1990), pp. 184–85.

Chapter Seven

1. Jeannie Oakes, "Tracking, Inequality, and the Rhetoric of Reform: Why Schools Don't Change," *Journal of Education,* vol. 168, no. 1 (1986), pp. 60–80; Jeannie Oakes, Amy Stuart Wells, Makeba Jones, and Amanda Datnow, "Detracking: The Social Construction of Ability, Cultural Politics, and Resistance to Reform," *Teachers College Record,* vol. 98, no. 3 (Spring 1997), pp. 482–510.

2. Robert E. Slavin, "Achievement Effects of Ability Grouping in Secondary Schools: A Best Evidence Synthesis," *Review of Educational Research,* vol. 60, no. 3 (Fall 1990), pp. 471–99; quote from p. 494.

3. David K. Cohen and Deborah L. Ball, "Relations between Policy and Practice: A Commentary," *Educational Evaluation and Policy Analysis,* vol. 12, no. 3 (Fall 1990), p. 334.

4. Robert E. Slavin, "Cooperative Learning," *Review of Educational Research,* vol. 50, no. 2 (Summer 1980), pp. 315–42; Fred M. Newmann and Judith A. Thompson, *Effects of Cooperative Learning on Achievement in Secondary Schools: A Summary of Research* (Madison, Wisc.: National Center of Effective Secondary Schools, September 1987); Steven A. Bossert, "Cooperative Activities in the Classroom," in American Educational Research Association, *Review of Research in Education,* vol. 15 (Washington, D.C.: American Educational Research Association, 1988), pp. 225–50.

5. Advocates disagree on how to structure cooperative learning. Robert Slavin believes a group reward structure is necessary to motivate student teamwork. David Johnson and Roger Johnson, arguing from a humanist educational philosophy, believe that cooperation without intergroup competition is superior. See Slavin, "Cooperative Learning"; Robert E. Slavin, "When Does Cooperative Learning Increase Student Achievement?" *Psychological Bulletin,* vol. 94, no. 3 (1983), pp. 429–45; David W. Johnson and others, "Effects of Cooperative, Competitive, and Individualistic Goal Structures on Achievement: A Meta-Analysis," *Psychological Bulletin,* vol. 89, no. 1 (1982), pp. 47–62.

6. Recent studies of school restructuring include: Fred M. Newmann and Associates, *Authentic Achievement: Restructuring Schools for Intellectual Quality* (San Francisco: Jossey-Bass, 1996), a study of authentic pedagogy and other reforms in a national sample of twenty-four schools. Nancy E. Jennings, *Interpreting Policy in Real Classrooms: Case Studies of State Reform and Teacher Practice* (New York: Teachers College Press, 1996), the story of three teachers and their responses to Michigan's state efforts to change reading instruction, making reading less "skills based" and more focused on "constructing meaning." Richard F. Elmore, Penelope Peterson, and Sarah J.

McCarthy, *Restructuring in the Classroom* (San Francisco: Jossey-Bass, 1996), case studies of three elementary schools altering organizational structures and instructional practice. Ann Lieberman, ed., *The Work of Restructuring Schools: Building from the Ground Up* (New York: Teachers College Press, 1995), case studies of several schools written by supporters of restructuring. Diana Tittle, *Welcome to Heights High: The Crippling Politics of Restructuring America's Public Schools* (Ohio State University Press, 1995), a reporter's story of an integrated high school's wrenching, failed experience with restructuring, including detracking. The author attributes the failure of tracking reform to the opposition of white parents and teachers. Patricia A. Wasley, *Stirring the Chalkdust: Tales of Teachers Changing Classroom Practice* (New York: Teachers College Press, 1994), case studies of teachers in schools restructuring along lines recommended by the Coalition of Essential Schools.

7. John I. Goodlad, *A Place Called School* (McGraw-Hill, 1984).

8. Research is beginning to shed light on heterogeneous classes. A recent study in Israel found that teachers of heterogeneous classrooms stress academic goals for high-achieving students and social-affective goals for low achievers. The different expectations lead to differential learning. Gad Yair, "Teachers' Polarisation in Heterogeneous Classrooms and the Social Distribution of Achievement: An Israeli Case Study," *Teaching & Teacher Education,* vol. 13, no. 3 (1997), pp. 279–93. Another Israeli study found that elementary school teachers of heterogeneously grouped classes stressed a balance of academic, personal, and social goals for students, while academic goals were paramount in ability-grouped classes. In junior high classes, academic goals dominated in all classrooms, probably in recognition of the responsibility to prepare students for high school. Yisrael Rich, "Educational Goals of Teachers in Heterogeneous and Homogeneous Classes in Elementary and Junior High School," *Teaching & Teacher Education,* vol. 9, no. 1 (1993), pp. 81–90.

9. Interviews were not tape recorded. Quotations are from field notes.

10. The term "the one best way" was popularized by David B. Tyack, *The One Best System: A History of American Urban Education* (Harvard University Press, 1974).

Chapter Eight

1. Press coverage of Proposition 227, a California initiative promoting English immersion over bilingual education, follows this pattern to a tee. Articles leading up to the proposition's passage were all about politics. Coverage after the election focused on problems with implementation. In the legislative arena, measures establishing educational standards and high-stakes tests receive similar treatment.

2. Deborah Stone, *Policy Paradox: The Art of Political Decision Making* (W. W. Norton & Co., 1997); Jeannie Oakes, *Keeping Track* (Yale University Press, 1985), p. xiv.

3. Joseph R. Gusfield, *Drinking, Driving and the Symbolic Order: The Culture of Public Problems* (University of Chicago Press, 1981).

4. Joyce L. Epstein and Douglas J. MacIver, *Opportunities to Learn: Effects on Eighth Graders of Curriculum Offerings and Instructional Approaches,* Report No. 34 (Baltimore: Center for Research on Elementary and Middle Schools, July 1992); Laura M. Argys, Daniel I. Rees, and Dominic J. Brewer, "Detracking America's Schools:

Equity at Zero Cost?" *Journal of Policy Analysis and Management,* vol. 15, no. 4 (Fall 1996), 623–45.

5. Linda Valli, "A Curriculum of Effort: Tracking Students in a Catholic High School," in Reba Page and Linda Valli, eds., *Curriculum Differentiation: Interpretive Studies in U.S. Secondary Schools* (SUNY Press, 1990), pp. 45–65; Margaret Camarena, "Following the Right Track: A Comparison of Tracking Practices in Public and Catholic Schools," in Reba Page and Linda Valli, eds., *Curriculum Differentiation: Interpretive Studies in U.S. Secondary Schools* (SUNY Press, 1990), pp. 159–82; Adam Gamoran, "Alternative Uses of Ability Grouping in Secondary Schools: Can We Bring High-Quality Instruction to Low-Ability Classrooms?" *American Journal of Education,* vol. 102, no. 1 (November 1993), 1–22.

6. I have criticized both NELS and HSB research for failing to accurately model school tracking policies. See Tom Loveless, "The Use and Misuse of Research," in Diane Ravitch, ed., *Brookings Papers on Education Policy, 1998* (Brookings, 1998), pp. 279–317. Also see Tom Loveless, "The Tracking and Ability Grouping Debate," *Fordham Report,* vol. 2, no. 8 (August 1998), pp. 1–27.

Index